Basic Condition Reporting

Basic Condition Reporting

A Handbook

5th Edition

Southeastern Registrars Association

Edited by Deborah Rose Van Horn, Corinne Midgett, and Heather Culligan

ROWMAN & LITTLEFIELD

Lanham • Boulder • New York • London

Published by Rowman & Littlefield
An imprint of The Rowman & Littlefield Publishing Group, Inc.
4501 Forbes Boulevard, Suite 200, Lanham, Maryland 20706
www.rowman.com

86-90 Paul Street, London EC2A 4NE

British Library Cataloguing in Publication Information Available

Library of Congress Cataloging-in-Publication Data

Names: Van Horn, Deborah Rose, editor. | Midgett, Corinne, editor. | Culligan, Heather, 1977- editor. | Southeastern Registrars Association.
Title: Basic condition reporting : a handbook / Southeastern Registrars Association ; edited by Deborah Rose Van Horn, Corinne Midgett, and Heather Culligan.
Description: Fifth edition. | Lanham : Rowman & Littlefield, [2021] | Includes bibliographical references and index.
Identifiers: LCCN 2021042841 (print) | LCCN 2021042842 (ebook) | ISBN 9781538150597 (cloth) | ISBN 9781538150603 (paperback) | ISBN 9781538150610 (ebook)
Subjects: LCSH: Museum registration methods—Handbooks, manuals, etc.
Classification: LCC AM139 .B38 2021 (print) | LCC AM139 (ebook) | DDC 069/.52—dc23
LC record available at https://lccn.loc.gov/2021042841
LC ebook record available at https://lccn.loc.gov/2021042842>

This book is dedicated to the Southeastern Registrars Association board and members. Thank you for your support on this project!

We would also like to dedicate this to our friends and family members who supported us while we worked on this project.

Contents

Acknowledgments

On behalf of the Southeastern Registrars Association, I'd like to thank you for purchasing *Basic Condition Reporting: A Handbook*, 5th Edition. Since 1982, *BCR* has been a SERA publication and labor of love. The ongoing popularity of the book is due to the expertise and practical tips offered by the many authors who have contributed their time and professional knowledge. Your purchase of *BCR* supports SERA's mission of encouraging high standards of museum practice and fostering professional growth. Practically speaking, SERA provides conference scholarships, networking opportunities, and professional awards to collections specialists in the southeastern United States.

Basic Condition Reporting was conceived as a training tool that could also provide a common vocabulary for condition reporting in museums and galleries. Despite the wide variety of free resources available on the internet, I still find it vital and helpful to have a practical, standardized handbook with material-specific terms right by my desk. Best of all, our authors—as well as all our SERA members—are incredibly responsive to questions and conundrums regarding condition reporting.

Our authors and my co-editors, Deborah Rose Van Horn and Heather Culligan, deserve tremendous thanks. Some of the authors are new to this edition, and I appreciate their willingness to try something new. Other authors have contributed to multiple editions of *BCR* and we're grateful for their continued support. This was my second time working with Deb and Heather, and just as before, they've been both enjoyable to work with and very hardworking, keeping the project on track and on time. I'd also like to thank our publishing partner, Rowman and Littlefield, for helping us make the switch from self-publishing with the fourth edition of *Basic Condition Reporting* and for supporting this fifth edition.

Lastly, Deb, Heather, and I would like to thank our families, friends, and co-workers for their support while we worked on this project. Without their support, the book wouldn't have happened.

Corinne Midgett
Southeastern Registrars Association
Chair and Co-editor

Preface

Basic Condition Reporting: A Handbook, 5th Edition, is a comprehensive guide to creating condition reports for museum artifacts. Condition reports are a vital part of the day-to-day operations in museum collections management. A good condition report can help with planning for exhibitions, loans, conservation, and insurance needs. This book is a great reference tool for museum staff members, volunteers, and students who are working with a variety of collection types. *Basic Condition Reporting* introduces the audience to the purposes of a good condition report, methods of examining a piece for a condition report, and a common vocabulary for recording the condition of an item.

This volume is intended to help create a standard vocabulary for all of the individuals in a museum that may be conducting condition reports. In an ideal world, everyone who does a condition report for an item would be trained in the exact same standards, use the same terminology, and use the exact same form, etc. However, the reality is that even if every registrar, collections manager, and curator in your institution does condition reports, each report will be slightly different. Then you throw in every intern, volunteer, or student who may assist and you will find a variety of methods and terminologies that appear. With this volume, we hope to provide you with a baseline that all these people can work from so that any person who opens the condition report can understand what the problems on a particular piece include.

Many texts include condition reporting as a small section of a larger discussion on collections care and management. This book breaks down the process of creating a condition report to the fundamental aspects of handling, examination, and documentation. Different types of materials may require specialized handling methods and vocabularies to adequately describe the current status of an object. This volume includes chapters on eighteen material types and their needs. The text also includes samples of condition report forms for various material types. Chapters include discussions of archaeological collections, basketry, ceramics, cultural heritage collections (ethnographic), furniture, glass, metals, mixed media objects, natural history collections, paintings, paper, photographs, plastics, sculpture, skin and leather items, taxidermy specimens, textiles, and wood.

In this expanded and updated edition, we have included a new chapter on digital condition reporting, and we have updated the information on condition reporting for incoming and outgoing loans. The last volume of this book was released in 2015; this expanded volume includes updated information and resources about the material types. We have also included images of some of the damage types to assist the reader with their understanding of the terminology used in the book.

Often, we are called upon as collections caregivers to examine pieces we are not familiar with. This book gives us the tools to examine an unfamiliar material type and document the condition issues that we see. Many of us have specialized training dealing with one collection type, but it is rare for a museum staff member to only handle that type of material. This book can assist museum staff members in learning about these different material types and the inherent vices of those materials.

The contributors to this book include collections specialists, including registrars, collections managers, and conservators. The authors have extensive experience in working with museum collections and are recognized leaders in collections care. The contributors each discuss a material type with which they are familiar and break it down so that novices, experienced museum staff members, and volunteers can use the volume to examine their collections.

The reader should be able to take away a general understanding of condition reporting, its purpose, and how to create a report. They will be able to use this book as a guide for future condition reports and keep it as a handy reference. Below you will find brief descriptions of the chapters and their contents.

CONDITION REPORTING: AN INTRODUCTORY PRIMER

This chapter defines the purpose of a condition report and goes over the basic components required in a report. The authors discuss various methods of examining pieces, tools for examination, methods of recording information regarding the condition of a piece, and a general vocabulary of terms to describe different types of damage. This chapter includes a sample condition report form that can be used with objects regardless of their composition.

CONDITION REPORTS FOR INCOMING AND OUTGOING LOANS

This chapter examines the purpose of condition reports during the loan process. The chapter discusses the importance of condition reports when filing an insurance claim on an item that is damaged in transit. The chapter also introduces topics such as the importance of condition reports in dealing with private lenders and traveling exhibitions.

DIGITAL CONDITION REPORTING

This chapter examines the processes and challenges of doing a digital condition report. As more collections caretakers move away from pencil-and-paper condition reports, this is becoming more and more common. The author looks at different aspects related to the topic, including software and applications that can be used. The chapter also introduces us to a recent poll of collections caretakers and shows how comfortable (or uncomfortable) we are as a field with doing digital condition reports.

ARCHAEOLOGICAL ARTIFACTS

This chapter examines the complex grouping of material types that make up archaeological collections. The chapter discusses types of damage that may be seen on ceramics, metals, glass, or other types of material after they have been buried in the ground. The chapter looks at damage that may have been caused by prior use, burial, and recovery. It covers the varying needs of these items and discusses their needs in depth. The chapter includes samples of condition report forms and maintenance forms, as well as instructions on how to use these forms.

BASKETRY

This chapter discusses the handling and examination of items that are woven into vessels such as baskets. The chapter looks at various damage types and provides a glossary of terms and photographs to help define the type of damage that has occurred to an item. The chapter has a condition report form that is designed to use with basketry collections.

CERAMICS

This chapter looks at the proper methods of handling and examining items made from ceramics. The chapter examines the different types of damage that can occur with ceramic items and provides a listing of terms to describe the damage. The chapter includes a sample form that is designed for use with ceramic items.

ETHNOGRAPHIC COLLECTIONS

This chapter examines the complexities of cultures and material types that make up cultural heritage (ethnographic) collections. It takes a look at issues such as cultural information, materials and treatments used with these collections, and proper handling. The chapter has several photographs to help illustrate issues that may relate to ethnographic collections and the chapter includes a glossary of terms that can be used to describe the condition of an object. This chapter includes a sample condition report form for ethnographic collections.

FURNITURE

This chapter looks at the examination and handling of furniture collections in a museum. The chapter has a glossary of damage types with photographs that help the reader identify certain damage types in furniture collections. The chapter includes a sample condition report for furniture collections.

GLASS

This chapter looks at the proper methods of handling and examining items made from glass. The chapter examines the different types of damage that can occur with glass items and provides a listing of terms to describe the damage. The chapter includes a sample form that is designed for use with glass items.

METALS

This chapter discusses various types of metals and their alloys that can be found in museum collections. The chapter goes over the proper handling and examination of metal objects in museum collections. It includes a glossary of terms related to the condition of metal objects and a sample condition report for metal objects.

MIXED MEDIA AND COMPOSITE OBJECTS

This chapter looks at the proper methods of examining and condition reporting objects made from mixed media or composite materials. The chapter reviews the interaction between different types of materials and how to complete a condition report for a mixed media or composite item.

NATURAL HISTORY SPECIMENS

The natural history chapter examines the wide variety of objects that can be covered under the umbrella term of *natural history*. The chapter discusses why condition reports are not always done when the specimen is collected and discusses the purpose of a condition report for these objects. The chapter looks at methods of examining different types of collections from two-dimensional herbarium sheets to three-dimensional items such as fossils and fluid-preserved specimens. The chapter includes a glossary of terms related to the condition of natural history specimens.

PAINTINGS AND FRAMES

The paintings and frames chapter examines the proper handling and examination of paintings and the frames in which they are placed. The chapter includes a glossary of terms relating to painting techniques and a glossary of terms related to potential damage to these items. A sample condition report form for paintings and frames is included with this chapter.

PAPER

The paper chapter takes a look at paper materials in museum collections, including items like prints, manuscripts, and books. The chapter discusses the proper handling and examination of paper items and includes a glossary of terms that describe the makeup and condition of paper items. A sample condition report for paper items is included in this chapter.

PHOTOGRAPHS

The photograph chapter includes a discussion of the composition of different photograph types and their handling and examination needs. The chapter incorporates several photographs that illustrate the damage that can occur to historic photographs and a glossary of terms used to describe the damage types. A sample condition report for photographs is also included in this chapter.

PLASTICS

The plastics chapter discusses the inherent vices of different types of plastics and gives a timeline for the manufacture of different types of plastics. The author discusses the different handling and examination requirements for materials made out of plastics and provides a detailed glossary of damage types that includes several photographs to help illustrate the types of damage. A sample condition report for plastic items is included in this chapter.

SCULPTURE

The sculpture chapter gives an overview of different material types that can comprise sculptures in museum collections. The chapter discusses handling techniques and provides listing of common materials and the condition issues to look for with these materials.

SKIN AND LEATHER

The skin and leather chapter covers a wide variety of materials that have been made from processed and treated animal skins. The chapter covers the processes by which these materials are made and the long-term condition issues that may be caused by the manner in which the skin is processed. The chapter includes a terminology section related to the processing of skin and leathers and a glossary of condition terms. The chapter also includes a sample condition report form for use with materials made from skin and leather.

TAXIDERMY

For the first time, *Basic Condition Reporting* is featuring a chapter that focuses on condition reports for taxidermy specimens. In the past, this was rolled into larger chapters and was often overlooked. The chapter will look at condition and safety issues while handling these specimens. The chapter also contains a terminology section related to the condition issues for these specimens.

TEXTILES

The textiles chapter discusses the proper handling and examination of artifacts composed of various types of fabric. The chapter includes a glossary of condition terms, including some photographs, to help describe the condition of textile artifacts. The chapter includes a sample condition report for textile collections.

WOOD

For the first time, *Basic Condition Reporting* will feature a chapter on wooden objects. In the past, the book contained a furniture chapter but overlooked other wooden items in collections. This chapter looks at different types of wooden objects in collections and the condition issues that are related to them. The chapter includes a glossary of condition terms, including some photographs, to help describe the condition of wooden artifacts.

Basic Condition Reporting is designed to be a resource for museum collections caretakers to use to learn the fundamentals of condition reporting for different materials. It is designed to help create a common nomenclature for the reports so that they can be useful whether you are a conservator, collections caretaker, student, or volunteer. We hope you will find this book to be a useful instructional tool and reference for creating great condition reports for museum collections.

1

Condition Reporting

An Introductory Primer

Deborah Rose Van Horn and Heather Culligan

Condition reports are one of the basic components of any collections record. The reports provide a lot of insight into the history of an object. Any good condition report "is an accurate and informative assessment of an object's state of preservation at a particular moment in time."[1] A condition report can be handwritten, typed into a database, recorded with a video camera, or inputted into an application on a tablet or computer. During the COVID-19 pandemic in 2020–2021, the field even moved to doing these reports for loans remotely over the internet, with one museum allowing the lender to see the loaned items live over video programs like Zoom, FaceTime, etc. Today, there are many ways of recording the condition of an object, but the fundamentals of the basic condition report remain the same.

A condition report should include this basic information:

- Information about who did the report and when it was conducted.
- Object information, such as the object title or type, the accession or loan numbers, and a brief description.
- The reason for the condition report, such as damage or consideration for an exhibit, loan, or conservation treatment.
- A description of the current condition of the object. This will include areas of damage, types of damage or deterioration seen, measurements, etc.
- Photographs, videos, drawings, or other visual information showing where the damage is and what it looks like.

There are many benefits to a good condition report, such as:

- Helping staff determine the stability of an object for exhibition or loan.
- Letting staff know what the concerns are about a piece and what they need to keep an eye on.
- Limiting how often an object is handled.
- Informing object handlers of unseen problems.
- Showing the condition of an object over time to determine the rate of deterioration.
- Setting priorities for conservation.
- Assisting staff in identifying similar objects.
- Aiding in the valuation process of an object for insurance purposes.

As much as we would all like to believe that our collections records are complete and accurate, we all know there are gaps in these records. Unfortunately, the condition report is often one of these gaps. In our careers in museums, we have seen too many records where the condition simply says "good" with the date the condition was observed. Unfortunately, this is incredibly unhelpful, because not only does it provide no real information about the condition, but it also uses terms that can be very subjective. Whether you believe something is in good or poor condition may be influenced by your familiarity with a particular type of object or the material with which it is made.

The guidelines provided in this chapter are meant to be used in conjunction with the information in the following chapters. While this chapter will give you the basics of the condition report, the other chapters will focus on specific types of reports (digital, loan reports, etc.) and specific material types (glass, ceramics, wood, plastic, metal, etc.). This book is designed to provide those that are new to the world of condition reporting with a primer on how to make a condition report. It is also a handy reference tool for those of us who have been in the field for many years, but may be dealing with a new medium for the first time.

TOOLS

The types of tools that you need to conduct a condition report may vary based on the type of object you are evaluating and the procedures at your institution. For example, some museums may prefer a pencil-and-paper report, whereas others will prefer to input straight into the database or use a condition-reporting application. This section contains suggestions as to the types of tools you may want to have on hand while creating a condition report. Many people make a condition-reporting kit that they can take with them so that they have everything they need while working in storage areas or galleries. The tools in the kits may depend on what type of collections you are working with. Please remember to inspect these tools from time to time to make sure that they are clean and are not damaged. This will help prevent harm to the object.

Documentation

- Soft lead pencils
- Paper
- Condition report examination forms
- Computer or tablet
- Camera (this can be on your phone or tablet)
- Past condition reports and photos for comparison

Measurement

- Cloth tape measure
- Calipers
- Rulers
- Scale

Handling/Support

- Gloves
- Acid-free, lignin-free board
- Buffered and unbuffered acid-free, lignin-free tissue paper
- Padded rolls, blocks, or weights
- Padded carts

Illumination

- Flashlight
- Pen or crevice light
- Portable worklights
- Ultraviolet lights

Magnification

- X10 hand lens
- Jeweler's loupe
- Microscope
- Head-mounted magnifier
- Computer-aided magnification devices

Miscellaneous

- Hand mirror
- Dental mirror
- Magnet (to identify ferrous materials)
- Brushes in a variety of shapes and stiffnesses
- Probes
- Tweezers
- Forceps

- Blower ball or brush
- Variable speed, high-efficiency particulate air (HEPA)–filtered vacuum
- Plastic screens for the vacuum

HANDLING

It is important to remember to minimize the number of times an object is handled. This best practice goes beyond condition reporting and really speaks to the overall goal of minimizing the risk of damage and preserving the objects. Prior to handling an object, remove any items such as jewelry, watches, or lanyards from your person. It is also recommended that loose clothing be removed, rolled up the arm, or restrained in some way. These types of items may interfere with your ability to handle the object properly, or can damage the object.

The topic of object handling often goes hand in hand with the topic of gloves. Museum professionals generally agree that whether or not to wear gloves depends on the object and type of material. Clean, dry hands are often preferable when handling ceramics, glass, paper materials, or textiles, while metal and wood objects should be handled with gloves. An object may be in such poor condition that gloves not only protect the object, but also protect the wearer's hands from getting soiled. Gloves should also be worn when handling objects with potential contaminants. If gloves are preferred, non-slip or nitrile gloves offer a tighter fit than cotton gloves and allow for a firmer hold on the object. It is important to consider what is best for the object and the handler when determining the necessity of gloves. When in doubt, gloves can be worn and will protect both the object and handler.

Be sure to conduct a visual inspection of the object prior to handling or moving it. Look for areas that are cracked, are weak, or hint at a previous repair. These areas will generally be the weakest and most vulnerable parts of the object. Take note of any loose, moving, or removable parts of the object. It is recommended that any removable part be unattached and moved separately. Keep in mind that an object may also be weakest at the points where it is typically handled. For example, a teapot is usually lifted by its handle, meaning the handle itself may be weak from use. Try to identify how an object is most likely handled, and then determine whether there is an alternate way to handle or move it safely.

Once the visual inspection is completed and the method of handling is determined, the next step is to transport the object. Planning ahead is key when transporting the object. Determine where the object will be placed. This area, preferably a sturdy table, should be clear of clutter and padded with polyethylene foam to protect the object and provide support. Plan the route the object will take and consider doorways, turns, thresholds, and lights along the path.

Use a cart to transport the object from its storage location to the examination location. The cart should also be padded with polyethylene foam and you may also have to use tissue or additional foam to support the object. If the object extends beyond the cart, make sure to protect that part of the object with foam or a clean moving blanket. Multiple people should be used when moving large objects. It is particularly important to have one person be the navigator and communicator to help those lifting the object move along the planned path. If you decide to carry an object, make sure it is supported with both hands and that the path can be navigated safely.

Other handling tips:

- Avoid sliding objects along a surface.
- Avoid moving objects over other objects.
- Be aware of shelf height when lifting objects.
- Lift objects slowly off surfaces to ensure they are not stuck to the foam, shelf, or other material.
- Place two-dimensional objects in an archival folder or between pieces of blueboard when transporting via cart or by hand.

- Do not place objects at the edge of a table or shelf.
- If using a cart, position the cart as close to the shelf or table as possible prior to moving the object.

EXAMINATION AND DOCUMENTATION

Examination of the object should take place once it has been safely transported to a clutter-free, padded table. Place any supplies you are using during the examination away from the object. Ensure that lighting sufficiently highlights the object. If it is inadequate, a headlamp or stand lamp can be used. Be cognizant of exposing the object to light for an extended period and make sure the light is not creating heat that can damage the object.

If available, read through previous condition reports prior to completing the new condition report. It is helpful to have previous reports with you and to conduct a brief examination of the object using those reports first. This will allow you to identify previous areas of concern and note any changes in the new report.

Whether the condition is documented on paper with a pencil, directly into a database, or through a condition report application, there are key things that should be documented:

- Accession number and/or loan number
- Object number
- Storage location of object
- Special handling and packing instructions
- Reason for condition report, i.e., new acquisition, loan, inventory, etc.
- Object name and description
- Current condition and damage
- Location and description of condition and damage
- Updates on previously recorded damage
- Previous repairs or conservation work
- Examiner's name and date of examination

It is common to see condition terms such as "Fair," "Good," or "Excellent" on condition reports. These terms are subjective and lend themselves to the creation of a generic condition report with little detail. Whether these terms are used at your institution or not, it is recommended that time be taken to complete a comprehensive and helpful condition report. Use bullet points or short sentences to describe the type and location of damage. Be brief, yet comprehensive.

The type of damage an object has usually falls under the categories of inherent vice, biological damage, physical/mechanical damage, or chemical damage. An inherent vice is when an object deteriorates because of incompatible materials or weak construction. Biological damage occurs from pests or mold, while physical/mechanical damage is the result of stress on an object and manifests itself by a crack, loss, or tear. Chemical damage occurs when there is a chemical reaction between the material and heat, light, or water. It is important to keep these types of damage in mind when creating the condition report. Check the object for each type of damage and note it if you find it. Remember, be specific, yet brief. For example, you may note that a textile has "carpet beetle damage on the cuff of the left sleeve."

Objects may have dust, dirt, or other debris on the surface. Should you encounter this, it is important to note it in the condition report, and, more importantly, note if any cleaning was performed by the examiner or conservator. For example, perhaps dust was removed from a teapot by the examiner with a clean cloth or brush. It may be found that certain debris should only be removed by a conservator. It is important to remember that more extensive cleaning should only be completed after consulting a conservator. Similar to moving objects, be cognizant of parts of the object that move or are reluctant to move. Do not force an object to move or open or operate in a way that can damage it without consulting a conservator.

Photographs of the object should be taken either as the examiner completes the condition report or once it is done. Make sure to take overall object photographs, and also photographs of specific examples of damage. It can also be helpful to note any damage, either physically or digitally, on the photograph and attach it to the final condition report.

TYPES OF DAMAGE

When doing your report, it is also important to record the types of damage found on the object. In some cases, we may know the reason for the damage, and it is important to record that, too. For example, if the piece is dropped or vandalized, it is important to record this information as both a part of the object's history and as information for future conservation work.

Sometimes artifact damage can be caused by inherent vice, or the object's own composition or nature. Some materials are more stable than others, and the more information you have in the report about the history (including materials) can help inform future caretakers whether it is something they need to watch.

Other types of damage may include damage from pests, physical contact, or biological materials, or it may be chemical in nature. If you are not sure of what type of damage it is, you should either call a conservator to look at the piece or you should use terms like *possible* when describing the damage.

It is also important to use common terms when describing damage. A glossary of damage terms may be helpful to your institution. This can be either an internal publication, a book like this one, or a website that has photographs showing damage types. The important thing is that your team uses common terms within the institution. It does not help anyone if you cannot understand what another person has described.

LOCATION

The location of the damage is just as important as the type of damage. If there is a fragile part of an object, it is helpful to everyone who follows you to know where that fragile spot is located. This should be described in clear and concise terms or through photographs so that the damage is easy to find. Sometimes this may be simple, like saying that a handle on a teapot is cracked near the bottom, but other times this is difficult, such as describing a spot on a larger piece like a tractor or a car.

For pieces like a painting or a quilt, you may want to consider using a *zone system* (Fig. 1.1). In this method, you will divide the piece into zones or sections and then describe where the damage is by the zone. Many times, the zones are set up as they are in the figure. This is a simple method that creates nine zones or areas. The areas can be given titles such as "top left," "center," or "bottom right." You can then describe where the damage is in the zone. For example, say you had an area of paint loss on an oil painting. You could say that it is in the "top left" zone on the left side next to

TL	**TC**	**TR**
CL	**C**	**CR**
BL	**BC**	**BR**

Figure 1.1. The zone system.
Source: Deborah Rose Van Horn

General Condition Report Form

Object ID Number Date

Evaluation by (Name/Title)

Object Name/Title

Description

Dimensions

Provenance

Previous Treatments or Conservation

Overall Condition (circle one):

Excellent Good Fair Poor

Overall Condition Notes (Please include location and description of damage, attach photos or sketches):

Figure 1.2. General condition report form.
Source: Deborah Rose Van Horn

the frame and that it is three inches from the top of the painting. This gives someone a very good idea of where the damage has occurred. It is also possible to mark a photo with the zones and mark the areas of damage on the photo. This gives a simple backup and helps future caretakers find the damage.

The *zone system* is extremely helpful for some types of objects, but it can be difficult to use on three-dimensional pieces. Sometimes it is better to use common terms to describe the location of the damage. For example, if you were condition reporting a car, it might be better to use terms like *driver's side* and *passenger's side* to indicate which side of the car the damage is on. For other three-dimensional pieces, you may be able to use other common terms like *rim*, *handle*, or *lid*.

Other methods include using terms like *proper-left* or *viewer's left* to help the report user orient themselves to where you started. You can also use *landmarks* to help someone find the damage. For example, say you are working on a piece with an inscription. You could use the inscription as a landmark on the piece and say the damage is located one inch above the letter *B* in the word *boy*. Again, this gives those who come after you a concrete place to look and find the damage.

EXTENT

Sometimes it is difficult to describe the extent of the damage to an object. This may be because the piece has some sort of damage that covers more of the piece. Examples are a book with foxing on the pages or a piece of farm equipment where the metal has rusted. In these cases, it may be better to describe the general location, such as the part of the page or the side of the damage.

Your institution may want to standardize some terms to help describe the severity of the damage. Some groups like collectors' organizations have come up with terms to describe damage on objects such as coins and stamps. These groups use terms like *negligible*, *slight*, *moderate*, *marked*, and *extreme*. As we discussed earlier with the terms *excellent*, *good*, *fair*, and *poor*, these terms can be very subjective, and it may be helpful to have your own internal definitions.

SPECIFIC TYPES OF REPORTS

Condition reports can be specific to the type of material or report being done. The amount of detail can be determined by the purpose of the report (loans, conservation, inventory, damage) or the material type. In the following chapters, we will look at several types of reports and their purposes. We will also look at how to do reports for specific types of materials and some terms that may be specific to the object type.

NOTE

1. Demeroukas, Marie. "Condition Reporting," in *Museum Registration Methods*, 6th ed. Lanham, MD: Rowman & Littlefield, 2020, 249.

BIBLIOGRAPHY

Demeroukas, Marie. "Condition Reporting." In *Museum Registration Methods*, 6th edition, edited by John E. Simmons and Toni M. Kiser, 249–60. Lanham, MD: Rowman & Littlefield, 2020.

Taylor, Joel. "Collection-Care Surveys for Preventative Conservation." In *Preventative Conservation: Collections Storage*, edited by Lisa Elkin and Christopher A. Norris, 99–111. New York, NY: Society for the Preservation of Natural History Collections, 2019.

Van Horn, Deborah Rose, Heather Culligan, and Corinne Midgett. *Basic Condition Reporting: A Handbook*, 4th ed. Lanham, MD: Rowman & Littlefield, 2015.

2

Condition Reports for Incoming and Outgoing Loans

Michelle Gallagher Roberts

Condition reports are created for a variety of reasons: documenting the condition of an object when it enters the museum's care and custody, tracking the condition of an object over time, as part of a damage report, and as part of the loan process. Condition reports are always important. However, during the loan process, they take on added significance. Condition reports for a loan document preexisting conditions of an object and assist in establishing the responsible party for any damage. The specific object type terminology and handling notes from the other chapters of this book will assist the reviewer with completing condition reports for loans.

Loss and damage during transit is the most frequent cause of insurance claims. As a result, museums file more insurance claims on loans than on permanent collection items. Museums are legally liable to pay for damage to loaned items, while a loss to a permanent collection object is often dealt with in-house. After the loan agreement, condition reports are the second most critical type of paperwork should an insurance claim need to be filed.

Detailed photographs are invaluable in documenting a preexisting condition and any subsequent changes to the object. High-resolution digital images will often record condition issues not easily seen by the naked eye. Should an issue be seen later, photographs can also be consulted to determine whether the reviewer missed the problem at first examination, whether the problem has worsened, or whether it is new.

There are no standards to the length or format of a condition report. The object type, purpose of the loan, current state, and conservation history of the object will dictate what information the condition report will contain and the format. At a minimum, the report needs to contain who completed the examination, when it was conducted, and the basic identifying information of the object (in order to distinguish it from other objects). Who is tasked with completing condition reports on loans is heavily dependent on staff availability. It is often the registrar, but it could be anyone from a curator to a conservator to the director. The title of the person is less important than their training and experience.

OUTGOING LOANS

Most loan agreements include a phrase similar to this: "The Lender represents and warrants that the loan is in such condition to withstand the ordinary strains of packing, transportation, and handling." The outgoing condition report is the lending institution's opportunity to document any preexisting conditions (or lack thereof), and to establish that the object is in acceptable condition to travel. The condition report is also a good opportunity to document any areas of concern that need to be closely monitored by the borrower. Measurements and detailed photographs should accompany all outgoing condition reports.

Many museums will conduct an initial condition assessment of objects requested for loan to highlight any conservation and/or framing needs that may need to be completed prior to the object traveling. These assessments are also the lending institution's opportunity to eliminate an object from being loaned based on condition. Some objects are just not capable of withstanding the physical stress of being packed and transported, even with conservation treatment. It might be better for a loan to be declined than to subject the object to this strain. Only the lending institution can make this decision.

These reviews could run the spectrum from a formal written report completed by a conservator to an informal assessment done by a collections manager, registrar, or curator. This will depend on the staffing and procedures of the lending museum. Either way, this initial review is the lending institution's chance to raise any issues that may need to be addressed prior to shipment. Any concerns should be communicated in writing to the borrowing institution in a timely manner. The borrower might not be willing or able to accept the costs or responsibility for an object in fragile condition.

A formal written outgoing condition report should be done as close to the point at which the object is packed and shipped. Ideally, this would be done no more than one month prior to the start of the loan. The official outgoing condition report should be completed after any conservation treatments or framing. The condition report should include an evaluation of the frame, even if it is new. Any damage or condition concerns that were resolved through conservation should be noted so they can be monitored during the course of the loan. Repaired damage can often resurface when an object is subjected to stress. However, any photographs attached to the condition report should include at least one post-treatment shot. An outgoing loan condition report is not the place for an in-depth conservation history. These reports should provide a succinct summary of the object's current condition with sufficient detail for another person to ensure no changes have occurred. This report is the lender's final snapshot of the object's condition from which all subsequent damage will be measured.

INCOMING LOANS

When a museum borrows an object, they are agreeing to take physical and financial responsibility for that object. A condition report should travel with any object being borrowed from another museum. However, this may not occur. In either case, the condition report, completed by the borrower, is the first step in defining the damage for which the borrowing museum will be held accountable.

The condition report on an incoming object starts before the object is even unpacked and ideally should occur on the loading dock or in the receiving area of a museum. The packing material for the object needs to be examined from top to bottom when it arrives. Any damage must be immediately brought to the attention of the shipper and should be noted on the bill of lading when it is signed for by the appropriate museum representative. Otherwise, it will be difficult to hold the shipper accountable. Photographs of the outside packaging showing any damage must be taken. The object should be carefully unpacked with photographs taken at every stage. Any damage to the object corresponding to the packaging damage should be carefully documented with photographs and written reports. These reports and images will need to be immediately sent to the lending institution, shipping agent, and any applicable insurance company.

Assuming most objects will arrive with no outwardly visible damage to the packaging, a condition report should be completed after an object is unpacked (Figure 2.1). If a condition report is supplied with the object, it is the responsibility of the

ABC MUSEUM

INCOMING LOAN CONDITION REPORT

Lender:

Description of Object:

Incoming Condition:

By: ______________________________ Date: ____________________

Outgoing Condition:

By: ______________________________ Date: ____________________

Figure 2.1. Incoming loan condition report form.
Source: Michelle Gallagher Roberts

borrowing museum staff to thoroughly compare the written report to their own observations. Different reviewers may see different areas of concern. Any significant additional condition issues identified should be communicated verbally and then followed up in writing to the lending institution. This is also the time to discuss any questions that might arise when reviewing the supplied condition report. Unclear notations or descriptions should be clarified to ensure a comprehensive report of the object is completed. Should no condition report accompany the object, it is even more important the borrowing museum complete a thorough and well-documented examination.

No matter how well an object is packed and by what means it is shipped, the object will undergo some stress during transit. This may exacerbate previous condition issues that need to be noted and perhaps mitigated at the borrowing institution. This can only occur in consultation and full agreement with the lender.

Throughout the duration of the loan, the borrowed object should be monitored. The nature of the object and purpose of the loan will dictate how often and comprehensive this monitoring will need to be.

At the conclusion of the loan, it is the responsibility of both the borrowing and lending institutions to complete condition reports. The borrowing museum should compare all previous reports to what is currently visible. This report should ideally be done just before the object is packed for return shipment. Hopefully, there will be no new comments to be made on the condition.

When the object is returned, it is important that staff at the lending museum go through the same procedure as when the object arrived at the borrowing museum. The packaging must first be examined and then the object should be compared to the three previous reports. Ideally, the person who first inspected the object should complete the return condition report. A consistent eye at each museum helps ensure a thorough and accurate examination. When the loan has been completed, the object should have been examined at least four times. These records should be maintained in the object's file as a history of the loan and as snapshots of the object's condition during that period.

On a loan agreement, there should be language regarding how long the lending institution has to register a claim regarding any damage that may have occurred while in the care and custody of the borrower. An example of this language is: "When the Loan is returned, the Museum will send a receipt to the Lender for the Lender's signature. If the signed receipt is not returned within fifteen (15) days of issue, the Museum will consider that the condition of the object(s) as noted and returned is acceptable to the Lender and the Lender waives any and all subsequent claims." Since the lending institution is working under a time limit, it benefits them to unpack and condition report the object promptly. Any deviations from their original condition report should be brought to the attention of the appropriate person at the borrowing institution.

PRIVATE LENDERS

Loans from private lenders can be fraught with hazards, making a thorough condition report invaluable. It is critical that a thorough condition report be completed before any agents of the borrowing museum touch the object. These agents could include a shipper, framer, packer, etc. Not thoroughly documenting a loan from a private lender could open a museum up to extensive liability if any damage is discovered later and cannot be definitively determined to have occurred prior to the borrower taking custody of the object.

If the object to be borrowed is not geographically close, some museums employ contract registrars in the lender's vicinity to complete a condition report. A staff member from the borrowing institution can also travel to the location of the object to complete the necessary condition report. While these can be added expenses, they may save the borrowing museum money in the long run. Many fine arts shippers can also complete condition reports for the borrower if they are also packing the item. This may be an additional cost, but it should be explored when packing arrangements are made. Many fine arts shippers complete brief condition reports as a matter of course to limit their own liability. Borrowers should request a copy of this paperwork for their own records if it is not supplied. If neither of these options are viable, then another alternative is to have the lender send current digital images of the object to the borrowing museum prior to the loan beginning. This is not ideal, but it is better than not having anything on record. With the proliferation of high-quality digital cameras available in cell phones, most lenders should be able to meet this request.

On most loan agreements, there is usually a clause discussing condition reports. An example of this language is: "A condition report of the loan shall be made by the Museum upon unpacking and repacking the loan. Upon request, a copy of the Museum's incoming condition report will be mailed to the Lender following receipt of the loan. The Lender must notify the Museum within fifteen (15) days after receipt of the Museum's condition report to discuss any discrepancy between the condition of the loan at the time of shipment and the loan at the time of unpacking. Any evidence of damage or loss at the time of receipt or while in the borrowing Museum's custody will be reported by that Museum to the Lender via telephone or email, which will be followed up in writing. No repair, restoration, or alteration shall be made by the borrowing Museum without the Lender's express written approval."

Any damage or areas of concern noted on the object upon the borrowing museum taking responsibility needs to be clearly communicated to the owner. However, sending a copy of the complete condition report to a private lender is a bit of a double-edged sword. Often, museum personnel will note condition issues that are not clearly visible to the naked eye or what the lender might consider significant. Private lenders can take offense to detailed condition reports noting every deficit or flaw of their prized possession. This can be a delicate balance between communicating with the lender and not overwhelming them.

TRAVELING EXHIBITIONS

There are usually numerous condition reports produced during a traveling exhibition. Since there are so many different formats for condition reports, the organizing museum will usually create a standard form to be used during the traveling exhibition schedule. Usually, these forms will have a section for incoming and outgoing condition notes from each venue that is signed and dated by each venue's staff (Figure 2.2). These forms usually supplement the original condition report supplied by the lender. It is best practice to have the same person complete the incoming and outgoing condition report of an object. This ensures a consistent eye is viewing the piece for each venue.

If a diagram or photographic condition report is supplied, it is standard to add any new observations to the preexisting notations. These additions should be initialed and dated (Figure 2.3). It is not uncommon for these addendums to be done in a different-colored ink. If the reviewer should choose to do this, these alterations should be done away from any object to ensure it is not inadvertently damaged by the pen. This allows all condition concerns and the date on which they were first observed to be seen in one quick and easily digested format.

Since these reports will be traveling to multiple locations and be viewed by many people, it is important that each person completing the reports not use abbreviations. Shorthand notations that are understandable within an institution can lead to confusion among staff at different museums, especially if the exhibition is traveling to different countries. Any abbreviations should be clearly defined for subsequent reviewers.

ABC MUSEUM

Exhibition Title:

Description of Object:
Maker
Title/Object Name
Date Made
Materials/Medium
Size (overall/framed/support)

Lender Information:

- -

Venue Name: ______________________________ Exhibition Dates: ______________

Incoming Condition:

By: ______________________________ Date: ______________

Outgoing Condition:

By: ______________________________ Date: ______________

- -

Venue Name: ______________________________ Exhibition Dates: ______________

Incoming Condition:

By: ______________________________ Date: ______________

Outgoing Condition:

By: ______________________________ Date: ______________

Figure 2.2. Condition report form for traveling exhibitions.
Source: Michelle Gallagher Roberts

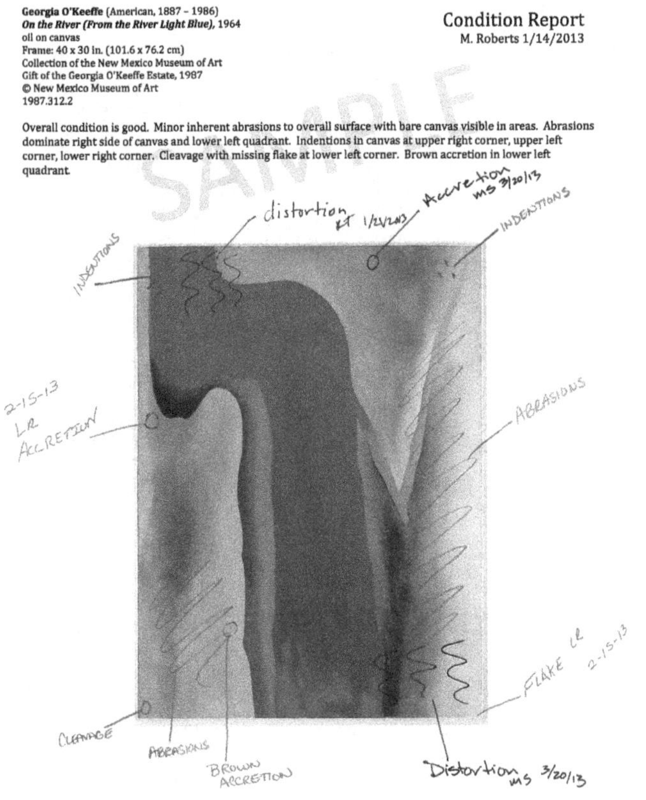

Georgia O'Keeffe (American, 1887 – 1986)
On the River (From the River Light Blue), 1964
oil on canvas
Frame: 40 x 30 in. (101.6 x 76.2 cm)
Collection of the New Mexico Museum of Art
Gift of the Georgia O'Keeffe Estate, 1987
© New Mexico Museum of Art
1987.312.2
Condition Report
M. Roberts 1/14/2013
SAMPLE
Overall condition is good. Minor inherent abrasions to overall surface with bare canvas visible in areas. Abrasions dominate right side of canvas and lower left quadrant. Indentions in canvas at upper right corner, upper left corner, lower right corner. Cleavage with missing flake at lower left corner. Brown accretion in lower left quadrant.
distortion
Accretion MS 3/20/13
INDENTIONS
ABRASIONS
FLAKE LR 2-15-13
CLEAVAGE
BROWN ACCRETION
Distortion MS 3/20/13

Figure 2.3. Completed condition report form with new damage noted and dated.
Source: Michelle Gallagher Roberts

Should any significant changes be noted on an incoming condition report or during the exhibition run, the organizing institution must be notified. The traveling exhibition contract will outline who should be notified. The contract may also stipulate whether a copy of the incoming and outgoing condition reports need to be sent separately to the organizing institution, and who should be completing the condition report—registrar, conservator, or courier. Before a traveling exhibition is onsite, the staff at the borrowing institution should review all sections of the exhibition contract related to object handling and conditions reports and make plans to fulfill any contractual obligations.

At the close of most traveling exhibitions, the organizing institution is responsible for ensuring that objects are safely returned to their owners. Similar to all outgoing loans, when the object arrives home, it is the responsibility of the lending museum to examine the object and report any issues to the organizer. Any condition problems that have arisen during the traveling exhibition should be addressed with the organizer. The successive condition reports can assist in pinpointing the origin and responsibility of any damage.

Condition reports play a vital role in the loan process. It benefits every party to the loan to complete a thorough examination when the object changes hands. These reports can also be used to track how the object is responding to the stress of packing, shipping, and a new environment. Along with the associated loan agreement, condition reports help establish financial and legal responsibility for any changes to the object. Documentation and communication are critical to the success of a loan.

BIBLIOGRAPHY

Buck, Rebecca A., and Jean Allman Gilmore. 2003. *On the Road Again: Developing and Managing Traveling Exhibitions*. Washington D.C.: American Association of Museums.

Malaro, Marie C., and Ildiko Pogany DeAngelis. 2012. *A Legal Primer on Managing Museum Collections*, 3rd edition. Washington, D.C.: Smithsonian Press.

Simmons, John E. and Toni M. Kiser, editors. 2020. *Museum Registration Methods*, 6th edition. Washington, D.C.: American Alliance of Museums.

3

Digital Condition Reporting

Tommie Rodgers

The incorporation of digital technology into the museum profession has been a slow progression. While registrars are armed with the basic tools of the trade as outlined in other chapters, many have incorporated a collections management software system to manage, document, and archive retrievable information that entails a comprehensive system for collection objects and archives. There are several systems on the market, and most have online components that allow the sharing of museum collections with the masses. All this technology comes with a price, and software companies typically charge an added annual fee for online availability.

Condition reporting is only one element of a collections management system, and the CMS can allow for multiple users on any one given system. The availability to multiple users is beneficial to the end goal of creating a storage warehouse for everything about a collection of objects.

With the need for instant documentation in the galleries, storage, and on the road, many registrars and conservators have longed to make condition reporting compact, instant, and simultaneously available across multiple devices. The software market has been slow to the punch, and the systems have tied most registrars and collections staff to their desks or doubled their efforts (if they even have a collections management system) when composing condition reports.

Ideally, a CMS would provide seamless sharing and editing of information between desktops, laptops, tablets, and cellular devices, but without some creative fixes, the flexibility is still a dream for most. While some collections management systems are moving to cloud-based storage and can be accessible from any device, the additional expense may be cost prohibitive for many, if not most institutions. A webinar titled "Dreaming of a New Collections Management System," hosted by the Balboa Park Online Collaborative in late 2020, provides just such a discussion on this topic.

The conversation in this webinar leads us to believe that software companies are lagging in upgrades for the high-functioning collections manager and registrar. This is a topic for another publication, but a well-designed CMS would be the ideal solution to digital condition reporting without the added expense and time-consuming learning curve that is sometimes required to perform this task.

Aside from time devoted in an office to create and complete a condition report, the most reliable way to tap in to one's CMS using a mobile device is through a remote desktop application. There are some free options as well as fee-based apps for using a remote system. To clarify the process, one can use the software to take over the use of one's computer from any location on a separate device such as a tablet or laptop. The user is manipulating the office computer exactly as one would if sitting in front of it. Assuming that the internet connection is strong, a vast amount of work can be achieved from other locations by remotely accessing one's computer.

While this chapter acknowledges that digital condition reporting can be performed in various ways, a recent survey conducted by the author to members within the Collections Stewardship Professional Network of the American Alliance of Museums in late 2020 shows that most registrars are not enamored with the products available. Some respondents shared that they use a variety of methods, which include a word-processed document converted to a PDF and manipulated in a PDF-editing app, while others use their tried-and-true paper-based forms.

One hundred percent of survey respondents (out of fifty-five responses) still send paper condition reports for their traveling exhibits, with a few sharing that they hope to go with a digital format in the near future. Some have tried the digital format in the past but may now only use it for specific traveling exhibitions.

Some respondents shared comments that referred to hindrances by going digital. Realized hindrances include poor internet service in a building or out on location, poor screen quality in the natural daylight when condition reporting outdoor sculpture, and budget restrictions that would impact the ability to purchase a subscription to a condition-reporting app. Perceived hindrances include time invested in researching multiple digital platforms and learning new applications, the inability to sketch and make freehand notations on paper, and finally, assuming the person on the receiving end of the digital report has the same knowledge and understanding of the software.

In addition to registrars, collection managers, and conservators, object professionals, which includes preparators, commercial gallery dealers, and shippers of fine art and historical objects, also must create condition reports. This group includes nonprofit as well as for-profit entities and creates a large pool of individuals who can and do make use of digital condition reporting. The author's survey only includes responses from museums, most of which are nonprofit and education-driven, thus limiting the pool of respondents. The very nature of being nonprofit continues to drive the use of time-saving, low-cost methods.

One would think that age, time invested in the profession, and time available on the job would drive the interest in digital condition reporting. These factors do not necessarily seem to be the driving force. Time, budgets, continuity, and the sheer fact that museum collections include a vast array of object types seem to be the main reasons that museum professionals are hesitant of the digital process. The concerns of using the digital platform parallel the issues that museum professionals encounter when using a collections management system. Object professionals would like to have a one-size-fits-all solution but find it hard to do so when comparing descriptive conditions for a painting, a suit of armor, a plant specimen, a kinetic sculpture, a historic house, a car, a railcar, a diamond brooch, etc. Some find it impossible to make their square object fit into a round hole, so to speak, while others find a pattern of statements or standardization to make the process work for a large group of objects.

A well-created condition report contains tombstone information about the object and images with markups indicating areas of change or concern. Other pertinent information that may be included can refer to an exhibition plan, shipping, and conservation work to be executed.

Digital condition reporting has encountered some growing pains throughout the object care industry. While many want an industry-wide standard, others still lack essential internet support, and just the time necessary to learn a new system. Experimenting with different systems requires a designated amount of time and the execution of multiple reports on the various platforms to enhance one's knowledge of the process.

AUTHOR'S NOTE

The registrar's condition reporting method is a personal or departmental choice, and while digital technology has been a part of record keeping for at least thirty years, mobile condition reporting is fairly new to the field. As of yet, the museum industry cannot deem one method superior to another, and the author recommends experimentation to determine preference.

The format of this chapter also does not allow for a step-by-step approach because each method can be varied. Software applications will change as updates are created and can therefore provide a language within the software that can streamline the process, and become synonymous or divergent from one another.

For example, in selecting a condition description such as the word *stain*, each application may provide a differing way of documenting the level of intensity, tonality, and degree of damage and/or allow the registrar to draw a freehand shape or drop a premade box or circle over the area of damage. While this difference is minor, it is still an element that requires familiarity from the user.

The author chooses not to recommend one software application over another to avoid the promotion of a commercial product. Most companies will offer interested individuals a few sample reports to complete so that one is not purchasing reports blindly.

DIGITAL CONDITION REPORTING METHOD OPTIONS

Non-Subscription-Based Options (Low or No Cost)

Create a document in a word processing application, save as a PDF, share with a PDF-editing application, and make notations. This document can be shared through multiple formats and saved for archiving or continual editing.

Collections Management System

Most collections management systems have a condition report component and can be used through the software's cloud-based sharing on a mobile device or through remote desktop access.

Subscription-Based Applications Dedicated to Condition Reporting

Articheck can be found at www.articheck.com.
Art Report can be found at www.artreport.fr.
Horus Condition Report can be found at https://horus-conditionreport.com.

Subscription-Based Exhibit Planning Applications That Include Condition Reporting

Exhibii can be found at https://www.exhibii.net.

TERMINOLOGY

App: Computer software or application (app) allowing one to perform a task.
Cloud: Data storage retrieved through the internet.
CMS: A Collections Management System stores museum or collection object information.
CSAAM: The Collections Stewardship Professional Network of the American Alliance of Museums is a professional museum group that provides a network for those in object care and management.
PDF: Portable Document File.
Remote Desktop: Describes a computer program that allows one to access or control a computer in another location.
Word Processing Document: A document created in a word processing application.

BIBLIOGRAPHY

Alex Kron, moderator. "Dreaming of a New Collections Management System." Webinar from

Balboa Park Online Collaborative, San Diego, CA, December 3, 2020. https://www.youtube.com/watch?v=lMzxR0A5eI4.

Rodgers, Tommie. Survey of the Collections Stewardship Professional Network of the American Alliance of Museums. December 2020.

4

Archaeological Artifacts

Elise V. LeCompte

Archaeological artifacts are, by definition, material remains recovered from burial in an earthly deposit by the process of excavation. Artifacts can be divided into three broad categories of material composition: *inorganic* (e.g., ceramic, glass, metal, stone); *organic* (e.g., wood, plant fiber, skin, textile); and *inorganic/organic composite* (e.g., bone, horn, antler, ivory, shell, modern synthetic). An artifact can be constructed of one single material, such as a stone projectile point, or it can be a combination of several different materials, such as a metal hoe found hafted to a preserved fragment of a wooden handle. Most archaeological artifacts, when recovered, represent only a small fragment of the original object.

The condition of an archaeological artifact is affected by several factors:

- *Prior Use*: Artifacts may have been damaged before deposition. Many objects are discarded because they are broken; once thrown away, they may survive to become part of the archaeological record.
- *Burial Conditions*: Material items suffer damage as a result of being buried. Archaeological artifacts are exposed to complex environmental variables. Soil and climatic characteristics of the archaeological deposit, such as pH and moisture content, determine which types of materials are preserved.
- *Excavation and Recovery*: For those remains that are preserved, the nature of the deposit also determines how deteriorated the materials are when they are recovered. The process of excavation itself often leads to subsequent deterioration of the item, especially organic remains. In a burial context, objects reach a certain equilibrium with the surrounding matrix. When excavated, they must adjust to an entirely new set of environmental conditions. In addition, poor handling during excavation may result in damage to the artifact.
- *Analysis and Curation*: Once recovered, artifacts may suffer damage when they are processed in the laboratory or during analysis. Again, this is often the result of readjustment to new environmental conditions or of improper or careless handling. Finally, methods of curation and exhibition can affect the condition of archaeological artifacts adversely.

Archaeological objects can be deceptively fragile. Depending on how an artifact reacts to conditions in a particular deposit and how it equilibrates with its curatorial environment, it may be quite well preserved or extremely fragile. Objects may look sound on the outside, but may be badly deteriorated on the inside. Wooden artifacts that come from waterlogged deposits are good examples. Their surface structure may appear intact, but

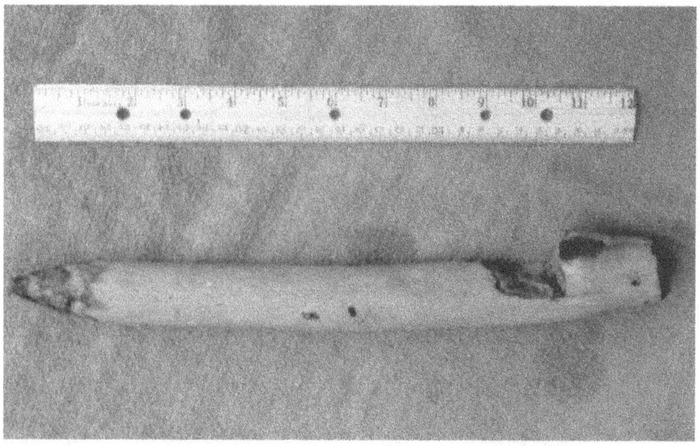

Figure 4.1. Preserved wooden stake from an archaeological deposit on Hontoon Island, FL (Site 8VO202).
Source: Elise V. LeCompte

underneath they have undergone a complex process of deterioration that leaves them vulnerable to complete collapse once they are removed from the waterlogged environment. Always assume that any archaeological artifact is more fragile than it looks. Objects are also subject to inherent vice, especially if constructed of more than one material. For example, the bone handle of a knife may be split by corrosion of the iron blade.

TERMINOLOGY

Because of the wide variety of items covered by the term *archaeological artifact*, it is impossible to list the many materials and manufacturing techniques exhibited by these objects. A few of the more basic terms and object definitions are included here. For further information, review the other chapters and bibliographies in this handbook as well as the sources listed in this chapter's bibliography.

Applied relief: Relief decoration attached to a surface after it has been formed. Common with ceramics, glass, and wood.

Artifact: Object that has been made or modified by humans, or is the result of human activity.

Bevelled: Cut or shaped to an angle other than a right angle. The area that is so shaped is called the *bevel*.

Burnished: Polished, smooth surface finish; done by rubbing a ceramic vessel before firing with a hard, smooth object such as a rock. Burnishing is also a technique applied to metals.

Carved: Technique in which material is cut away from the surface or the body of the object. It can refer to a decorative treatment or a manufacturing technique.

Cast: A manufacturing technique in which a shape is formed by pouring a liquid material into a mold. Can apply to ceramics, glass, and metals.

Cordage: Any cord, rope, or string that is made by twisting fibers together.

Cutting Edge: The edge of the tool that is used to do the cutting.

Debitage: Waste left from toolmaking. Commonly used to refer to lithic, shell, and bone toolmaking remains.

Effigy: An object bearing the likeness of an animal or human.

Embossed: Decorated with designs and patterns that are raised in relief above the surface of the object.

Engraved: A decorative technique in which designs are cut into the surface of an object by a sharp instrument.

Etched: A decorative technique in which designs are produced by coating the surface with an acid-resistant material, scratching the designs into the surface, and then exposing them to the acid.

Facetted: A process in which small, polished planes are cut on the object's surface. A *facet* is one of these cuts; it can be round, oval, ovoid, or rectangular. Common to glass, stone (especially gems), and some shell.

Firebloom, Firecloud: Darkened area on a ceramic vessel's surface resulting from uneven firing and the deposit of carbon in the pores during firing.

Flash: Narrow ridge of metal that protrudes from the object along the mold line. It occurs on cast or molded objects. Same as *joint-line* or *casting-seam*.

Fragment: Archaeological term for the broken piece of any object, except ceramics (see *potsherd* below).

Gilded: A technique in which goldleaf, gold paint, or gold dust is applied to the surface of an artifact. *Gilt* is the term used to refer to the applied gold itself. Common to ceramics, glass, and wood.

Impressed: Decorative technique used on ceramics in which the imprint of a tool is pressed into the surface of the object. The tool can be natural (e.g., shell, reed, corncob, animal teeth or bone, finger, fingernail) or manufactured (e.g., piece of mat, textile, string). Common types include *cord marked, fabric impressed, net marked*, and *cob marked.*

Incised: Decorative treatment in which lines are cut with a pointed implement.

Inclusion: Particulate matter present within the body of the object. It can be either an intentional addition or an accidental occurrence.

Lithics: Archaeological term for stones and stone tools.

Maker's Mark: The mark or symbol placed on an object by the maker or manufacturer. It identifies the individual who, or the factory or company where, the object was created.

Molded: The process of forcing a material (e.g., clay, glass) into a mold to create a desired shape. Done with air pressure (as with mold-blown glass) or with pressure exerted by a plunger (as with mold-pressed ceramics and glass). Can apply both to the body of the object and to its decoration. Common to ceramics and glass.

Mounted: Description of an object attached to a support and arranged or assembled for use, examination, or display.

Potsherd, Sherd: Broken fragment of pottery. Sometimes spelled *shard.* A *rimsherd* is a potsherd that includes a portion of the rim of the original vessel. A *body sherd* comes from the body of the vessel.

Projectile Point: Stone tool hafted (i.e., lashed) to a spear, dart, or arrow. Terminology used to describe its parts are as follows: *apex* or *tip*; *base*; *blade* (i.e., the body); *shoulder*; *stem* or *tang*; *blade edge* or *lateral edge*; *notched (corner*, *side*, or *basally)*; *flute* or *hafting channel* (i.e., rounded groove that extends from the base up to about the midsection of the point); and *beveled* or *serrated edge*.

Punctated: Decorative treatment used on ceramics in which depressions are punched with a sharp or pointed instrument.

Seam: Area where two pieces of material are joined together. With a *lap seam*, the two pieces overlap. In a *folded* or *grooved seam*, the two pieces are folded around each other.

Silvering: A technique in which the surface of an object is covered with a silver amalgam.

Stamped: Surface decoration produced by striking the object with a die or a carved or textured object, such as a fabric-wrapped or carved paddle. Common types include *simple stamped, check stamped, complicated stamped, roulette stamped*, and *rocker stamped.* Used on ceramics, metals, leather, and wood.

Stippled: A decorative technique in which the surface is covered with a series of small dots.

Tinned: A technique in which the surface of an object is covered with a fine layer of tin. Mostly used on other metals, but sometimes found on wood, as well.

Temper: Mineral or organic material added to clay to improve its working, drying, or firing properties. Different types of temper include bone, chalk, plant fibers, shell, sponge spicules, limestone, mica, quartz, grog (crushed or ground-up prefired clay or potsherds), sand, and grit.

Transfer: Surface-applied design. Common to ceramics and glass. Called *transfer print* when used with ceramics.

Type: Formal classification scheme that specifies a set of inclusive, associated attributes, and results in the creation of a class of objects.

Type Specimen: Specimen on which a formal classification scheme (or definition) of a type is actually based.

Working Edge: The edge of a tool that is used to shape another material (e.g., the bit of an adze or celt, the pounding edge of a hammer, the cutting edge of a knife or axe).

HANDLING

As mentioned, archaeological artifacts can be deceptively fragile. Therefore, it is important to follow the standard guidelines for proper handling of museum objects (see the chapter on general condition reporting).[1]

Some objects, especially ceramics, may be reconstructed by cross-mending excavated fragments in the laboratory. The seams between the mended fragments, called *joins*, are highly susceptible to failure and separation. Therefore, it is important to examine reconstructed objects carefully before picking them up in order to determine which areas may be unstable and need extra support. It is not a good idea to hand-carry mended or reconstructed objects; instead, put the item in a padded tray or box. Some lithic remains can be extremely heavy. Try to assess the weight of the object before moving it and get extra help if needed.

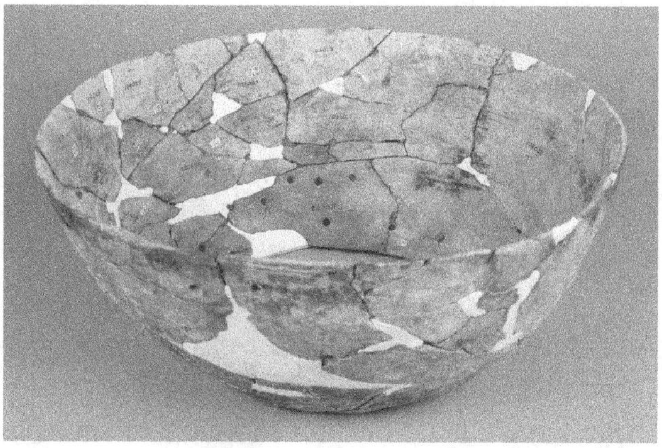

Figure 4.2. St. Johns plain pot reconstructed by cross-mending individual sherds.
Source: Florida Museum of Natural History

Surface decorations, such as slip-on ceramics, and accretions of associated materials, such as fibers of basketry preserved in corrosion products on metal artifacts, are often fractured and friable. They may be easily dislodged by rubbing or the application of pressure. Chemical and physical weathering of the surface often leaves archaeological artifacts cracked, crizzled, splintered, powdery, or flaky. Some conservation treatments, such as the electrolysis of metal pieces, leave the surface rough and uneven. In these cases, objects require careful handling to avoid abrasion and loss of the original surface material.

The practice of wearing gloves when handling archaeological material is one not often observed by archaeologists during excavation and laboratory processing. Unfortunately, this has led to a very casual attitude regarding the use of gloves when handling curated items. Many archaeological materials such as metal, porous stone, or unglazed ceramics, once cleaned, are easily damaged from oils on the skin. Therefore, it is good policy to require that archaeological artifacts in museum collections be handled with gloves. Due to the nature of their deteriorated surfaces and the possible presence of toxic residues and additives, archaeological objects are best handled with nitrile gloves.

EXAMINATION

It is important to examine all surfaces of archaeological artifacts. Look for surface decorations, finishes, and construction techniques. Identify old repairs or restorations, which are often frail and subject to failure. Check for tool or use marks, maker's marks, inscriptions, and labels. Use a flashlight to look into crevices, underneath handles and rims, and underneath bases. This examination is crucial for metal artifacts, since these are areas where active corrosion is likely to occur.

Ultraviolet light can reveal the presence of adhesives, resins, or fills that are not part of the original artifact.[2] Infrared light can be extremely

Figure 4.3. A sixteenth-century brass clasp prior to conservation, displaying areas of active corrosion.
Source: Elise V. LeCompte

helpful in detecting designs or decorations barely visible or imperceptible to the naked eye.[3] Xeroradiography (sometimes called x-radiography) can reveal the presence of underlying cracks and voids, and invisible inscriptions and decorations.[4] Although examination with ultraviolet, infrared, and X-ray lighting is outside the realm of basic condition reporting, it may be advisable for particular archaeological artifacts. This is especially true if they are going to be subjected to the stresses of traveling or if underlying designs are suspected to have been preserved.[5]

It is important to measure and record the weight of an artifact, since any change in weight indicates a change in the object's condition. This is especially true for organic materials (e.g., wood, bone, skin) where weight gain or loss can indicate fluctuations in moisture content and thus changes in structural condition. Archaeological convention dictates use of the metric system of measurement.

DOCUMENTATION

In general, it is standard practice in condition reporting to record each object on a separate form. Due to the size and scope of most archaeological collections, this is not a realistic proposition. To save time and effort, artifacts with the same catalog number that match in description and condition can all be recorded on the same form; make sure to indicate the number of items being examined. For loans and exhibits, each artifact should have its own individual condition report. This is especially important for traveling exhibitions, where each condition report serves as a cumulative record of what happened to the artifact as it traveled.

The artifact name listed in the condition report should conform to common classification and typological schema developed by the archaeological community. For example, there are extensive regional classifications for naming Native American ceramics and stone projectile points. Historic period ceramic types are known by the names given to them by their manufacturers.

Since most archaeological artifacts, when recovered, are fragments of the original item, they can be difficult to identify or describe. In this case, consult references, such as those listed in the bibliography, covering that specific type of object or material to help identify the artifact. If an artifact is broken, it should be recorded as one object with *x* number of fragments.

The material composition of the artifact should be identified as specifically as possible. For example, list the type of stone or metal or the species

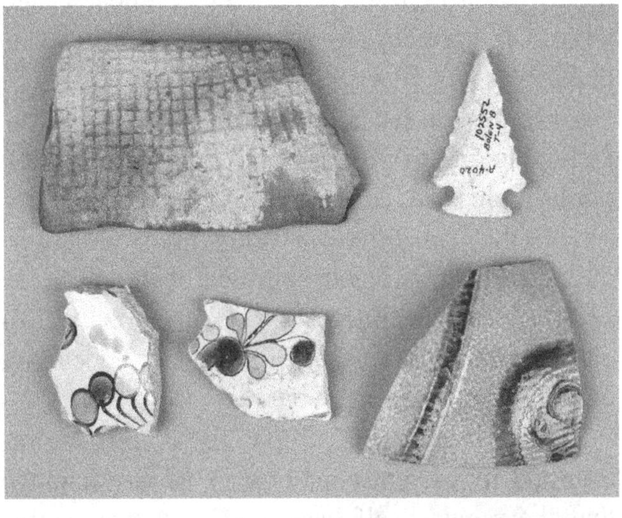

Figure 4.4. A St. Johns checked stamped sherd and a Boien-beveled projectile point (common ceramic and stone projectile points found in Florida). An Abo polychrome majolica sherd.
Source: Florida Museum of Natural History

of plant or shell. If a material cannot be identified exactly or the identification is uncertain, the examiner should use the generic class name of the material with a modifier, such as "unidentified metal" or "wood, unknown species," or a question mark, such as "earthenware, faience?"

When describing surface decorations, finishes, or construction techniques, use the terms that are standard for that particular class of artifact. Common terms for surface decorations on pottery are incised, punctated, and stamped. The word *patina* describes a surface finish on glass and metals. Standard terms for ceramic construction include *coiled* and *wheel-thrown.*

Construction terms for glass include *blown* and *molded.* Consult references (either within this handbook or its bibliographies) covering a specific type of object or material to help identify these features.

Many archaeological artifacts have some kind of tool or use marks on them. These kinds of distinctive patterns can tell a lot about the construction and prior use of an individual artifact. Maker's marks, inscriptions, and labels provide important historical data about an artifact. It is important that such marks with their descriptions and their locations be recorded on the condition report. Consult references, such as those listed in the bibliography, to help identify tool marks, maker's marks, inscriptions, and labels.

Make sure to list all colors present on an artifact, including variations of the same color if they exist.[6] Prehistoric ceramics provide a good example; as they are often unevenly fired, variations in color occur across the surface of the piece. In addition, the substrate of a sherd may be a different color than the surface of the sherd, depending on the firing temperature.

Record the nature of any repair or restoration and its current condition. Note any damage that the repair itself has caused, such as stains or adhesive residues. If easily identifiable, note what materials were used to conduct the repair or restoration. Common types of adhesives and

Figure 4.5. The sherd on the left shows a firebloom; the sherd on the right shows the differences in color that can occur between the substrate and the outer surface of a ceramic sherd.
Source: Florida Museum of Natural History

coatings used on archaeological objects include the following: animal glue; cements (e.g., Duco); cyano-acrylic glues (e.g., Krazy Glue); epoxies; gums; shellac; varnish; and white glues (e.g., Elmer's). Plaster fillings, metal rivets, and metal staples are sometimes found in ceramic and metal artifacts. If a material cannot be identified specifically, use terms such as *resin-like substance* or *glue-like material*.

Archaeological artifacts often have no obvious point of reference (that is, no proper left and right or obverse and reverse). In these cases, it is up to the examiner to set a standard point of reference. It may be helpful to use the location of a label or a catalog number as the standard point of reference. The location of an appendage, such as a handle, can be arbitrarily designated as the proper left or right side of an object. Make sure to record whatever decision is made in the condition report, for future reference.

For small artifacts such as potsherds, projectile points, and glass fragments, drawings can be made by tracing the outline of the artifact and then sketching in damage and other relevant details. With certain artifacts, it is better to make a good line drawing than to rely on photographs. For example, with wet organic remains, photographs are unable to adequately capture detailed features like surface decoration, small cracks, dents, tears, or old repairs.

As is done when describing their condition, similar types of artifacts should always be drawn or photographed with the same orientation. For example, a projectile point is best illustrated with the base of the point at the bottom of the image.

Several different methods for describing the location of defects and damage can be adapted for use with archaeological artifacts. A zone system (see the chapter on general condition reporting) works well for two-dimensional artifacts such as projectile points, potsherds, and some metal and glass fragments. Another technique is to trace the artifact on graph paper and use the printed grid to set up a zone or matrix. Details of construction, identification, and condition can be marked on illustrations with crosshatching, shading, or other codes. A key to their meaning should be provided either on the illustration itself or somewhere in the body of the condition report (Florian et al. 1990:212).[7]

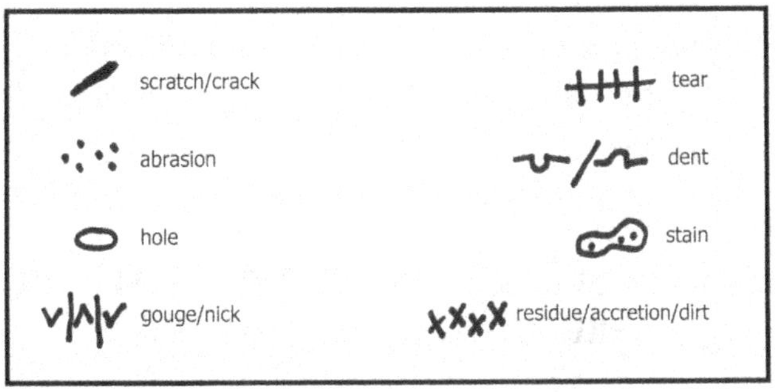

Figure 4.6. Examples of condition codes.
Source: Elise V. LeCompte

One of the easiest and clearest methods used in the past to show the location of damage on a three-dimensional archaeological artifact was the use of a transparent overlay placed on top of a photograph. Defects and damage were then traced right on the overlay. In order to indicate where the overlay should be placed on the photograph, the overlay was marked in some manner—either by marking the outline or corners of the photograph on the overlay or by marking where the top and bottom of the pictured artifact should be centered. For an artifact with extensive damage, a series of overlays (each showing one area of damage or one defect) were placed over one photograph. With the advent of digital photography, this technique was revolutionized. Defects and damage can now be marked directly on a digital image using photo-editing software (e.g., Adobe Photoshop), or by importing the image into a word-processing program (e.g., Microsoft Word) or presentation program (e.g., Microsoft PowerPoint). Using drawing tools available in the software (e.g., circle, square, oval, line, arrow), damage and defects can be easily identified.

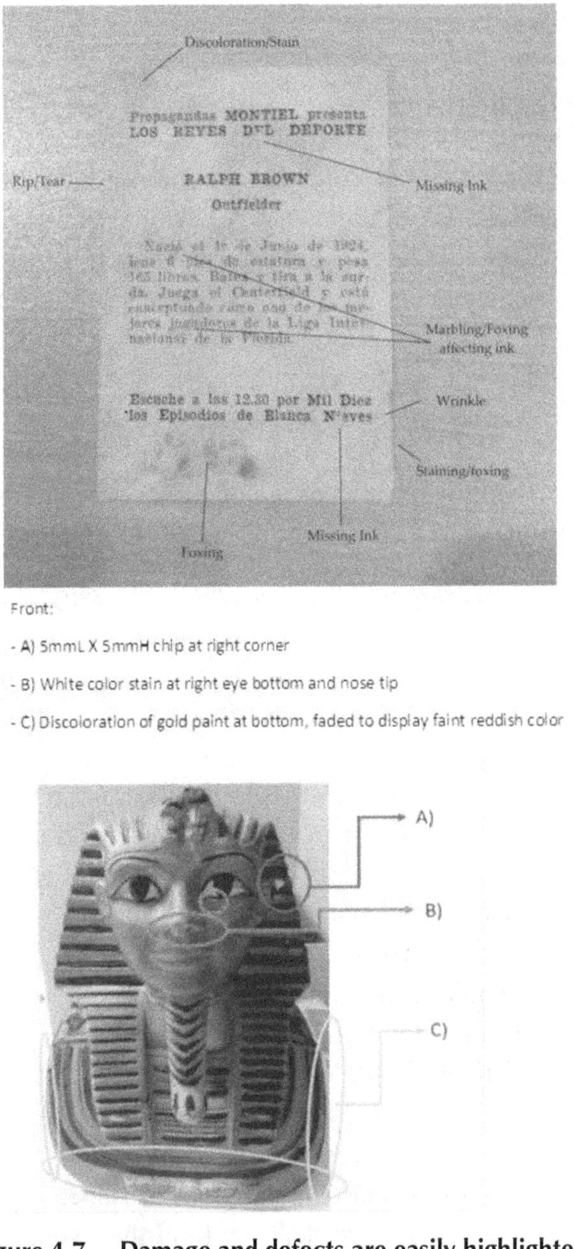

Figure 4.7. Damage and defects are easily highlighted using the drawing tools in Microsoft Word.
Source: Elizabeth McCoy and Lim Xin

Photographs should be printed in a large format so that areas of damage can be seen clearly, and should include any identifying numbers (e.g., catalog number), a metric scale, and a color standard card.

CONDITION REPORT FORMS

The sample condition report forms included with this chapter are the ones used by the Anthropology Division of the Florida Museum of Natural History.[8] They show a typical format for condition report forms for archaeological collections. The FLMNH-AD Artifact Condition Report Form is used for the original condition report. The FLMNH-AD Maintenance Addendum to Original Artifact Condition Report Form is used to record subsequent condition reports on the same artifact. It is especially useful for traveling exhibitions, where incoming and outgoing condition reports have to be generated at each venue.

Condition report forms for archaeological artifacts should contain the following information:

- *Accession and Catalog Data*: Accession number; catalog number; field number; site number; site name; intrasite provenience; other numbers (indicate what they mean and their source, if known).
- *Object Description*: Artifact name; number of pieces (if fragmented); number of items (if more than one); types and number of attachments and appendages (e.g., handles, lids); measurements; weight; material composition; technique of construction; types of surface decoration or finish; tool or use marks; other distinctive marks (e.g., maker's marks or inscriptions); color(s).
- *Condition/Damage/Problems*: Overall condition of object; condition of surface; accretions or surface deposits (and their source if determinable); condition of substrate; areas of weakness or instability; any indications of insect activity; location and size of any kind of defect or damage; areas that may become problematic in the future.
- *Previous Repairs or Restorations*: Presence of surface coatings, infilling, adhesives, or added pigments; presence of any added supports; stability of surface coatings, old mends or joins, and added supports; whether repairs are "native" or a result of post-collection restoration or conservation treatments, if determinable.
- *Details of Examination*: Use of any special type of lighting (e.g., ultraviolet, infrared, x-radiography); type and power of magnification.
- *Attached Records*: Photographs; slides; drawings; sketches; any other kinds of illustrations or relevant documents.
- *Other*: Recommendations or special requirements for handling, packing, display, and storage; indication of whether artifacts need to be examined by a conservator; examiner's name or initials; date of examination.

SAMPLE CONDITION REPORT FORMS AND INSTRUCTIONS FOR COMPLETION

Instructions

1. *Acc. No.* stands for accession number.
2. *Cat. No.* stands for catalog number.
3. *Prov.* stands for intrasite provenience.
4. *Other Nos.*: If other numbers are present, indicate what they mean and their source if known.
5. *Frags.* stands for fragments. *Pcs.* stands for pieces.
6. *Artifact Name*: Use proper typological terms.
7. *Dimensions and Weight*: Use metric conventions.
8. *Construction Technique*: Describe the construction technique using terms appropriate to the specific class of artifact. (See the glossary.)

FLMNH-ANTHROPOLOGY DIVISION
Artifact Condition Report Form

Acc. No. ________ Cat. No. ________ Field No. ________ Site No. ________ Site Name ________

Prov. ________ Other Nos. ________ No. of frags./pcs. ________

Artifact Name ________ Dimensions ________ Weight ________

Artifact Description:

A. Materials
Inorganic
Metals
___ copper, brass, bronze
___ gold
___ iron, steel
___ lead, pewter
___ silver
___ tin
___ other ________

Nonmetals
__ ceramic, type ________
___ glazed, type ________
___ slipped
___ unglazed
___ clay, terra cotta
___ stone, type ________
___ glass
___ other ________

Inorganic/Organic
___ bone, species ________
___ shell, species ________
___ antler, species ________
___ horn, species ________
___ ivory, species ________
___ daub
___ rubber
___ plastic
___ celluloid
___ other ________

Organic
___ wood, species ________
___ bark, ____ root, species ________
___ cordage, fiber species ________
___ plant, species ________
___ leather or skin, type ________
___ cloth or textile, type ________

B. Construction Technique:

C. Surface Decoration/Finish:

D. Distinctive Marks
___ Tool marks ________
___ Use marks ________
___ Maker's marks ________
___ Other ________

Figure 4.8. Artifact condition report form.
Source: Florida Museum of Natural History

9. *Surface Decoration/Finish*: Describe the type of surface decoration and/or finish using terms appropriate to the specific class of artifact. (See the glossary.)
10. *Distinctive Marks*: Describe the marks and record their location.
11. *Color(s)*: If more space is needed, attach an additional page.
12. *Condition*: A brief description of the extent of the damage can be noted beside the checked condition/damage in this section. If more space is needed, use section I instead.
13. *Comments, Recommendations, Requirements*: Use this section for any general comments or notes, and to record recommendations or special requirements for handling, display, and storage.
14. *Location and Extent of Damage*: Describe the location and extent of the damage in this section. Use this space for sketches also.
15. Attach any photographs, illustrations, or other relevant documents to the condition report as necessary.

INSTRUCTIONS FOR COMPLETING THE FLMNH-ANTHROPOLOGY DIVISION MAINTENANCE ADDENDUM TO THE ORIGINAL ARTIFACT CONDITION REPORT FORM

1. *Acc. No.* stands for accession number.
2. *Cat. No.* stands for catalog number.
3. *Loan No.*: This could be an incoming loan number, an exhibit loan number, or an outgoing loan number. The loan type will be obvious by the form of the loan number.
4. *Artifact Name*: Use proper typological terms.
5. *Location and Extent of Damage*: Describe the location and extent of any additional damage that has occurred since the last condition report was completed. (This could be the original condition report or a prior maintenance addendum condition report.)

FLORIDA MUSEUM

FLMNH-ANTHROPOLOGY DIVISION
Maintenance Addendum to the Original Artifact Condition Report Form

Acc. No. _______________ Cat. No. ____________________________ Loan No. __________________

Artifact Name: ____________________________________ Original Condition Report Date:________________

Comments, Recommendations, Requirements:

Structural:

Surface:

Biological Activity:

Condition:

Location and Extent of Any Additional Damage:

Recommendations:

Other:

DATE: _______________ RECORDER: ___________________ RECORDING INSTITUTION: ____________________________

cont. Page #_____

Figure 4.9. Addendum to the original artifact condition report form.
Source: Florida Museum of Natural History

FLMNH-AD Artifact Condition Report Form (cont.)

Date Examined ____________________

Name of Examiner ____________________

E. Color (s)

Munsell Reading ____________________ Location ____________________

Munsell Reading ____________________ Location ____________________

Munsell Reading ____________________ Location ____________________

F. Condition

Structural

___crack(s), dimensions ____________________

___ corroded
___ holes
___ split
___ warped, checked

___ other ____________________

Surface

___ flaking

___ crizzled

___ powdery
___ abraded
___ gouged, nicked
___ scratched
___ stained
___ accretions, deposits, type ____________________
___ Native ___ non-Native
___ salts present
___ other ____________________

Biological Activity
___ insect, type ____________________

___ mold, mildew
___ other ____________________

Mends/Repairs/Restorations

Type

___surface coatings, type ____________________

___ infilling, material ____________________

___ adhesive, type ____________________

___ added pigments ____________________

___ other ____________________

Source

____ Native ____ non-Native
____ restoration ____ former conservation treatment

Condition
____ stable
____ unstable, location ____________________

G. Examination
___ Special lighting, type ____________________

____ Magnification, type ____________________

H. Comments, Recommendation, Requirements:

I. Location and Extent of Damage

Figure 4.9. ***(continued)***
Source: Florida Museum of Natural History

6. *Date*: Record the date of examination here.
7. *Recorder*: Record the name of the examiner here.
8. *Recording Institution*: Record the name of the institution where the object was located when the recorder filled out the maintenance addendum condition report.
9. *Cont. Page #*: Record the next page number here if there are any previous condition reports. If this is the first maintenance addendum condition report, the page number will be "2."
10. Attach any photographs, illustrations, or other relevant documents to the condition report as necessary.

CONDITION GLOSSARY

Abrasion: Mechanical wearing away of the surface caused by scraping, rubbing, grinding, or friction.

Accretion: Accumulation of extraneous material on the surface of an artifact. Can be a result of burial or accidental deposits.

Adhesive Residue: Dried or tacky remains of pressure-sensitive tape (e.g., masking, cellophane) or other bonding substances whether organic or inorganic, natural or synthetic.

Blister: Convex bulge or separation of layers appearing as an enclosed, bubbled area. Used to refer to metal corrosion.

Break: Fracture or split resulting in the separation of parts.

Bronze Disease: Appearance of powdery, light green spots (copper chloride) resulting from exposure to moisture; attacks copper and copper alloys (e.g., bronze, brass).

Byne's Disease: Reaction between calcareous specimens (e.g., shell, eggshell) and the acetic and formic acids outgassed by some storage and exhibit materials. Results in the formation of calcium acetate-formate salts, which replace the calcium carbonate. Appears as a white, crystalline, or powdery surface deposit. Specific to shell and bone.

Chalky: Like chalk in texture. Surface of the object is soft and easily damaged by scratching or rubbing. Not characterized by crystalline or powdery surface deposits. Common to shell and bone.

Charred: Burned. Some wooden artifacts (e.g., poles, posts, construction elements) often have charred areas.

Check: Partial split, usually along the grain. Often results in squarish patterns of tiny cracks. Sometimes referred to as an *alligatored finish*. Common to wood, bone (especially burned bone), rubber, plastic, and other modern synthetics.

Chip: Defect in the surface caused by material that has been broken away.

Coating: Any covering of the surface that alters its appearance, feel, and/or composition.

Coil Fracture: Smooth-edged circumferential breakage characteristic of coiled vessels in which the coils were poorly bonded, resulting in planes of weakness. Specific to ceramics.

Corrosion: Chemical alteration of a metal surface caused by agents in the environment. Corrosion may only affect an object's color and texture without altering the form, such as silver tarnish, or it may add to the form, producing blisters or crusts, such as rust on iron.

Crack: A surface fracture or fissure across or through a material. A *hairline crack* is a tiny fissure; an *open crack* is a larger fissure.

Crazing: Fine network of cracks in the surface layer of an object. Common to ceramic glazes and glass (cf., crizzling).

Crizzling: Network of fine interior cracks. Common to glass (cf., crazing).

Crease: Line of crushed or broken fibers. Common to leather, skin, and woven artifacts (e.g., basketry, textiles).

Crossmended: Archaeological term referring to the part of an object where two or more fragments have been joined back together or to a whole object thus mended.

Crumbly: Apt to crumble; easily crumbled; crumbling.

Crushed: Misshapen by pressure; having been squeezed out of shape.

Crystalline Deposit: Compound or residue that is made up of crystals or has crystallized, and is deposited on or in the object.

Delamination: Separation or splitting of layers. Common to organic artifacts (e.g., wood, leather, skin), organic/inorganic composite artifacts (e.g., bone, horn, antler, ivory, shell), and artifacts with a surface coating.

Desiccated: Completely dried.

Dirt: General term denoting any material that soils, sullies, or smirches an object. *Dust* is loose dirt generally distributed on surfaces. *Grime* is soil tenaciously held on surfaces (a *smear* and a *fingerprint* are types of local grime). A *spatter* or *run* is the result of dried droplets or splashes of foreign material.

Discoloration: Change of hue or color, often unevenly distributed.

Distortion: Warping or deformation of the original shape. Common to organic remains (e.g., basketry, leather, skin, textiles).

Dry Rot: Decay of wood caused by fungi that consume the cellulose of the wood. Leaves a soft, spongy skeleton that can collapse into a powder.

Efflorescence: Powdery or crystalline crusts on the surface. Formed when transmigrating water reacts with an artifact's chemical makeup or extraneous deposits, such as salts, in the artifact. Common to ceramics, clays (e.g., daub, adobe), porous stones, wood, bone, and shell.

Embrittlement: Decline in the pliability and suppleness of a material to the degree that damage may result from the condition. The artifact may be crumbling or fragile to the point of easily snapping or breaking. Common to organic artifacts.

Encrustation, Incrustation: Crust or hard coating.

Eroded: Surface wear due to chemical and mechanical processes.

Fading: Loss of color.

Finger Marks: Areas on an object that have been damaged by the oils in fingerprints.

Flaking: Lifting and sometimes loss of flat areas of the surface layer. Flakes are often oblong or rectangular in shape, and very thin. Common to artifacts with thin surface coatings (e.g., glazed ceramics, painted and gilded artifacts).

Fold: Turning over of the material on itself so that the front or back surface is in contact with itself. The line of flexing may or may not be creased. Common with leather, skin, and woven artifacts (e.g., basketry, textiles).

Fossilized: Condition of an object wherein minerals have replaced the original material of the object, thereby making it a fossil. For example, some bone tools may be made out of fossilized bone.

Fraying: Raveled or worn spot indicated by the separation of strands of material. Common with archaeological textiles, cordage, and basketry remains.

Gouge: Defect in the surface where material has been scooped out. A *nick* is smaller in area and depth.

Haft Wear: Surface erosion or abrasion on the haft area of a tool.

Hole: Area of missing material; a void, an opening, a hollow in or through the artifact. Often spherical in shape.

Impact Scar: Lengthwise broken area (scar) on the working edge of a tool, resulting from impact of the tool with another object. Produced by a combination of shear and tensile stress. Found mostly on tools like hammers, adzes, celts, and projectile points. Common to stone and shell tools.

Infill: Material used to replace areas of loss. Infill is often inpainted. Also called *fill*.

Inpainting: Introduction of new pigment into areas of loss in an original construction. Used to restore design or color continuity. Common on restored or reconstructed artifacts.

Iridescence: Color effect due to the partial decomposition of the surface and the formation of innumerable thin scales. Results in an uneven, flaky surface. Common to glass and some ceramic glazes. Natural iridescence (i.e., not due to decomposition) is common to some species of shells.

Loss: General term for missing areas or holes.

Mold, Mildew: Biological in nature, mold or mildew can be seen as colored, furry, or weblike surface accretions. Sometimes detected as a musty odor. Can be a problem with all archaeological collections, especially organic artifacts and waterlogged remains that have not been treated.

Patina: Colored, chemically altered surface layer (e.g., corrosion, oxidation, discoloration) caused by chemical reactions between the artifact's surface and the burial environment.

Perforation: A hole or void that penetrates through an object. Can be produced intentionally or accidentally.

Pest Damage: Surface loss, tunneling, holes, deposits, fly specks, and frass (a coarse powder made up of insect excrement and food remains; looks like sawdust) caused by insects or other pests.

Pitting: Small, irregular, shallow, pinhole-sized losses scattered over the surface of an artifact and caused by a chemical reaction such as acid erosion. Although used mostly in reference to metal corrosion, it can occur on all types of archaeological artifacts.

Powdery: Crumbling or pulverized condition. The loss of very fine, dry particles from the coating, surface, or body of the artifact.

Reconstructed: Term for an object that has been rebuilt. Missing areas are often infilled. Missing elements are often replaced with modern replications. Reconstructed objects are not restored to their original appearance (as opposed to restored objects).

Red Rot: Powdery red substance found on vegetable-tanned objects resulting from chemical reactions. Common to leather and other skins.

Residue: Accumulation or deposit of extraneous material on the surface of an artifact. May be remains from use of the object (e.g., cooked food remains). These "native" residues often provide clues about use patterns. They may also come from the burial environment or from post-excavation handling and treatment.

Restored: Object that has been rebuilt. Missing areas are often inbuilt. Missing elements are often replaced with modern replications. Restored objects are repaired so that their appearance is close to the object's original appearance or its appearance at a particular time period (as opposed to reconstructed objects).

Rust: A corrosion product found on iron. Can be brown, reddish-brown, or orange in color.

Salts: Chemical compounds produced by the combination of water with other compounds or elements. Appear as tiny crystals or powder deposits; may sparkle under bright light or magnification. Common to ceramics, clays (e.g., daub, adobe), porous stones, wood, bone, and shell.

Scratch: Linear surface loss due to abrasion with a sharp point.

Shrinkage: Distortion that causes a material to become compacted or smaller.

Snap Break: Complete break, usually along the midsection or at the haft area of a tool. Caused by the forces of impact. Common to stone and shell tools.

Spalling: Spherical or conical losses of material from the surface. Common to ceramics, glass, and stone.

Splintered: Broken or split into thin, sharp pieces.

Split: Rupture running along the grain. Common to wood, bone, and modern synthetics like rubber and plastic.

Stain: Color change as a result of soiling, adhesives, pest residue, food, oils, etc.

Stiffness: Loss of flexibility and suppleness of fibers, offering resistance to bending. Common to leather, skin, cordage, and woven artifacts (e.g., basketry, textiles).

Tarnish: A dullness or blackening of a metal surface. Used in reference to metal artifacts (e.g., silver tarnish).

Tear: Break resulting from tension or torsion. Common to organic remains such as basketry, leather, skin, and textiles.

Use Wear: Polish, striations, battering, breakage, or minor flaking that develop on a tool's edge during use.

Warping: Structural distortion in which a material is turned, twisted, or bent out of shape and is no longer flat or in plane (i.e., planar deformation of an artifact). Can be convex or concave. Most common to organic artifacts such as wood, leather, skin, and textiles.

Weathering Rind: Outer layer of an object produced by chemical reactions between the object's material and compounds in the burial deposit. Common to stone.

Wear: Surface erosion due to repeated handling.

Weeping: Reaction between water and acid that produces a wet, dripping surface. Specific to glass.

NOTES

1. Many references on basic collections care discuss the proper handling of artifacts. Nancy Odegaard's book, *A Guide to Handling Anthropological Museum Collections* (Tucson: The Western Association for Art Conservation, 1992), is

especially helpful and easy to use. Dixie Neilson's DVD, *From Here to There: Museum Standards for Object Handling*, is another excellent resource (Gainesville, FL: Art Care Tutorials, 2012; available from the *Welcome to Art Care Tutorials* webpage, http://www.artcare.biz/Pages/default.aspx).

2. For examples, see Andrew Oddy, "Introduction," in *The Art of the Conservator*, edited by Andrew Oddy (Washington, D.C.: Smithsonian Institution Press, 1992), 17–18; H. J. Plenderleith and A. E. A. Werner, *The Conservation of Antiquities and Works of Art*, 2nd ed. (London: Oxford University Press, 1971), 71, 72, 181, and 322–23; and Israel Shenker, "A Celebrated Roman Vase Has Become a 20th-Century Phoenix," *Smithsonian* 20 (July 1989): 62.

3. For examples, see Oddy, "Introduction," in *The Art of the Conservator*, 17–18; and Plenderleith and Werner, *The Conservation of Antiquities and Works of Art*, 71, 72, and 181.

4. For example, a metal disk in the archaeological collections of the Florida Museum of Natural History has the imprint of a coin's inscription preserved in the surface corrosion. Although the coin itself no longer exists, the type (and therefore the time period) of the coin was identified from the preserved inscription. This information then allowed archaeologists to estimate the date of the deposit in which the disk and other associated archaeological remains were found (a factor that was extremely important in determining the cultural history of the archaeological site). This example is reported in Jonathan Max Leader's master's thesis, "Metal Artifacts from Fort Center: Aboriginal Metal Working in the Southeastern United States" (M.A. thesis, Department of Anthropology, University of Florida, Gainesville, 1985), 54–59. For additional examples see John Larson, "Statue of the Bodhisattva Guanyin," in *The Art of the Conservator*, 180–81; N. A. North, "Conservation of Metals," in *Conservation of Marine Archaeological Objects*, edited by Colin Pearson (London: Butterworths, 1987), 210, 231, 246, and 248–49; Oddy, "Introduction," in *The Art of the Conservator*, 18–19; Elizabeth E. Peacock, "Archaeological Skin Materials," in *In Situ Archaeological Conservation*, edited by Henry W. M. Hodges, Proceedings of meetings sponsored by the Institute Nacional de Antropologia e Historia de Mexico and the Getty Conservation Institute (Marina del Ray, CA: J. Paul Getty Trust, 1987), 123–24; Plenderleith and Werner, *The Conservation of Antiquities and Works of Art*, 158, 181, 190, 228, and 285, and plates 21 and 36; Anna O. Shepard, *Ceramics for the Archaeologist* (Carnegie Institution of Washington, Publication 609. Washington, D.C.), 183; and Nigel Williams, "The Sutton Hoo Helmet," in *The Art of the Conservator*, 74–75.

5. Sources of these types of lighting are often available at local institutions such as hospitals or university chemistry and materials science departments. Many times, these institutions are more than willing to help a museum or repository with the examination of artifacts.

6. One trait that is very hard to qualify in a systematic manner is color. Standardized color descriptions can be determined by using the *Munsell Book of Color*; a specialized edition of this book, the *Munsell Soil Color Charts*, is very easy to use. Macbeth Division of Kollmorgen Corporation, *Munsell Book of Color*, 2 vols., and *Munsell Soil Color Charts* (Baltimore: Kollmorgen, 1976). A wide range of colors makes these books adaptable to most artifacts, and there is usually one copy of them in every natural history museum.

7. Mary-Lou Florian, Dale Paul Kronkright, and Ruth E. Norton, *The Conservation of Artifacts Made from Plant Materials* (Marina del Rey, CA: J. Paul Getty Trust, 1990), 212.

8. The FLMNH-Anthropology Division Artifact Condition Report Form was created by the author, using two other report forms as examples: one developed by Katherine Singley, archaeological conservator, and one printed in Carolyn Rose, "Ethnographic Materials," in *Caring for Your Collections*, edited by Harriet Whelchel (New York: Harry N. Abrams, Inc., 1992), 141–42. The

FLMNH-Anthropology Division Maintenance Addendum to Original Artifact Condition Report Form was created by Donna L. Ruhl, FLMNH collections manager for North Florida Archaeology and Bioarchaeology, with input from the author.

BIBLIOGRAPHY

Abbott, R. Tucker. *American Seashells*. 2nd ed. New York: Van Nostrand Reinhold Co., 1974.

Acton, Lesley, and Paul McCauley. *Repairing Pottery & Porcelain, A Practical Guide*. 2nd ed. Guilford: Lyons Press, 2003.

Bordaz, Jacques. *Tools of the Old and New Stone Age.* Garden City, NY: Natural History Press, 1970.

Brennan, Louis A. *Artifacts of Prehistoric America.* Harrisburg: Stackpole Books, 1975.

Cambron, James W., and David C. Hulse. *Handbook of Alabama Archaeology.* Pt. 1, *Point Types*, rev. ed. Birmingham: Archaeological Research Association of Alabama, 1975. http://www.gutenberg.org/ebooks/39974.

Canadian Conservation Institute. Various Dates. *CCI Notes.* Ottawa: Canadian Conservation Institute. http://www.cci-icc.gc.ca/resources-resources/ccinotesicc/index-eng.aspx.

Culberson, Linda Crawford. *Arrowheads and Spear Points in the Prehistoric Southeast.* Jackson: University Press of Mississippi, 1993.

Deagan, Kathleen. *Artifacts of the Spanish Colonies of Florida and the Caribbean, 1500–1800.* Vol. 1, *Ceramics, Glassware, and Beads.* Washington, D.C.: The Smithsonian Institution Press, 1987.

Deagan, Kathleen. *Artifacts of the Spanish Colonies of Florida and the Caribbean, 1500–1800.* Vol. 2, *Portable Personal Possessions*. Washington, D.C.: The Smithsonian Institution Press, 2002.

Denker, Ellen, and Bert Denker. *North American Pottery and Porcelain.* New York: Main Street Press, 1982.

Fennimore, Donald L. *Silver & Pewter.* The Knopf Collectors' Guides to American Antiques. New York: Alfred A. Knopf, Inc., 1984.

Florian, Mary-Lou, Dale Paul Kronkright, and Ruth E. Norton. *The Conservation of Artifacts Made from Plant Materials.* Marina del Rey, CA: J. Paul Getty Trust, 1990.

Gardner, J. Starkie. *Ironwork.* Pts.1–3. Photolitho impression with supplementary bibliography compiled by Marian Campbell. London: Crown, 1978.

Gayle, Margot, David W. Look, and John G. Waite. *Metals in America's Historic Buildings.* Washington, D.C.: Preservation Assistance Division, National Park Service, 1980.

Gilbert, Miles B. *Mammalian Osteology.* Laramie: Modern Printing Co., 1980.

Grattan, David W. *Saving the Twentieth Century: The Conservation of Modern Materials*. Ottawa: Canadian Conservation Institute, 1993.

Hiller, Bevis. *Pottery and Porcelain, 1700–1914.* New York: Meredith Press, 1968.

Hodges, Henry. *Artifacts: An Introduction to Early Materials and Technology*. 5th ed. London: John Baker Publishers, Ltd., 1981.

Keegan, William F. "Pattern and Process in Strombus gigas Tool Replication." *Journal of New World Archaeology* 6(2): 15–24, 1984.

Ketchum, William C., Jr. *Pottery & Porcelain.* The Knopf Collectors' Guides to American Antiques. New York: Alfred A. Knopf, Inc., 1983.

Kidd, Kenneth E., and Martha A. Kidd. "A Classification System for Glass Beads for the Use of Field Archaeologists." Occasional Paper in *Archaeology and History*, No. 1. Ottawa: Canadian Historic Sites, 1970.

Kovel, Ralph M., and Terry H. Kovel. *Dictionary of Marks: Pottery and Porcelain.* New York: Crown Publishers, Inc., 1953.

Kuttruff, Jenna Tedrick, et al. "Investigations of Early Cordage from Bayou Jasmine, Louisiana." *Southeastern Archaeology* 14(1): 69–83, 1995.

Larson, John. "Statue of the Bodhisattva Guanyin." In *The Art of the Conservator*, edited by Andrew Oddy, 177–89. Washington, D.C.: Smithsonian Institution Press, 1992.

Leader, Jonathan. "Metal Artifacts from Fort Center: Aboriginal Metal Working in the Southeastern United States." Master of Arts thesis, Department of Anthropology, University of Florida, Gainesville, 1985.

Luer, George M., ed. *Shells and Archaeology in Southern Florida.* Florida Anthropological Society, Publication 12. Tallahassee, 1986.

Macbeth Division of Kollmorgen Corporation. *Munsell Book of Color*, 2 vols., and *Munsell Soil Color Charts*. Baltimore: Kollmorgen, 1976.

MacDonald-Taylor, Margaret, ed. *A Dictionary of Marks: Ceramics, Metalwork, Furniture. The Identification Handbook for Antique Collectors.* New York: Hawthorn Books, Inc., 1962.

Marquardt, William H. "Shell Artifacts from the Caloosahatchee Area." In *Culture and Environment in the Domain of the Calusa*, edited by William H. Marquardt. Gainesville: Institute of Archaeology and Paleoenvironmental Studies, Florida Museum of Natural History, 1992.

Masson, Marilyn A. "Shell Celt Morphology and Reduction: An Analogy to Lithic Research." *Florida Anthropologist* 41(3): 313–35, 1988.

McKearin, George S., and Helen McKearin. *American Glass.* New York: Crown Publishers, Inc., 1948.

McKee, Harley J. *Introduction to Early American Masonry: Stone, Brick, Mortar and Plaster.* Washington, D.C.: The Preservation Press, 1973.

National Park Service. Various Dates. *Conserve-O-Gram.* Washington, D.C.: Curatorial Services Division, National Park Service. http://www.nps.gov/museum/publications/conserveogram/cons_toc.html.

National Park Service. *Museum Handbook.* Pt. 1, *Museum Collections*, rev. ed. Washington, D.C.: Curatorial Services Division, National Park Service, 1990. http://www.nps.gov/museum/publications/MHI/mushbkI.html.

Neilson, Dixie. *From Here to There: Museum Standards for Object Handling*, DVD format. Gainesville, FL: Art Care Tutorials, 2012.

Nelson, Lee H. "Nail Chronology as an Aid to Dating Old Buildings." *Technical Leaflet* 48. Nashville: American Association for State and Local History, 1968.

Neumann, George C. *The History of Weapons of the American Revolution.* New York: Bonanza Books, 1957.

Noel Hume, Ivor. *A Guide to Artifacts of Colonial America.* New York: Alfred A. Knopf, 1969.

North, N. A. "Conservation of Metals." In *Conservation of Marine Archaeological Objects*, edited by Colin Pearson, 207–52. London: Butterworths, 1987.

Oddy, Andrew. "Introduction." In *The Art of the Conservator*, edited by Andrew Oddy, 7–27. Washington, D.C.: Smithsonian Institution Press, 1992.

Odegaard, Nancy. *A Guide to Handling Anthropological Museum Collections*. Tucson: The Western Association for Art Conservation, 1992.

Olsen, Stanley J. "Fish, Amphibian and Reptile Remains from Archaeological Sites." *Papers of the Peabody Museum of Archaeology and Ethnology* 56, no. 2. 1968.

Painter, Floyd. "Pointed Weapons of Wood, Bone, and Ivory: Survival Tools of Early Man in North America." *Central States Archaeological Journal* 33(1): 62–76, 1986.

Peacock, Elizabeth E. "Archaeological Skin Materials." In *In Situ Archaeological Conservation*, edited by Henry W. M. Hodges, 122–31. Proceedings of meetings sponsored by the Institute Nacional de Antropologia e Historia de Mexico and the Getty Conservation Institute. Marina del Rey, CA: J. Paul Getty Trust, 1987.

Pearson, Colin, ed. *Conservation of Marine Archaeological Objects.* London: Butterworths, 1987.

Perry, Kenneth D., ed. *The Museum Forms Book*, rev. ed. Austin: Texas Association of Museums and the Mountain-Plains Museums Association, 1990.

Peterson, Harold L. *Arms and Armor in Colonial America, 1526–1783.* New York: Bramhall House, 1956.

Plenderleith, H. J., and A. E. A. Werner. *The Conservation of Antiquities and Works of Art*, 2nd ed. London: Oxford University Press, 1971.

Powell, John. *Points and Blades of the Coastal Plain: A Guide to the Classification of Native American Hafted Implements in the Southeastern Coastal Plain Region.* West Columbia, SC: American Systems of the Carolinas, Inc., 1990.

Purdy, Barbara A. *Florida's Prehistoric Stone Technology.* Gainesville: University Presses of Florida, 1981.

Quimby, George Irving. *Indian Culture and European Trade Goods.* Madison: University of Wisconsin Press, 1966.

Rice, Prudence M. *Pottery Analysis: A Sourcebook.* Chicago: University of Chicago Press, 1987.

Rose, Carolyn. "Ethnographic Materials." In *Caring for Your Collections*, edited by Harriet Whelchel, 138–55. New York: Harry N. Abrams, Inc., 1992.

Rowell, Roger M., and R. James Barbour, eds. *Archaeological Wood.* Advances in Chemistry Series 225. Washington, D.C.: American Chemical Society, 1990.

Schwartz, Marvin D., and Robert E. DiBartolomeo, eds. *American Glass.* Vol. 1, *Blown and Molded*, and Vol. 2, *Pressed and Cut.* New York: Weathervane Books, 1974.

Shenker, Israel. "A Celebrated Roman Vase Has Become a 20th-Century Phoenix." *Smithsonian* 20(4): 52–64, 1989.

Shepard, Anna O. *Ceramics for the Archaeologist.* Carnegie Institution of Washington, Publication 609. Washington, D.C., 1976.

Spillman, Jane Shadel. *Tableware, Bowls & Vases* and *Bottles, Lamps & Other Objects.* Vols. 1 and 2, respectively, of *Glass.* The Knopf Collectors' Guides to American Antiques. New York: Alfred A. Knopf, Inc., 1983.

Stewart, Hilary. *Indian Fishing: Early Methods on the Northwest Coast.* Seattle: University of Washington Press, 1977.

Walker, Karen Jo. "Bone Artifacts from Josslyn Island, Buck Key Shell Midden, and Cash Mound: A Preliminary Assessment for the Caloosahatchee Area." In *Culture* and *Environment in the Domain of the Calusa*, edited by William H. Marquardt. Gainesville: Institute of Archaeology and Paleoenvironmental Studies, Florida Museum of Natural History, 1992.

Whelchel, Harriet, ed. *Caring for Your Collections.* New York: Harry N. Abrams, Inc., 1992.

Williams, Nigel. "The Sutton Hoo Helmet." In *The Art of the Conservator*, edited by Andrew Oddy, 73–88. Washington, D.C.: Smithsonian Institution Press.

5

Basketry

Rachel Shabica

A basket seems like such a simple item. We all likely have them in and around our homes and don't think twice about what we put into them. Yet they serve a variety of functions. In her book *Who Is Afraid of Basketry?*, Willeke Wendrich defines the *basket* as "a class of artefact made out of vegetable fibres of limited length or with a shape which is specific to the raw material. Basketry thus defined comprises baskets; bags and mats . . . sandals; hats, and belts." Thus, a basket can be where you place your laundry, something to wear on your head, or what you take with you on a picnic. While baskets today can be made out of many things, including plastic, for the purposes of this chapter we will be focusing on the specific baskets that you are likely to find in museum collections—those that are woven without the use of looms or frames to tension the elements.

A part of Wendrich's definition that rings the most clearly is that baskets, while sometimes decorative, are more often made to be *used*. By this, then, baskets are naturally exposed to all varieties of light, heat, dry conditions, physical stress, and other elements that will evidence changes in their condition. These changes may be chemical, biological, physical, or even mechanical. Writers of condition reports on baskets therefore may need to be aware of the basket's previous function as it will often indicate how or why it is in a certain condition.

STRUCTURE

There are considered to be three basic weave structures that are commonly used to create baskets, though these are utilized in myriad combinations:

Coiling is a sewn technique in which stationary warp elements are sewn together with moving weft elements. A coiled basket often starts in the center and is sewn in successive circles.

Twining is a technique in which rigid warps are woven with multiple flexible weft strands. Variations can be made by changing the number of any of the elements at any time. Wicker work is a common variation of twining in which there is only one, flexible, and often thinner, weft element.

In *plaiting*, the warp and the weft often have similar thickness and pliability. They are woven over and under each other so that it is impossible to tell which is which.

Something to note when considering structure is that a basket is an integrated system; the integrity of the basket is intimately related to the integrity of the weave. This becomes important when documenting any structural damage, as we'll see below.

HANDLING

Many baskets look sturdy and strong. Some are, but others can be extremely fragile. Ensure that you have a safe and clean workspace that is clear of clutter and potential hazards. Because of the nature of the plant fibers that make up most baskets, it is often helpful to have a light-colored cloth on the table so you can see if the basket is shedding. Ideally wear nitrile gloves when handling, and be sure to remove all jewelry, buckles, badges, or anything else that might abrade or snag on elements of the basket.

Attempt to identify areas of potential weakness prior to moving so you may avoid them. Even if a basket has handles, always fully support it from the bottom to avoid any surprise shifting or breakage. If a basket has a detachable area such as a lid, remove it prior to moving the object and move it separately. Depending on the size and shape of the basket—for example, if it has a rounded base—you may want to ensure you have bolsters handy to keep it in place. A bolster should be made of a firm, but neutral, material such as a polyethylene foam, like Ethafoam or Volara, that won't further damage the basket. If moving the basket farther than a few feet, consider using a padded tray or cart. Always follow any handling and use policies that have been established by conservation staff at your institution.

EXAMINATION AND DOCUMENTATION

As baskets are three-dimensional, it is prudent to develop a consistent system by which all examinations will be done. Break the basket down into sections, if you will, and then systematically address each section in turn. Move from left to right, turning the basket a similar distance each time. Work from top to bottom. Measure as you go. You should take an overall measurement (height, width, diameter) with a soft tape measure—metal can cause accidental abrasion. You can also use measurements in your documentation—measure from a particularly noteworthy point such as a decorative element. In the days before ubiquitous digital photography and cell phone cameras, a sketch to provide orientation was helpful. Today, photographs can be key to helping navigate a more complete examination of your basket (but I'm still a fan of the rough sketch).

Intimate knowledge of the basket's maker or origin is not a requirement to writing a complete condition report, but it can be helpful to know the cultural group from which a basket came. It can allow you to be more precise about the materials used to create the basket as well as the manner in which it was used—both of which can inform any damage you may be documenting. Most Indigenous baskets are made with a variety of plant fibers (willow, yucca in the Southwestern United States; bamboo in the Far East), depending entirely on the environment of those creating the basket. Contemporary baskets can be made from various types of materials, including plastic, and decorative items on both types of baskets are often made from beads, shells, feathers, or other materials.

As mentioned above, since a basket is an integrated system, it is important to document the severity of any structural damage as it may indicate potential further damage to surrounding areas. Note any losses, splits, or tears in the materials. If there is an area of loss, for example, is it just one coil stitch or is it an entire row?

While knowing where a basket originates can help you identify the materials, knowing what it was used for can often help you identify sources of damage. Some damage may be structural: A burden basket may have splits or tears at handles from holding heavy loads. Other types of damage are on the surface, such as staining in a basket used for berry picking or charring on a basket used for cooking. Additional types of surface damage to look for are abrasions to fibers, accretions, mold, bloom, loss of decorative elements, or fading or discoloration of dyed or natural materials.

TERMINOLOGY

Abrasion: A wearing away of the surface, frequently caused by rubbing or friction.

Accretion: An accumulation of material, such as dirt, on the surface.

Bloom: A cloudy area on the surface that looks similar to mold.

Charring: A darkened area caused by contact with heat or fire.

Discoloration: A change to the original color of the natural materials. This could be from a stain or wear over time.

Embrittlement: A lack of flexibility and pliability caused by a breaking down of the fibrous structure, often due to water or heat damage.

Fading: A loss of color frequently associated with light exposure.

Fold: A pleat or line resulting from one part having been doubled over for an extended time.

Hole: An area in which fibers from both the warp and weft are missing.

Loss: A more general term for an area of missing fibers.

Mold/mildew: Microbial activity often observed as stains and/or furry growth, often accompanied by a musty odor.

Sheen: A polished or shiny area likely caused by oils from hands when an object is frequently handled.

Split: A crack that runs through an entire element.

Stain: An area of soiling or discoloration.

Tear: An irregular break in a woven element.

With sincere thanks to Kelly McHugh, Caitlin Mahony, and Tessa Lummis.

BIBLIOGRAPHY

Adovasio, J. M. "Textile and Basketry Impressions from Jarmo." *Paléorient* 3 (1975): 223–30.

Bernstein, Bruce, ed. *The Language of Native American Baskets: From the Weavers' View*. Washington, D.C.: National Museum of the American Indian, 2003.

Canadian Conservation Institute. "Care of Basketry." Accessed April 14, 2021. https://www.canada.ca/en/conservation-institute/services/conservation-preservation-publications/canadian-conservation-institute-notes/care-basketry.html.

Demeroukas, Marie. "Condition Reporting." In *Museum Registration Methods*, 6th edition, edited by John E. Simmons and Toni M. Kiser, 249–60. Lanham, MD: Rowman & Littlefield, 2020.

James, George Wharton. *Indian Basketry*. New York: Dover Publications, Inc., 1972.

Newman, Sandra Corrie. *Indian Basket Weaving: How to Weave Pomo, Yurok, Pima and Navajo Baskets*. Flagstaff, AZ: Northland Press, 1974.

Tanner, Clara Lee. *Indian Baskets of the Southwest*. Tucson: University of Arizona Press, 1983.

Wendrich, Willeke. *Who Is Afraid of Basketry?* Leiden, The Netherlands: Leiden University Centre of Non-Western Studies, 1991. Retrieved from https://escholarship.org/uc/item/7p51v5jz.

Young, Holly. "Basketry." In *Basic Condition Reporting: A Handbook*, 4th edition, edited by Deborah Rose Van Horn, Heather Culligan, and Corinne Midgett, 31–37. Lanham, MD: Rowman & Littlefield, 2015.

6

Ceramics

Erica Hague

CREATION

Despite being prone to breaking if mishandled, ceramics are some of the easiest pieces to care for due to their chemical stability and corrosion-resistant materials.

Ceramics are made of clay. All clay is made up of three things: silica, aluminia, and flux. Potters will vary the ratio of these three to give clay certain desirable characteristics, for instance, being less prone to cracking. Once the potter has the ratio they desire, they then form the clay into a clay body, which they will finish into a ceramic piece. The varieties of ceramic pieces can be broken down into four categories: adobe, earthenware, stoneware, and porcelain.

Adobe is an unfired and unglazed clay mixture often used for building (mud bricks), or for writing surfaces, such as cuneiform tablets.

Earthenware is a low-fired (950–1100°C) clay mixture that can be either glazed or unglazed. The unglazed pottery is soft, porous, and easily damaged. Typical colors are red, brown, black, or yellow from naturally occurring minerals in the clay, and any glazed areas are immediately recognizable. Glazes on low-fired ceramic objects form a physical, not chemical, bond with the clay.

Stoneware is a medium-fired (1100–1350°) clay mixture where the clay is often naturally vitrified or glazed. These objects are typically less porous than earthenware, much denser, and less prone to scratches. Typical colors are buff, brown, or gray in color, and if tapped with a finger, they have a distinctive ring. Glazed areas are recognizable, and the glaze undergoes temperatures high enough that they are bonded chemically to the object.

Porcelain is a high-fired (1300°C+) special clay mixture called kaolin. It must be fired under precise conditions, but it results in a completely vitrified and non-porous object, which is usually white and translucent. Porcelain objects can be made in much more complex structures, and they will ring at a higher tone than stoneware when tapped with a finger.

The firing process changes the chemical composition of the clay body by burning away carbon, sulfur, and other matter, making it hard and brittle. Objects can undergo multiple firings, and many do. Glazed ceramics typically undergo at least two firings at varying temperatures. The first firing is a "bisque" firing at about 600°C to strengthen the object, and the second firing occurs at a higher temperature to vitrify the glaze to the object.

HANDLING

Before handling any ceramic object, a workspace should be prepared. Ideally, a worktable should be padded with a soft and smooth material that is thin enough to provide the objects with stability, but thick enough to provide proper support. Polyethylene foam (Volara, Ethafoam) or clean packing blankets covered in muslin are good options. Cotton gloves are not ideal for handling glazed ceramics. Non-slip gloves (nitrile) or clean and dry hands will ensure a grip on the objects as they are moved, examined, and stored. Jewelry should be removed to prevent the objects from being scratched.

Prior to attempting to move an object, prepare a padded box or cart with which to move the object to the workspace. Take time to examine the object prior to moving and note any repair work or weak spots. Remove any loose pieces and parts such as lids, stoppers, and other pieces at this time. Do not lift the object by its handles or other protrusions, but instead, support the object from the base. Always use both hands to lift and support the object, regardless of size.

If working on or moving multiple objects on the same cart or in the same box, be sure to provide ample space and padding between the objects. If stacking plates, bowls, or cups, they should always have padding (Volara, Ethafoam) between each piece, and should be approximately the same size and weight, as well as being undamaged. Ideally, stacked items should be only two pieces high to reduce the weight and pressure on the bottom-most item, although this is not always practical for storage and transport. Be especially careful of raised decorations, gilt, and/or decorative work when handling, moving, and examining items.

EXAMINATION AND DOCUMENTATION

Each component of an object should be handled and examined separately. Take particular care with areas that appear damaged and handle the object as little as possible. Always ensure the stability of the object. If an object is top heavy or unstable, place it in a way that will increase its stability without putting more pressure on delicate areas. Repairs and adhesives sometimes fluoresce differently under black light or transmitted light. Be sure to wear UV eye protection when using a black light. Other details to document during examination include chipping, flaking, glazes, gilding, staining, and scratches.

When examining the object, be consistent and always finish examining one side before moving to the opposite side. It is easiest to find a significant detail to designate as the twelve o'clock. Work clockwise around the piece noting damage, repairs, and other details in reference to where they fall in relation to the twelve o'clock detail in a concise and precise way. Location, extent, and specifics of a damaged area should be clearly written, and include measurements, when possible, to clarify the extent of the damage. If there are no clear distinguishing marks or features to help orient the report, the accession number may be used as an orientation location, as long as this method is noted in the report.

While most collection management software packages include a digital form or entry, they should be used similar to hardcopy condition reports. Both methods should contain all of the basic information on a piece, such as the item name, accession number, creator, date of creation, dimensions, date of examination, reason for examination, and who examined the piece. A brief description, the current condition, additional notes, and a space for the examiner to sign should also be included. If applicable, space for lending/borrowing institutions to sign, along with the loan information, can be added. Any special handling instructions or additional information that does not fit within these categories should default to the additional notes section. Photographs of the object, along with detailed images of any damaged areas, should be taken and added to the database. If the object database requires additional information on items, it should be gathered at this time.

Item Name:

Creator: Accession #: Storage Location: Current Location:

Dimensions: Date of Creation: Description:

Evidence of:

○ Crazing ○ Efflorescence ○ Kiln Fault ○ Spalling ○ Vitrification

Previous / Outgoing Condition:

○ Excellent ○ Very Good ○ Good ○ Fair ○ Bad

Reported by: Date:

Current / Incoming Condition:

○ Excellent ○ Very Good ○ Good ○ Fair ○ Bad Reported by: Date:

Figure 6.1. Ceramics condition report form.
Source: Erica Hague

TERMINOLOGY AND CONDITION GLOSSARY[1]

Adobe: An unfired and unglazed clay.

Bisque: Unglazed ceramic that will be glazed and re-fired.

Bone China: Also known as semiporcelain, imitation porcelain, or soft paste porcelain. Hard, white, glassy, occasionally translucent, but composed of white clays and a glassy frit.

Clay Body: A formed, undried, and unfired ceramic object.

Crazing: Unintentional network of fine cracks in a glazed ceramic object.

Earthenware: A low-fired clay mixture that can be either glazed or unglazed.

Efflorescence: A crusty formation on a ceramic or glass object that can be powdery or crystalline. This is caused by hygroscopic salts and moisture being drawn to the surface of a piece. The moisture then evaporates, leaving the salt on the surface.

Enameling: Decorative finish painted and fired onto a glass or ceramic object.

Flux: Material added to glaze to aid in fusing the glaze to the ceramic object.

Glaze: A thin layer of silica and flux that is painted onto a ceramic object, which is then fired, resulting in the finished ceramic being impervious.

Greenware: Formed and dried ceramic objects that have not been fired.

Inpainting: Duplication or repair of damaged original decoration on ceramics or glass.

Kiln Fault: Imperfections in a ceramic object due to a deficiency in the original firing of a ceramic object.

Lead Oxide: Otherwise known as red lead, a basic flux used in early ceramic glazes.

Overglaze: Decorative glaze that has been applied over the base glaze and fired.

Press Molding: Clay that has been formed by being pressed into a mold.

Salt Glaze: A kiln-finishing technique used for stoneware that results in a thin vitreous film.

Stoneware: A medium-fired clay mixture where the clay is often naturally vitrified or glazed.

Slip: A mixture of clay and water used to cover or decorate a clay body prior to firing.

Spalling: Weakness in a ceramic object that results in the chipping off or exfoliation of the layers running parallel to the surface.

Sprigging: Molded clay ornaments that are applied onto an unfired clay body.

Terracotta: Natural clay objects that are unglazed, but once fired, have a pink to deep red color.

Transfer Printing: Technique in which an engraved copper plate is used to print a design onto thin tissue paper, which is then used to transfer the design onto a previously fired ceramic body prior to glazing.

True Porcelain: A high-fired special clay mixture called kaolin that results in a completely vitrified and non-porous object that is usually white and translucent.

Tin Oxide: An additive to lead glaze that renders the glaze opaque, such as in delft ware ceramics.

Underglaze: Decoration applied to a ceramic object prior to firing.

Vitrify: To become glassy through fusion of melting ceramic particles. Objects that are vitrified are non-porous and non-absorbent.

NOTE

1. These terms are pulled from various sources, such as (Bivins 1972); (Hamer and Hamer 1986); (National Park Service 2000); (Newman 1977); and (Phillimore 1976).

BIBLIOGRAPHY

American Institute for Conservation of Historic and Artistic Works. "Caring for Your Treasures: Caring for Ceramic and Glass Objects."

American Institute for Conservation. Undated. https://www.culturalheritage.org/docs/default-source/resources/outreach/glassandceramics.pdf?sfvrsn=14ac8810_2 (accessed 02/19/2021).

Bivins, John, Jr. *The Moravian Potters in North Carolina*. Chapel Hill, NC: University of North Carolina Press, 1972.

Buys, Susan, and Victoria Oakley. *The Conservation and Restoration of Ceramics*. London: Taylor & Francis, 2016.

Cohen, David Harris, and Catherine Hess. *Looking at European Ceramics*. Malibu, CA: J. Paul Getty Museum, 1993.

Deck, Clara. *The Care and Preservation of Glass & Ceramics*. The Henry Ford Museum. 2016. https://www.thehenryford.org/docs/default-source/default-document-library/the-henry-ford-glass-amp-ceramics-conservation.pdf/?sfvrsn=2 (accessed 02/19/2021).

Hamer, Frank, and Janet Hamer. *The Potter's Dictionary: Of Materials and Techniques*. 2016.

National Park Service. "National Park Service Museum Handbook, Part I." National Park Service. 2000. http://www.nps.gov/museum/publications/MHI/AppendP.pdf (accessed 02/19/2021).

Newton, Charlotte, and Judy Logan. "Care of Ceramics and Glass—Canadian Conservation Institute (CCI) Notes 5/1." Minister of Public Works and Government Services, Canada. 2007. https://www.canada.ca/en/conservation-institute/services/conservation-preservation-publications/canadian-conservation-institute-notes/care-ceramics-glass.html (accessed 02/19/2021).

Phillimore, Elizabeth. *A Glossary of Terms Useful in Conservation*. Ottawa: Canadian Museums Association, 1976.

Rhodes, Daniel. *Clay and Glazes for the Potter*. 2015.

———. *Stoneware & Porcelain: The Art of High-Fired Pottery*. New Zealand: Pitman, 1978.

7

Ethnographic Collections

Nicole Passerotti

The term *ethnographic collection* historically refers to the scientific description and systematic recording of people and material culture. As museum professionals shift away from terminology rooted in colonialism, the title *Cultural Heritage Collection* reflects a broader understanding of the material culture and the people who make/made, use(d), value(d), and preserve(d) these materials.

Collections that fall into this category are typically labeled by regional location and/or historical time frames. Examples include, but are not limited to, Native North American, Pre-Columbian, Oceanic, and Sub-Saharan African. While these descriptions can be useful tools for grouping cultural materials together, it is important to remember that many of these labels do not reflect the nuances of culture, time, and values. Collections that fall into this broad category also represent both historic and contemporary Indigenous groups from across the globe.

Indigenous groups have their own perspectives in the care and preservation of their cultural materials, which generally have not been recognized by standard museum practices, although this is changing. One major shift in museum practice is the consideration of the point of view of the originating source communities. This can open the door for nuanced discussions about collections care practices and a more expansive understanding of what it means to be a steward of a collection.

Cultural Heritage Collections can be decorative, utilitarian, or both, designed for everyday or ceremonial use, created to be used within a community, or sold/traded outside of the community. The value of an object can be in its function and the active use of it, or an intangible sentiment related to a song, story, or memory. Certain objects are meant to stay pristine while others are created with the explicit intent to decompose with time. Another consideration is that objects could have specific handling guidelines or restrictions, language preferences, as well as storage preferences, like facing a specific cardinal direction or whether an object should be covered from view. While many of these questions may remain unknown as you write a condition report, it is still worthwhile to consider them as you look closely at an object and record its details for future reference. In the instances where a dialog with a source community member can happen, there are online resources available for working with communities, such as the *Guidelines for Collaboration* compiled by the School for Advanced Research.

TYPES OF MATERIALS

The first step in assessing the condition of an object is attempting to identify the materials. Cultural Heritage Collections encompass a large variety of materials, many of which are covered in this book in detail, and can include baskets, ceramics, glass, metals, paint, paper, plastics, sculpture, skin and leather, and textiles, among others. You may find lists of material description such as ceramics, glass, and wood found in other chapters in this book to be helpful.

A single object may consist of a multitude of materials or a single material. It may be impossible to determine all the materials present on an object, and that's okay. Broadly speaking, material types fall into three categories: organic, inorganic, and composite.

Organic

When looking at a museum collection, *organic* refers to carbon-based materials made from:

1. *Plants* (cellulose-based): includes bark, cotton, linen, paper, plant fiber, wood, etc.
2. *Animals* (protein-based): includes claws, feathers, fur, skin, hair, horns, intestines, leather, quills, silk, wool, etc.
3. Other carbon-based materials made by chemical reactions like synthetic fabrics or plastics.

This category also includes dyes, oils, resins, waxes, etc., that are plant-, animal-, and carbon-based.

Inorganic

When looking at a museum collection, *inorganic* can be broken up into two further categories:

1. *Metal*: includes both pure and alloyed aluminum, copper (brass, bronze), gold, iron (steel), lead, silver, tin, titanium, zinc, etc.
2. *Non-Metal*: includes ceramics (glazed, unglazed), clay, glass, pigment, paint, plaster, minerals, stone, etc.

Composite

Composite refers to the mixture of both inorganic and organic materials. Examples include antler, bone, shell, teeth, and ivory, which are all predominantly inorganic materials with some organic elements like collagen.

PESTICIDE RESIDUES

Another important consideration when handling and examining objects is what may have been applied to them in the past. Museums and collectors have a well-documented history of preserving their organic (plant- and animal-based) materials with pesticides to keep unwanted pests like moths, beetles, and termites away. This type of collection was often treated with chemicals such as heavy metal arsenic compounds, mercuric chloride, and the insecticide DDT (dichlorodiphenyltrichloroethane), among others. Residues from these chemicals may remain in or on objects for decades. In addition, point tips found on arrows may have been dipped in poisons, and those residues may still exist, too. It is important to wear protective equipment such as nitrile gloves and lab coats when handling objects that may have been treated in the past with toxic chemicals. Cotton gloves are not recommended because they do not offer the protection of nitrile gloves, and the texture of the cotton can snag protruding materials. Make sure to properly discard your gloves after use.

EXAMINATION

When examining an object, it is important to have a dedicated workspace such as a padded table or cart with a clean surface and good light. Additional tools that you might find useful include: a flashlight, a soft tape measure, tweezers, long porcupine quill or bone folder, magnifying glass or optivisor, clipboard, pencil (never ink, you do not want to accidentally put a mark on the object you are examining), small plastic bags for disassociated pieces like beads or buttons, a fine-tip marker to write information on the plastic bags, and support boards or cushions for the object.

When handling an object, be aware of all the parts, including attachments, protruding elements, fringe, feathers, beads, etc., and the overall condition of each element. The goal is to record materials and condition issues without causing any further damage to the object, so being aware of areas with loose beads, brittle hair or feathers, or shattered silk will aid in your careful handling.

MATERIAL IDENTIFICATION AND DESCRIPTIONS

As noted above, the first step in examination is to identify and describe the material composition. Record the materials that you see. In instances when it is unclear, you can write "unknown" or "looks like . . ." If it is not clear, then keep the descriptions general, like "metal" instead of "silver," "stainless steel," or "lead," if you do not know. You can further describe the metal by color, shape, size, or anything else that might distinguish it further. Descriptions can include dimensions, shape, colors, whether a component is hard or soft, whether it is reflective or transparent, to name a few. It can also be useful to describe the way an object is constructed, as well as the techniques used. For example, you may notate whether a textile has machine stitching versus hand stitching, or whether a wooden tool is constructed from a single piece of wood versus three pieces nailed together.

Take a moment to consider if there is evidence of use. This could be noted in a depression or smoothness in a handle, loose seams in a particular area of a garment, or soiling patterns related to use. Evidence of use plays a role in understanding context as well as condition issues. If there is a notable repair, consider when and how it was made and what types of materials were used. The repair could be from original use and might be made with similar or contemporaneous materials, while a more recent repair might use different types of materials.

CONDITION ASSESSMENT

The materials, construction, past use, environment, storage, and display history all contribute to the current physical state of an object. When accessing the physical state or condition of an object, it is helpful to review the ten agents of deterioration:

1. *Water* exposure can cause distortion, warping, swelling, discoloration, delamination, and mold growth.
2. *Fire* exposure can cause changes to the surface, soot deposits, and discolorations.
3. *Light* exposure can cause fading, yellowing, and/or the disintegration of materials.
4. *Temperature* fluctuations and extreme highs and lows can cause chemical and physical changes depending on the type of materials, ranging from melting to brittleness.
5. *Relative humidity* fluctuations and extreme highs and lows can create mold, corrosion, and other issues.
6. *Physical force* from direct or indirect impact can cause deformation, stress, breaks, and abrasions.
7. *Dissociation* is the loss of information related to the object, including physical and intangible value.
8. *Pollutants* can deposit and collect on the surface of an object causing surface discoloration.
9. *Thieves and vandals* can remove an object from a collection, which means written and photographic records are incredibly valuable.
10. *Pests* can include, but are not limited to, rodents and insects, which can cause damage by eating materials.

A condition assessment can be broken into three main sections: an overall condition summary, the structural condition, and the surface condition of an object.

CONDITION SUMMARY

The summary addresses the overall condition of an object, how it should be handled, and answers the question: Is it stable? For consistency, it is recommended that you define the descriptive terminology used for your specific collection. Below is a general example of descriptions for an overall summary of the physical state of an object.

An object in *excellent* condition is like new and/or has no visible damage, can easily be displayed, and therefore is in stable condition.

An object in *good* condition may have minor visible damage, but is in stable condition and can still be displayed.

An object in *fair* condition has minor to moderate damage, and some issues may prevent it from being easily displayed.

An object in *poor* condition is likely unstable, cannot be displayed, and needs to be considered for conservation treatment or deaccession. Cleaning or conservation treatment should be done by or in consultation with a conservator or trained collections care specialist who is aware of the cultural ramifications, or source community members who are familiar with the materials and object.

STRUCTURAL CONDITION

Structural condition issues refer to damage that may jeopardize the structural integrity of a material or object. The goal is to describe the type of condition you see, the location and severity (major/large or minor/small), and whether the condition is active or passive.

Types of structural condition issues include brittleness, broken or missing pieces, bulges, cracks, corrosion, creases, delamination, dents, fraying, gouges, insect damage or activity, iridescence, lifting, losses, pitting, previous repairs or restorations, rusting, shattering, shrinking, splitting, tears, warping, and wear/worn. This list is not exclusive to only structural issues nor is it exhaustive.

SURFACE CONDITION

Surface condition issues refer to damage that appears on the surface, but does not jeopardize the structural integrity of the object. Surface condition issues can be aesthetically unpleasing and benign, but certain issues can develop from surface to structural issues if left unchecked. The goal is to describe the type of condition you see, the location and severity (major/large or minor/small), and whether the condition is active or passive.

Types of surface condition issues include abrasions, accretions, bleeding, corrosion, cracking, delamination, dirt, discoloration, distortions, efflorescence, fading, flaking, paint loss, mold or mildew, powdering, previous repairs or restorations, residues such as a yellowing coating, rust, scratches, soiling, stains, shedding, and tarnishing. This list is not exclusive to only surface issues, nor is it exhaustive.

DOCUMENTATION

Recording materials, condition issues, and observations from examining an object can be done in several ways. Documenting this information is a critical part of tracking and understanding the long-term needs and changes of an object. This can be achieved by words, drawings, photographic images, and annotated images. Types of condition reports range from long-form descriptive paragraphs to checklists created for a specific collection with space for notes. Reports can be handwritten on paper, created in a program like Excel, or recorded in a museum's database.

Digital photography is an excellent tool for recording and documenting current information about an object and can be used as a comparative tool in the future. As with examining an object, make sure you have a clean and clear space with the necessary boards or cushions to support the object if you need to move it around to photograph it. For the photography, including a photography scale or a small ruler aids the viewer in understanding the size of an object. Likewise, including a label in the photograph, such as a catalog number and date, is also useful for archiving. To highlight and point out specific condition issues, you can print a digital image and annotate it with colored pencils or digitally annotate it in Photoshop or similar programs. All written and photographic documentation can be stored as hard copies or digital files. Regardless of the format, all the data should be backed up.

EXAMPLE OF A CONDITION REPORT FORM

The type of collection and its priorities will guide the specific headings you will want to include in your report. This example may include headings that you might choose to exclude.

Condition Report for Cultural Heritage Collections

Accession or Catalog #:

Date Written:

Written by:

Identifying Marks:

Dimensions: L x W x H (cm or inches)

Provenance:

Cultural Affiliation:

Artist or Manufacturer:

Type of Object or Title:

Material Description: Include number of components, types of known and unknown materials with descriptions.

Previous Treatment or Repairs: Either from catalog records or noted from your observations.

Summary of the Overall Condition: Structurally stable/unstable? Can it be displayed safely? Does it require conservation treatment?

Structural Condition: Include descriptions about the type of damage, the location, the severity (major/large or minor/small), and whether it is active or passive.

Surface Condition: Include descriptions about the type of damage, the location, the severity (major/large or minor/small), and whether it is active or passive.

Include Drawings, Digital Images, and Annotated Images

Figure 7.1. Condition report for cultural heritage collections.

REFERENCES

Clavir, Miriam. 2007. *Preserving What Is Valued.* Vancouver: UBC Press.

"Guidelines for Museums | Guidelines for Collaboration." 2021. *Guidelinesforcollaboration.Info*. https://guidelinesforcollaboration.info/guidelines-for-museums/.

Institute, Canadian. 2021. "Agents of Deterioration—Canada.ca." *Canada.ca*. https://www.canada.ca/en/conservation-institute/services/agents-deterioration.html.

"ObjectsWiki." 2021. *Conservation-Wiki.com*. 2021. https://www.conservation-wiki.com/wiki/Objects#Ethnographic_Objects.

Odegaard, Nancy, Marilen A. Pool, and Alyce Sadongei. 2001. *Old Poisons, New Problems*. Tucson, AZ: Arizona State Museum, 2021.

Ogden, Sherelyn. 2004. *Caring for American Indian Objects*. St. Paul: Minnesota Historical Society Press, 2004.

Passerotti, Nicole, Caitlin Mahoney, and Beth Holford. 2019. "Condition Reporting for Museum Collections." Presentation, Cultural Survival in the 21st Century, International Conference of Indigenous Archives, Libraries, and Museums (ATALM), Temecula, CA, 2019.

Rose, C. 1992. "Ethnographic Materials." In *Caring for Your Collections: Preserving and Protecting Your Art and Other Collections*, edited by H. Whelchel, 138–222. New York: Harry N. Abrams.

"Visual Glossary—Australian Institute for the Conservation of Cultural Material." 2021. *Australian Institute for the Conservation of Cultural Material*. https://aiccm.org.au/conservation/visual-glossary/.

8

Furniture

Kathleen McClain Jenkins, revised by Misty Tilson Jackson

Furniture can be complex due to the nature of production and variety of materials that may be used in construction. When completing condition notes, one must also consider the piece's original intended function. When one thinks of furniture, one primarily thinks of wood, because the aesthetic quality of most furniture is based on the natural beauty of wood. However, many other materials, both organic and inorganic, may be used, such as marble, metal, glass, fabric, and plastic.

Most furniture falls into three basic categories based on construction and use: seating, tables, and case pieces (cabinets). Within each category, one can find a variety of specialized object types that fall within recognized stylistic periods. Specialized texts on furniture design should be consulted for construction information. Beds are a category unto themselves, but have components and characteristics in common with objects from the three other categories.

In its most basic definition, seating means a piece of furniture constructed with a seat that is raised on legs. Seating generally exhibits a greater history of abuse than other types of furniture, because it is the most heavily used. Upholstered seating routinely undergoes the wear and replacement of textiles or leather due to the fragile nature of these materials.

A table is basically a flat top supported on a base or legs. It may have a jointed frame with legs at each corner or a pedestal base with a tilting top. A table may also have a folding top or a drop-leaf top with swinging gate legs. Tables exhibit considerable variety in the types of materials used for tops or top coverings, from wood to marble to leather.

Cabinet furniture consists of freestanding objects with an enclosed space for storage. They are basically boxes fitted with doors, lids, or drawers that are accessible from the front, sides, or top. Mainly built with frame-and-panel construction, cabinets can also be made of solid slabs of wood joined together. Because many cabinets have moving components, they exhibit the stress history of their use in warped doors, sticking drawers, and damaged hinges and drawer pulls.

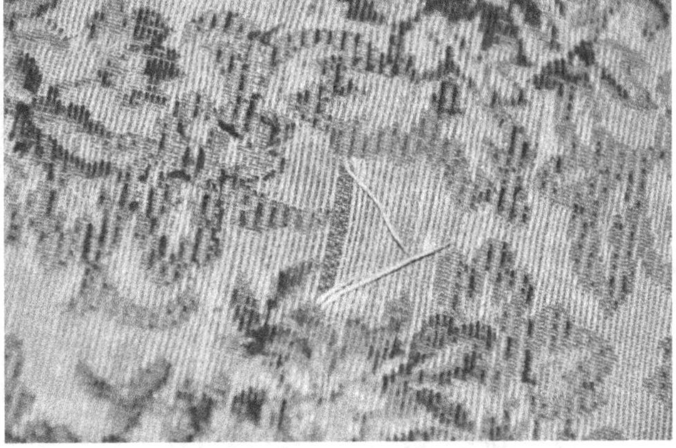

Figure 8.1. Example of upholstered fabric exhibiting fading and fraying.
Source: William H. Jackson

As an organic material, wood has a hygroscopic tendency, meaning wood will expand and contract across the width of its grain with the addition or subtraction of moisture. This tendency can cause a great deal of problems in regard to a piece of furniture's condition. The methods by which a piece of furniture is created can also affect its future condition.

Different cuts of wood react differently to environmental conditions and physical stress. Quarter-sawn boards are cut radially from the center of a log and tend to remain flat over time, but shrink in width. Through-and-through or plain-sawn boards are cut straight across the entire width of the log and have a tendency to cup. An alternative to the use of solid wood is laminated wood like plywood, which is built up of thin wood layers glued together. Plywood is better able to resist warping and cracking. Veneered wood is made up of a thin sheet of exotic wood glued over a more common wood. Veneered wood is susceptible to damage from stress movement between the veneer and the structural wood below.

Figure 8.2. Lifting of veneer on seat of bench coat rack.
Source: William H. Jackson

Fine furniture often combines organic materials with insets of inorganic materials that have very different responses to environmental conditions. One example of this is boullework, an elaborate inlay of brass or other materials into a wooden surface. The uneven environmental responses of the inorganic decoration and its surrounding organic surface make these inlays prone to lifting.

The glues and hardware used to join pieces can also affect furniture. Glues can deteriorate over time. Hide glue, a protein or animal derivative, is water soluble; fluctuating humidity can cause joints to weaken. Synthetic glues are generally not susceptible to humidity; they sometimes cause stress damage as the more hygroscopic materials around them shrink and expand. Ferrous nails and screws can rust, staining wood and weakening joints.

A finish is generally applied to a furniture piece as a decorative or protective surface treatment. These applications are highly vulnerable to change and damage, especially in their simplest forms as applications of wax or oil. The most common finishes are paint, varnish, gilding, French polish (built-up layers of shellac), graining, ebonizing (an opaque black polish), and lacquering. Varnish is susceptible to alligatoring, a crackle appearance brought on by improper drying of the finish or old age. As these coatings age, they become more brittle.

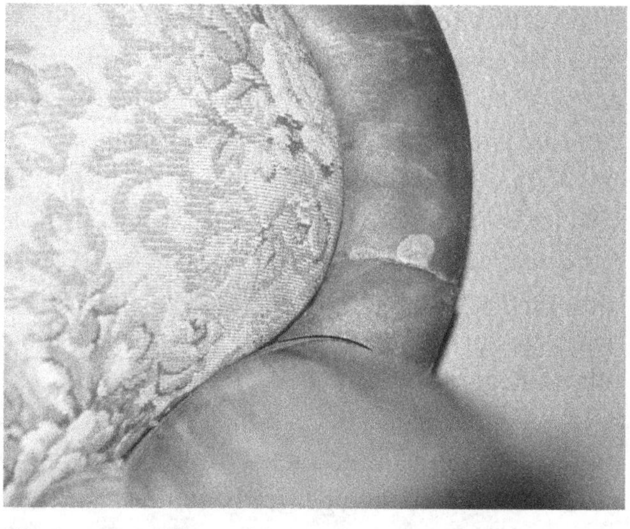

Figure 8.3. Alligatoring can be seen at the top of the settee arm.
Source: William H. Jackson

Many seating pieces are upholstered. Upholstered furniture is susceptible to light damage, which can be seen in the fading of colors and weakening of fibers.

TERMINOLOGY

The following are a few of the more technical terms involved in describing the component parts of furniture. For further information, see the bibliography.

Batten: Thin strip of wood used to support shelves inside cabinet pieces.

Bearers: Parallel wood strips attached to the bottom of a tilt tabletop to position it on its pivot; also, a cross-rail carrying a drawer.

Bevel: The slanted edge of a pane of glass or mirror.

Block: Wood piece glued onto the frame of furniture to build up thickness or to provide support.

Chevron: Any *V*-shaped pattern.

Composition: Aggregate material formed of two or more substances. Historically refers to gesso; recent furniture makers have begun to use a composite of pressed wood pieces in a binder as a substitute for solid wood. Sometimes called compo.

Drawer Stop: Internal block to keep a drawer from being pushed in too far.

Dust Board: Cover piece of wood used underneath a cabinet or between drawers.

Finial: Carved ornament at the top of a cornice or pediment on a case piece or the top of a bed post.

Frame: Rigid structural support, usually made of wood, which is the base for a piece of furniture; also, the surrounding member in a frame-and-panel construction, used as an alternative to solid wood pieces.

Fretwork: Open design, usually of geometric interlacings, cut into a piece of wood that can be solid or laminated. Types are blind fret, which is applied onto a solid wooden back, and pierced open fret, such as is found on the top of a cabinet or under the apron of a table.

Gilding: Surface decoration usually consisting of a thin layer of goldleaf or gold dust (adhered by water or oil) on a gessoed, carved surface.[1] In a silver gilt finish, silver or silverleaf is applied.

Glazing Elements: Clear glass panels, or lights, found in bookcase doors or a glass mirror over a chest of drawers. Sometimes glass elements have a beveled, or sloped, edge. Other elements include either the putty or the glazing bead, a convex molding nailed against a pane of glass to hold it in place.

Gesso: A type of plaster made from powdered chalk and size. When many layers are applied to wood, provides a hard, smooth base for painting or gilting and can be carved.

Hardware, Fittings: Usually made of brass, iron, or steel. They include castors, the small, solid wheels found beneath the legs of some furniture; catches, which hold the top down on a pedestal table; escutcheons, decorative keyhole surrounds; drawer pulls; handles; hinges; knobs; and locks.

Inlay: A decorative layer of fine material that fills specially shaped and routed surface cuts in the furniture surface. Inlays are made of materials such as mother-of-pearl, ivory, tortoiseshell, and fine woods. Boullework interlays are made of brass or horn veneers. Patterns of wood inlays include marquetry, geometric patterns in colored veneer; *parquetry*, abstract natural forms in colored veneer; and stringings, long, thin strips of contrasting woods (or sometimes brass) inlaid near an edge of a piece.

Joint: Connection between pieces of wood that can be hand-cut or machine-made, fixed or movable, held by glue or screw. Pegs or wedges are sometimes inserted to prevent movement in the joint. Common joint types include the *butt joint*, in which two pieces of wood are joined end to end, often with nails and glue without overlapping; *chamfered joint*, in which a thick wood panel fits into a frame grooved all around; *dovetail joint*, in which a dove tail-shaped part that is cut into the edge of a piece of wood fits into a corresponding cut-out shape on the piece that it joins; *dowel joint*, in which a round wooden peg fits into a hole in the adjoining piece; *halving joint*, which allows two parts to close flat against one another; *knuckle joint*, which resembles a door hinge opening on a pivot pin and is often used on swing legs below tables; *miter joint*, in which two pieces meet smoothly at a 45-degree angle in a corner; *mortise-and-tenon joint*, the strongest and most common type of joint, with a projection (tenon) fitting into a corresponding recess (mortise) in another piece and often using a wedge as a tightening mechanism; and *rule joint*, usually used for drop-leaf tables, with a half-round that disappears when the leaf is raised.

Lopers: Wood pieces that extend out to support the writing surface of a drop-front desk; also called fall-board supports.

Molding: Continuous band of decoration that can be either applied, made separately and glued on, or integral, cut on the wooden edge of the piece itself. Beading, a raised half-round, is one of the most common types of molding: closing bead molding seals the center connection between two doors on a cabinet piece, and cock bead molding is a continuous half-round applied to each edge of a drawer front. A cornice at the top of a cabinet piece is another type of molding, usually a composite of several parts. Other molding types include cross-grains, with veneer applied as molding with the graining running across its short width; gadrooning, a rope of curved flutings; ovolo or quarter-round molding; and reeding, a series of vertical, parallel, half-round moldings.

Mounting Block: Point at which a tilt-top table pivots on top of the pedestal.

Ormolu: Type of ornamented or gilded metal; an amalgam of mercury and gold applied over brass or bronze that is washed and burned, leaving only the gold on the surface.

Panel: A thin, flat piece of solid wood or plywood, used to form the "box" of a cabinet piece.

Pendant: Carved ornament hanging down from a piece, as from the edge of a table apron.

Pilaster: Wood ornamentation cut into the shape of a partial column and applied against a flat surface, such as the front corners of a case piece.

Rail: Horizontal element of furniture framing. Examples include the side rails of beds; the back rail, tenoned into the back legs of chairs; the cresting rail, doweled onto the top of the back legs of chairs; the crossrail, holding the side rails of a table together at midpoint; a hooped rail, steam bent for use in bentwood furniture; seat rails (front, back, and side), tenoned into the legs of chairs; stretcher rails, set at a low level between the legs of chairs, and H-stretcher rails, turned rails joining chair legs in an *H* configuration.

Rebate: Horizontal channel or groove along the edge of a piece.

Seat: Predominant horizontal element of a seating piece. Varieties include caned seats, rush seats, solid wooden seats, and upholstered seats. The latter includes the drop-in seat, a webbed frame padded with hair and wadding; a pincushion seat, a shallow pad on a seat frame, finished with nails or braid; and a stuffed-over seat, webbed underneath with coil springs and layers of stuffing shaped by an edge roll. Wooden seats can be solid, like a saddle seat of a Windsor chair, or a panel seat of molded or pressed plywood.

Serpentine Front: Found on a case piece, a convex curve with concave curves on either side. Also seen as a serpentine edge on tabletops.

Shoe: Piece of wood fitted along the seat rail on a chair back at the base of the splat.

Socket: Round hole in a wood chair seat; receives the spindle or leg.

Spindle: Turned piece of wood used vertically, such as on the back of a Windsor chair.

Splat: Thin wood panel placed vertically in the center of a chair back.

Stain: Pigment applied to a wood surface beneath a transparent finish.

Stile: Vertical element of a panel frame or chair back.

Turned Leg: Shaped on a lathe; the leg may be weak where it is reduced in diameter.

Upholstery: Use of fabric, leather, synthetic material, etc., to cover seats, backs, and arms of furniture. Parts of upholstered pieces include the cover or "show" fabric; the dust cover, which protects the cover from soil; an edge roll, which creates a firm edge on a chair seat; the Hessian or scrim panel, which supports the stuffing; the lining fabric, which covers and shapes the stuffing; decorative piping, which traces the seams of covers; the steel-wire double-cone coil springs; the stuffing, made of animal hair, vegetable fibers, or synthetic materials; assorted types of trim, braid, gimp, or decorative nails; wadding, a bulky layer of loose cotton beneath the show fabric; and webbing, interwoven support strips nailed to the wood seat frame.

HANDLING

Prior to moving a piece of furniture, always evaluate how it is constructed. Identify the sturdiest point. To retain a firm grip, it is best to use clean, bare hands when handling large pieces. Do not wear keys or jewelry that could scratch the finish. Any fingerprints left on the wood should be buffed out with a soft cloth immediately after handling. Gloves may snag on splinters, loose veneer, carving, or gesso. However, wear cotton or nitrile gloves when touching metals or fabrics. Also, if moving, always know the final destination and route.

Remove all detachable parts from a piece of furniture, such as drawers or marble top, before examining it. This will also lessen the weight if the piece needs to be moved. Inspect the piece for unstable or damaged portions before moving it. Be aware of vulnerable surfaces, such as gilding, inlay, and lacquers.

When a heavy piece must be moved for examination, it should always be carried with its weight distributed evenly to avoid damage. Be aware of the center of gravity. Never put a point of weakness under tension. Have an adequate number of people on hand to handle the object, being careful not to put uneven stress on its legs. Do not drag a heavy piece across the floor; dragging places horizontal pressure on joints that were designed to accept only vertical forces. Instead, lift the piece, even one that has castors, to avoid breaking joints or splitting legs. Always lift by a low part of the main case or frame, not by an attached part or ornament.

Lift chairs by the seat, not the arms. The seat rail is normally the strongest part. Use a carpeted furniture dolly whenever possible. Marble tabletops or large pieces of glass should be carried in a vertical position to avoid a stress fracture across the center. Also, old glass and mirrors are extremely brittle and should be handled with extra care.

A table should be lifted by its base. If the table is large, it can be lifted by its apron, the wooden panel that connects the tabletop and legs.

Either lock a cabinet's doors before moving it or tie twill tape around it to keep doors from unexpectedly coming open. Make sure the tape is secure but does not cut into the piece; pad corners with clean cotton padding or polyethylene foam. Pad the floor with blankets if it is necessary to lay an object on its back. When examining the upper section of a large cabinet, make sure the top is screwed to the base before opening the doors, as the redistribution of weight may pull the piece forward.

EXAMINATION

Visual examination will become easier with experience and familiarity with furniture pieces. Visual examinations aid in identifying materials and construction techniques, as well as provide a baseline condition from which to note any changes since previous repairs and treatments. Before beginning the examination, make sure you have an appropriate and adequate workspace. One of the basic tools for examining furniture is a bright handheld lamp or flashlight. Pad sharp or hard edges of tools to avoid scratching the piece. Other handy tools include:

- Pencil
- Cloth measuring tape and a pair of calipers for measuring cracks
- Small hand mirror or dental mirror for checking inaccessible areas
- Magnifying glass for closer examination of items
- Magnets, which are useful for identifying iron or iron alloys such as steel
- Spool of wide twill tape for securing cabinet doors
- Ample supply of blankets or other padding if pieces need to be laid on the floor for further examination
- Digital camera
- Webbing slings to lift large pieces of furniture or marble tops

A piece of furniture should be examined for structural soundness in each of its members and in the joints. Look for strain and structural damage from rough handling or inappropriate use. Examine joints for failure due to bad design or construction, environmental stress, poor usage, or deterioration of glue.

To check joints in a chair, stand at the front of the piece and carefully try to rock it from front to back or from side to side. Rocking or movement indicates weakness in the joints.

Case furniture may have loose joints, broken or missing pieces, or damage to panels. Examine dovetail joints for slight unevenness along the edge, which would indicate shrinkage that may be partially hidden under veneer. A line of unfinished wooden surface along the edge of a panel indicates shrinkage, as does a split if the panel edges have become adhered permanently to the frame on the edges and prevented from expanding and contracting.

Look behind bracket feet to make sure the interior cornerblock is not missing, causing the weight to be held entirely by the decorative brackets. Case pieces have the most moving parts, and thus, the greatest possibility of wear and breakage. Drawers often have broken or loose joints, worn sides and runners, and shrunken bottoms. Check the structural stability of the drawer itself. See if drawer stops are missing or have loose nails.

Cabinet doors may shrink, expand, or become distorted. Examine the hinges for proper connections. The hinged writing surface of a drop-front desk is also susceptible to distortion. Loose supporting lopers can result in unnecessary stress on the writing surface, allowing it to fall below the horizontal level. Examine the connected pieces of feet and cornices for structural stability. On glazed pieces, check the putty or glazing beads around the edge of the glass for soundness.

Look for problems resulting from environmental conditions, such as veneer damage and bleaching and fading of textiles from sunlight. Rub a white cotton cloth over hardware to check for red rust corrosion on ferrous (iron-based) pieces or green corrosion on brass or copper. Other problems that should be noted include sticking or jamming of doors and drawers, buckling of veneer, glue failure in joints, and a dull, discolored finish. Look for mold or mildew growth inside closed pieces or behind large pieces, where the dark, unventilated conditions are optimal for fungal

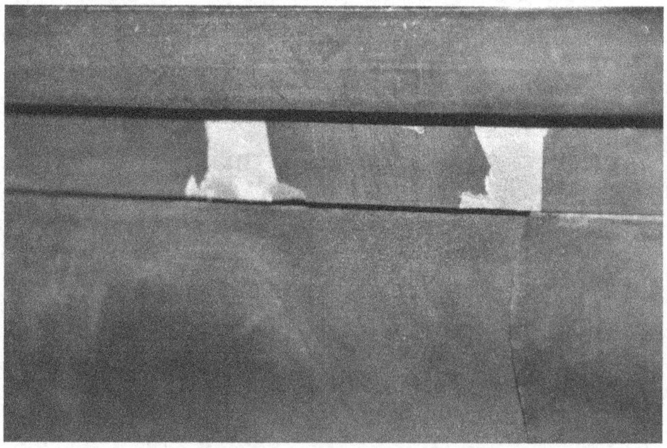

Figure 8.4. Sections of lost veneer.
Source: William H. Jackson

growth. Previous mold and mildew growth can also stain wood and upholstery fabric.

Examine all types of ornamentation. Functional and decorative finishes (e.g., shellac, graining, gilding) may be discolored, abraded, or flaking. Molding and other applied details, whether solid wood or composites, may be separating or have missing elements. The upholstery and trim (e.g., fabric, tassels, decorative nails) may be stained, torn, or corroded.

Figure 8.5. Broken and missing element.
Source: William H. Jackson

Because of its history as a functional object, a piece of furniture has a high likelihood of having been repaired at some point. Note any replacement parts or hardware. Look for signs of previous repairs such as patching and retouching. The presence of metal brackets, plates, screws, staples, straps, or nails to repair joints are usually evidence of amateur work.[2]

Figure 8.6. Surface scratches and missing hardware on cabinet drawers.
Source: William H. Jackson

Wood-boring insects may infest any piece of wood furniture, but they are especially partial to plywood and the unfinished wood behind cabinet pieces. In a raking light, it is sometimes possible to identify whether exit holes are new (light in color, with sharp edges) or old (dark in color, filled with dirt or wax). Closely check nearby pieces for signs of damage or infestation, as well as windowsills, for signs of adult beetles, cigarette beetles, clothes moths, cockroaches, or silverfish. Look for evidence of chewing damage, frass, insect carcasses, or larval cases.

DOCUMENTATION

A condition report for furniture should include the specific object name, the object's catalog or accession number, the date of examination, the name of the examiner, and a detailed overall description of the piece. The description should include material(s), provenance, date, place of manufacture, inscriptions, stamps, etc. The examiner should also record its overall dimensions in length, width, and height. The units of measure should be consistent. If there are other measurements taken, such as size of drawers, this should be noted, as well. Terms such as *good, fair*, and *poor* are often used, but these terms can be problematic. What one person views as good may only be fair to another; therefore, these general terms should be followed up with a more detailed description of the condition.

The next section of a condition report should record notations about the structural frame of the furniture, any surface treatments, hardware, and upholstery. Any losses, splits, or damage should be described and measured and detailed photographs taken. The photographs will provide the most detailed means of observing changes over time. Digital photography provides a way to take as many condition photographs as necessary to document every angle of an object. Close-up images of problem areas that need to be monitored are especially helpful. Conditions can then be noted and highlighted on these photographs. The photographs should contain notation of date, size, location, and extent. The written description accompanied by the photographs will provide a more complete record. Condition reports can be kept in hardcopy files and should also be entered into the collections database to complete each object's record.

The use of laptops and tablets connected directly to the data management system can accelerate the condition reporting process. In recent years, a number of condition-reporting apps have been created. These apps offer the ability to record condition notes directly to digital photographs. In addition to apps, other software can be used to create digital condition reports. One will need image-editing software, file-sharing capabilities, remote access to the data management system, and document-editing software, in addition to a good wifi connection. When considering digital condition reports or an app, one will want to consider individual needs and workflow.

CONDITION GLOSSARY

Glossary terms can assist in providing a basis for consistent terminology used within an institution. Because furniture can be composed of many materials, such as wood, fabric, metal, and leather, it may be useful to refer to other chapters within this handbook for more material-specific glossary terms.

Abrasion, Scuff: Signs of mechanical scraping or wear in a surface finish.

Accretion: Gradual accumulation of layers. Can include loose deposits, greasy dirt, mold, stains, exudations; dirt firmly adhered to a surface.

Alligatoring: Series of hairline cracks in old varnish, creating the appearance of alligator hide.

Bleaching: Fading of pigment, which is evidence of light damage, in organic materials such as textile colors or dark woods, usually from direct exposure to sunlight.

Blister: Raised bubble indicating a detached portion of wooden veneer.

Bloom: White discoloration on the surface of wood; indicative of moisture penetrating the surface.

Figure 8.7. Small bloom spots on top of a side table.
Source: William H. Jackson

Buckling: Overall uneven veneer surface resulting from shrinkage in the base wood below.

Checking: Slight gapping between wood cells that creates a checkerboard-like pattern; found where wood is cut straight across the grain for carving, such as in a ball-and-claw foot.

Chipping: Loss of small pieces of wooden veneer around edges resulting from a blow.

Compression: A flattening or concavity in the stuffing of upholstered pieces; caused by overuse.

Cracks: Splits, surface fractures that run across surface pieces of wood or in wooden framing members. They may also appear in marble, glass, or gessoed gilding. A radial crack is a crack in a cross-section of wood running from the center of a log out.

Cupping, Dishing: Warping across the width of a board, usually with the upper surface developing a concave curve.

Cutdowns: Furniture components, such as table legs, which have been altered from their original size.

Darkening, Yellowing: Seen in light woods and finishes as a result of light damage.

Delamination: A separation of layers; splitting.

Disjoin: Partial or complete separation of a joint between two members of an object.

Dry Rot: Wood decay caused by a certain type of fungi.

Embrittlement: Decline in firmness, pliability, and suppleness, causing a material to snap when bent or curled; the effect of low relative humidity on wood or glue.

Etching: Deterioration of the smooth surface on a marble top from a spill of acidic liquids.

Flaking: Loss of small portions of surface treatment (e.g., paint, gesso) due to the formation of air pockets beneath the surface as the wood below shrinks.

Fraying: Partial loss of textile upholstery or trim due to mechanical forces, such as wear, or environmental deterioration, such as embrittlement.

Gouge: A defect in the surface where material has been scooped out.

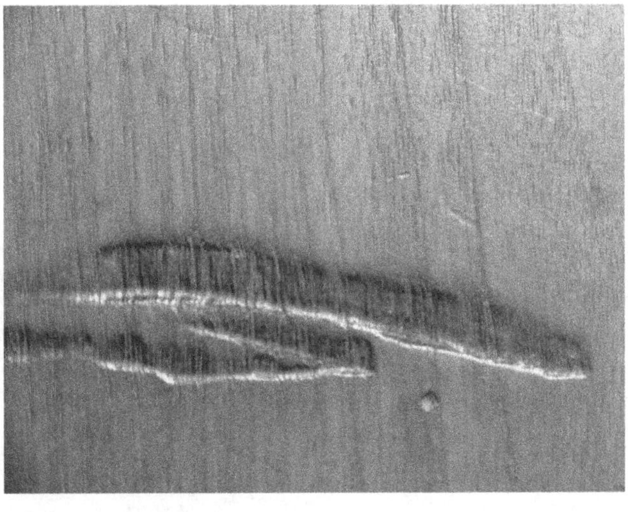

Figure 8.8. Example of gouge in the surface of wood.
Source: William H. Jackson

Infestation: Presence of woodworm or other insects, evidenced by fresh frass, the powdered wood that falls out as the insects chew through the wood. Exit holes, made on the exterior of wood by adult beetles as they leave the furniture, could be a sign of earlier insect damage.

Lifting: Raising of inlaid surfaces or veneer away from the surrounding wooden surface.

Looseness, Slack: Indication of failure in furniture joints.

Mold, Mildew: Fungal infestations that can occur on any organic material at high levels of relative humidity. Seen as dark or light stains, especially with powdery or fluffy surfaces.

Patina: Natural, aged appearance of a finished wood surface.

Sagging: Furniture part, such as a shelf, that has warped from the pull of gravity, so that its shape is no longer true to its original design.

Scratch: Accidental mark in the surface finish caused by abrasion with a sharp point.

Shrinkage: In organic materials, such as wood, a loss of mass or size in response to dry relative humidity conditions.

Softening: Malleable effect of high relative humidity on some glues in furniture joints.

Split: Crack that runs through an entire surface, such as veneer.

Stain: Any of several types of discoloration. On wooden furniture, it can take the form of white rings resulting from spills of alcohol or water. On a marble top, it can be the result of a porous absorption of grease, liquid, or dirt.

Sticking, Binding: Impaired motion of a drawer or door from swelling due to high relative humidity.

Tear: Textile rip without significant loss of material.

Warping: Irregularities in wood as a result of shrinkage over time in response to relative humidity. It can take the form of cupping or twisting.

Wear: Surface erosion, usually at edges, due to repeated handling.

Basic Condition Report - Furniture

Inventory #: ____________________ **Object:** ____________________

Object Description: ____________________
____
____

Materials: ____________________
____
____

Dimensions:
________ Length
________ Width
________ Height

Details: ____________________
____
____
____

Identifying Photograph

Additional Detailed Condition
Photos Should be Attached

Overall Condition: ____________________
____
____
____
____
____
____
____
____

Surface Treatments:

________ Varnish	________ Gesso/Gilding	________ Scratch
________ Wax	________ Unfinished Wood	________ Loss
________ Painted	________ Stain	________

Hardware/Decorative Materials:

____ Drawer pull(s)	____ Key holes	____ Glass damaged	____ Original
____ Door pull(s)	____ Castors	____ Mirror damaged	____ Replaced
____ Hinges	____ Loss		

Upholstery:

________ Original	________ Abraded	________ Dirty	________ Repaired
________ Replaced	________ Torn	________ Discolored	________ Trim Loss

Photo Date: ____________________

Examined by: ____________________ **Date:** ____________________

Figure 8.9. Furniture condition report form.
Source: William H. Jackson

NOTES

1. A telltale sign of old gilding over in gesso is a series of small cracks running across its short width.

2. Although conservation standards for museum objects discourage cosmetic repairs, the physical integrity of broken structural parts should always be restored to avoid further stress on other parts. Always bag, label, and save loose pieces for later conservation.

BIBLIOGRAPHY

Applebaum, Barbara. *Guide to Environmental Protection of Collections.* Madison, CT: Sound View Press, 1991.

Considine, Brian. "Furniture." In *Caring for Your Collections*, edited by Harriet Whelchel. New York: Harry N. Abrams, Inc., 1992.

Forrest, Tim. *The Bulfinch Anatomy of Antique Furniture: An Illustrated Guide*. London: Little, Brown & Company, 1996.

Jackson, Albert, and David Day. *Care and Repair of Furniture*. London: HarperCollins, 2006.

Klim, Susan. "Furniture Conservation." In *Conservation Concerns: A Guide for Collectors and Curators*, edited by Konstanze Bachmann. Washington, D.C.: Smithsonian Institution Press, 1992.

Lindsay, Helen. "Evidencing the Case for Preventive Conservation: The Role of Collections Care Documentation." *Studies in Conservation* 63 (September 2018), 175–80. doi:10.1080/00393630.2018.1504516.

McGiffin, Robert F. *Furniture Care and Conservation.* Nashville, TN: American Association for State and Local History, 1983.

National Park Service. "Upholstered Furniture: Agents of Deterioration." *Conserve-O-Gram*, Number 7/4. Washington, D.C.: National Park Service, 1993.

Rivers, Shayne, and Nick Umney. *Conservation of Furniture*. Butterworth-Heinemann Series in Conservation and Museology. Amsterdam: Elsevier Butterworth Heinemann, 2005.

Smithsonian Museum Conservation Institute. "Furniture Care and Handling." Smithsonian Institute. Accessed March 6, 2021. https://www.si.edu/mci/english/learn_more/taking_care/index.html. Photographs courtesy of William H. Jackson. Furniture courtesy of Jan Jackson.

Thickett, David. "Frontiers of Preventive Conservation." *Studies in Conservation* 63 (September 2018), 262–67. doi:10.1080/00393630.2018.1504455.

9

Glass

Erica Hague

CREATION

Although prone to breaking, glass is one of the easiest materials to care for in a stable environment, as it is generally chemically stable and resistant to most corrosion.

Glass is a silica or quartz sand and mineral mixture that is melted into a liquid at high temperatures (1500–2315°C) in a heat-resistant crucible. Various minerals help to lower the required temperature and allow for decorative features. Molten glass is then shaped by blowing/pressing it into a mold, or by freeform blowing. Many glass pieces are then heat-treated to strengthen the object in a process called annealing.

HANDLING

Before handling any glass object, a workspace should be prepared. Ideally, a worktable should be padded with a soft and smooth material that is thin enough to provide the objects with stability, but thick enough to provide proper support. Polyethylene foam (Volara, Ethafoam) or clean packing blankets covered in muslin are good options. Cotton gloves are not ideal for handling glass. Non-slip gloves (nitrile) or clean and dry hands will ensure a grip on the objects as they are moved, examined, and stored. Jewelry should be removed to prevent the objects from being scratched.

Prior to attempting to move an object, prepare a padded box or cart with which to move the object to the workspace. Take time to examine the object prior to moving and note any repair work or weak spots. Remove any loose pieces and parts such as lids, stoppers, and other pieces at this time. Do not lift the object by its handles or other protrusions, but instead, support the object from the base. Always use both hands to lift and support the object, regardless of size.

If working on or moving multiple objects on the same cart or in the same box, be sure to provide ample space and padding between the objects. If stacking plates, bowls, or cups, they should always have padding (Volara, Ethafoam) between each piece and should be approximately the same size and weight, as well as being undamaged. Ideally, stacked items will be only two pieces high to reduce the weight and pressure on the bottom-most item, although this is not always practical for storage and transport. Be especially careful of raised decorations, gilt, and/or enamel work when handling, moving, and examining items.

EXAMINATION AND DOCUMENTATION

Each component of an object should be handled and examined separately. Take particular care with areas that appear damaged, and handle the object as little as possible. Always ensure the

Item Name:

Creator: Accession #:

Storage Location: Current Location: Dimensions: Date of Creation:

Description:

Evidence of:

- ○ Crizzling ○ Devitrification ○ Efflorescence ○ Glass Disease ○ Iridescence

Previous / Outgoing Condition:

○ Excellent ○ Very Good ○ Good ○ Fair ○ Bad

Reported by: Date:

Current / Incoming Condition:

○ Excellent ○ Very Good ○ Good ○ Fair ○ Bad Reported by: Date:

Figure 9.1. Glass condition report form.
Source: Erica Hague

stability of the object. If an object is top-heavy or unstable, place it in a way that will increase its stability without putting more pressure on delicate areas. Repairs and adhesives sometimes fluoresce differently under black light or transmitted light. Be sure to wear UV eye protection when using a black light. Other details to document during examination include chipping, flaking, glazes, gilding, staining, and scratches.

When examining the object, be consistent and always finish examining one side before moving to the opposite side. It is easiest to find a significant detail to designate as the twelve o'clock. Work clockwise around the piece noting damage, repairs, and other details in reference to where they fall in relation to the twelve o'clock detail in a concise and precise way. Location, extent, and specifics of a damaged area should be clearly written, and include measurements, when possible, to clarify the extent of the damage. If there are no clear distinguishing marks or features to help orient the report, the accession number may be used as an orientation location as long as this method is noted in the report.

While most collection-management software packages include a digital form or entry, they should be used similar to hardcopy condition reports. Both methods should contain all of the basic information on a piece, such as the item name, accession number, creator, date of creation, dimensions, date of examination, reason for examination, and who examined the piece. A brief description, the current condition, additional notes, and a space for the examiner to sign should also be included. If applicable, space for lending/borrowing institutions to sign, along with the loan information, can be added. Any special handling instructions or additional information that does not fit within these categories should default to the additional notes section. Photographs of the object, along with detailed images of any damaged areas, should be taken and added to the database. If the object database requires additional information on items, it should be gathered at this time.

TERMINOLOGY AND CONDITION GLOSSARY[1]

Blown Glass: Glass that has been shaped by free blowing or by being blown into a mold.

Crimping: Decoration done on a viscous glass object that results in a wavy pattern.

Crystal Glass: Brilliant, colorless glass with a high proportion of lead.

Crizzling: Network of fine cracks on glass caused by hydration of the salts leaching excess alkali from the object.

Cut Glass: Glass that has a decorative pattern cut with a grinding wheel.

Devitrification: Loss of transparency in glass caused by the crystallization of the object.

Efflorescence: A crusty formation on a ceramic or glass object that can be powdery or crystalline. This is caused by hygroscopic salts and moisture being drawn to the surface of a piece. The moisture then evaporates, leaving the salt on the surface.

Enameling: Decorative finish painted and fired onto a glass or ceramic object.

Glass: A silica or quartz sand and mineral mixture that is melted into a liquid at high temperatures in a heat-resistant crucible.

Glass Disease: Also known as sick glass or weeping glass, an inherent chemical weakness in the glass resulting in moisture being drawn out of the object and causing the object to feel damp or slimy.

Inpainting: Duplication or repair of damaged original decoration on ceramics or glass.

Iridescence: Partial decomposition of the surface into thin scales, resulting in a lustrous color effect and an uneven flaky surface in a glass object.

Lead Glass: Glass with lead oxide used as flux.

Molded Glass: Molten glass that has been blown, cast, or pressed into a mold to form a finished object.

Pontil Mark: Rough point on the bottom of a glass object where the pontil rod was broken away.

Pressed Glass: Molten glass that has been shaped by pressing it into a mold.

NOTE

1. These terms are pulled from various sources, such as (Bivins 1972); (Hamer and Hamer 1986); (National Park Service 2000); (Newman 1977); and (Phillimore 1976).

BIBLIOGRAPHY

American Institute for Conservation of Historic and Artistic Works. "Caring for Your Treasures: Caring for Ceramic and Glass Objects." American Institute for Conservation. Undated. https://www.culturalheritage.org/docs/default-source/resources/outreach/glassandceramics.pdf?sfvrsn=14ac8810_2 (accessed 02/19/2021).

Brill, Robert H. "The Use of Equilibrated Silica Gel for the Protection of Glass with Incipient Crizzling." *Journal of Glass Studies* 20 (1978): 100–18.

Davison, Sandra, and R. G. Newton. *Conservation and Restoration of Glass*. Abingdon, Oxfordshire: Routledge, 2020.

Deck, Clara. *The Care and Preservation of Glass & Ceramics*. The Henry Ford Museum. 2016. https://www.thehenryford.org/docs/default-source/default-document-library/the-henry-ford-glass-amp-ceramics-conservation.pdf/?sfvrsn=2 (accessed 02/19/2021).

Koob, Stephen P., N. Astrid R. van Giffen, Jerzy J. Kunicki-Goldfinger, and Robert H. Brill. "Caring for Glass Collections: The Importance of Maintaining Environmental Controls." *Studies in Conservation*. 63, no. sup1 (2018): 146–50.

National Park Service. "National Park Service Museum Handbook, Part I." National Park Service. 2000. http://www.nps.gov/museum/publications/MHI/AppendP.pdf (accessed 02/19/2021).

Newman, H. *An Illustrated Dictionary of Glass: 2,442 Entries, Including Definitions of Wares, Materials, Processes, Forms, and Decorative Styles, and Entries on Principal Glass-Makers, Decorators, and Designers, from Antiquity to the Present*. London: Thames and Hudson, 1998.

Newton, Charlotte, and Judy Logan. "Care of Ceramics and Glass—Canadian Conservation Institute (CCI) Notes 5/1." Minister of Public Works and Government Services, Canada. 2007. https://www.canada.ca/en/conservation-institute/services/conservation-preservation-publications/canadian-conservation-institute-notes/care-ceramics-glass.html (accessed 02/19/2021).

Phillimore, Elizabeth. *A Glossary of Terms Useful in Conservation*. Ottawa: Canadian Museums Association, 1976.

Phillips, Phoebe. *The Encyclopedia of Glass*. New York: Crescent Books, 1987.

Reilly, Julie A., and Martin Mortimer. "The Care and Conservation of Glass Chandeliers." *Journal of the American Institute for Conservation* 27 (1998): 149–72.

Zerwick, Chloe. *A Short History of Glass*. Corning, NY: Harry N. Abrams, 1990.

10

Metals

Mary D. LaGue

Throughout the ages, metal, with its unique qualities of durability, strength, and a variety of forming methods, has been the material of choice for many types of objects. Metallic forms are therefore found in many museums' collections, whether they be history-, art-, or science-related. The majority of metals, except pure gold and platinum, are processed from rock-based ores, and their inherent tendency is to corrode or oxidize back to their original chemical form. Many metals are combined, or alloyed, to enhance a resulting object's strength and resistance to oxidation, but ore-based metals are never completely free of the tendency to go back to their original state. Thus, caretakers of metallic objects must look for and protect against this chemical reversion.

COMMONLY FOUND METALS AND ALLOYS

Base Metals

Copper

Reddish-orange-colored in its refined state, malleable copper has been used as a base for enameling, for printing plates, and in coinage. Its oxidized form is a blue-green color and is termed *verdigris*.

- *Copper Alloys*
  - *Brass*: Copper combined with tin, or later zinc. Golden-yellow, it can be either cast or beaten into form.
  - *Bronze*: Copper combined with a small proportion of tin, sometimes zinc and phosphorus. It varies from brown to gold in color, depending on the copper to tin ratio, and is generally cast.

Iron

Dark gray in its refined state, iron is relatively easy to melt and/or beat into shape after heating. It has been used to make a wide variety of household goods, architectural elements, and weapons. Its oxidized form is reddish-orange and is termed *rust*.

- *Iron Alloy*
  - *Steel*: Iron combined with carbon, and now other heavy metals. Industrial and mild steel are medium gray and susceptible to rust. Corten steel allows an even coat of stable rust to develop and therefore is often used for outside decorative purposes. Stainless steel is combined with other metals so that it neither rusts nor is magnetic.

Silver

Light, shiny gray in its refined state, silver is used in jewelry, dining utensils, and coinage. It is quite often alloyed because it is inherently very soft. Its oxidized form is dark, iridescent brownish-to-bluish gray and is termed *tarnish*.

- *Silver Alloy*
  - *Sterling Silver*: Silver combined with copper for durability, it can be cast, beaten, and sometimes electroplated over a copper base. Looking very much like pure silver, this alloy is commonly used in the United States and western European countries; other types of silver alloys have been developed in other areas such as Japan and eastern Europe.

Tin

Silvery-gray in its refined state, tin has been used to make useful objects like lanterns, dining utensils, and ventilation panels in furniture such as pie safes. Its oxidized form is whitish-gray and termed either *tin pest* or *tin disease*.

- *Tin Alloys*
  - *Britannic Metal*: A silver-like combination of tin, antimony, and copper, often including zinc and bismuth.
  - *Pewter*: A light gray alloy of tin, copper, antimony, and sometimes lead in lower-quality ware.
  - *Zinc*: Also silvery gray in its refined state, zinc is used for printing plates and as a sanitary table- or countertop. Its oxidized form is a medium gray.

METAL TECHNIQUE TERMINOLOGY[1]

Alloy: Mixture of two or more metals formed when melted.

Annealing: Process of heating then cooling sheet metal to relieve stress and return it to a malleable state.

Burnishing: Type of surface polish created by rubbing with a hard and smooth material.

Casting: In this context, the act of forming objects by pouring melted metal into a mold.

Chasing: Process of adding detail or ornamentation by indenting the metal with a non-cutting-edged tool and hammer.

Coating: Protecting barrier, usually a synthetic resin or wax, applied to a surface.

Damascene: Process of annealing layers of iron and steel together, creating strong implements characterized by wavy patterns; and also, to ornament with inlays of precious metals.

Electroplate: Process of coating one metal with another by running an electric charge through a solution.

Embossing: Process of creating a raised design on a surface by working from its reverse with a punch.

Enamel: Process of melting and fusing a glass-based powder over a metal base, either for protection or decoration.

Engraving: Process of removing lines from a metal surface using chisel-like tools termed *graves*.

Etching: An acid bath being used to eat away unprotected areas of a design.

Filigree: Fine wire formed into delicate openwork designs.

Finishing: Cleaning, polishing, patinating, and/or coating a surface.

Forging: Beating or hammering metal with or without heat to create a form.

Gilding: A gold or gold-toned overlay on a surface.

Inhibitor: Material that reduces formation of rust or corrosion.

Inlay: Insertion of a material into a concavity of another base material. Also, the reinforcement of silver-plated objects with an additional coating of silver.

Lacquer: Spirit-based varnish used as a finish coating.
Mold: A form used for casting metal objects.
Niello: Technique using black-colored mixture of silver, copper, or lead, with sulfur to oxidize them. The resulting alloys are used as inlay material.
Patina: A deliberate layer of color on a metallic surface, often a copper alloy, which may either be natural or artificial.
Piercing: Puncturing or perforating metal to produce an openwork design.
Planishing: Similar to burnishing; done with a smooth hammer.
Plating: Depositing a thin layer of a metal or alloy over another base metal.
Raising: Creating a three-dimensional design.
Repoussé: A raised form made by embossing.
Soldering: Joining separate metal elements with relatively low-melt alloys, also termed *fluxes*.
Tensile Strength: A metal's ability to stretch or bend without breaking.
Tinning: Plating a base metal with tin.
Welding: Joining separate metal elements by fusing at near-melting point.
Wrought: Object shaped by beating with a hammer.

HANDLING METALS

Wear gloves, preferably powder-free nitrile or vinyl gloves, to handle metals, as the fatty acids and salts found on human hands will hasten corrosion. However, as some nitrile has sulfur in its makeup, which will not be indicated on the packaging, standard cotton gloves should be worn to work with silver and silver-plated artifacts. Some metals, whether by virtue of constituent elements (such as lead or rust) or form (such as weaponry), pose a risk to those who handle them. Gloves will serve to protect both the wearer and the object handled.

Though metals are initially durable, they can often be dented, scratched, and abraded and so must be protected with soft, inert, and acid-free materials. As previously noted, most metals tend to oxidize back to their original ore forms and thus become brittle—if signs of corrosion are noted, brittleness is also likely. Do not attempt to remove corrosion from an object, as doing so may cause irreparable structural damage or diminish its aesthetic or historic qualities. Similarly, if an examiner wishes to brush or vacuum debris from an object to clear it for evaluation, he or she should first consult a conservator and/or curator before taking any action.

EXAMINING METALS

Since different metal alloys often resemble each other, or possibly an elemental metal, finding out about the history and composition of a metal object is valuable. Such information will help an examiner determine whether a given object is corroded, or whether the surface is patinated; whether a work is made to be taken apart, or whether it is broken. Moving from the general to the particular, check the object's overall structure, paying attention to the state of any joined areas and loose parts.

Also evaluate the surface to determine what techniques may have been used to embellish or protect it. Look for surface alterations, which may often be flaky, patchy, and loosely adhered. Corrosion in a base layer of metal may cause gilded or painted surfaces to bubble, lift, and/or flake. Watery-looking or powdery areas may indicate serious corrosion. Objects with decorative or protective coatings can still corrode.[2] An imperfectly applied coating may exhibit dark areas with sharp borders, indicating no coating material was adhered to those places. Some coating materials may become brittle and crack, allowing exposed areas of metal to oxidize. Incompletely removed residue from a previous cleaning may have left deposits or even promoted corrosion.

DOCUMENTING CONDITION

The standard type of condition report has been a paper-based form, which may include check-off boxes, narrative description, and a drawn illustration of an object's condition specifics. However, with the advent of electronic aids such as digital photography and computer-based collections management databases, several options for condition reporting have become available. An object can be photographed and the resulting digital-image output full-page sized, then areas of damage circled or pointed to, with notations in borders around the image; there are also apps available that allow a user to electronically mark on an image. Many databases allow output of text condition reports typed into a given object's record, and some allow design of a printable form that will include the typed information as a baseline condition for a working hard-copy report. Some newly designed databases have enhanced tools to aid in condition reporting.

Whatever form is chosen, the following methods will lead to an accurate, detailed condition report:

- Include areas for positive identification of the object to be examined, such as identifying number, title/name, artist/maker, measurements, and medium.
- Note any specific handling instructions.
- Have an area for noting the examiner's name and the examination date.
- If historical condition data is available, note previous repairs and their time frame.
- The usual order of examination is from top to bottom, exterior to interior, and obverse to reverse.
- If the report is not an initial report, note any variations to the previously reported status.
- To provide damage location in a narrative form, use a zoning system—for two-dimensional objects or elements, the nine-part zone described in chapter 1 can be used; for rounded/three-dimensional forms, a clock-base zoning system may be more helpful. Include measurements both to locate the damage within the zone system and to note the dimensions of the damage itself.
- Allow blank areas for comments if the form is a checklist type.

CONDITION GLOSSARY

Abrasion: Friction damage such as wear, grinding, or rubbing away of a surface.

Accretion: An extraneous material that has adhered to the object's surface; examples are bird droppings, dirt, grime, unremoved casting materials, or splattered paint.

Bronze Disease: A type of copper corrosion, generally found on unearthed archaeological objects, and characterized by powdery green spots. Chloride is the catalyzing agent.

Checking: Surface cracking that resembles a grid and is often associated with a degrading protective coating.

Copper Stearate Corrosion: Found at points of contact between copper-based metals and leather, this type of corrosion forms when fatty acids arising from leather-tanning processes react with the metal.

Corrosion: Chemically induced formation of mineral encrustations as the metal reverts to its constituent materials.

Dent: Concave deformation of a surface caused by hitting.

Inclusions: Impurities in cast metals such as molding materials or slag.

Loss: Missing element or portion of a surface.

Missing Element: A lost component that at one time was part of a complex object.

Condition Report

Object Number: **1970.097**
Artist/Maker:
Object Name/Title: I: PATERA, -350
Medium: bronze
Dimensions: handle- 4.75'x 1.25'diam.: 1 3/4 x 8 3/4 in. (4.4 x 22.2 cm)
Credit Line: Roanoke Public Library; transfer of the Francis W. Collins Collection

---

SURVEY INFORMATION — Survey Type: **Initial Condition**

Survey Date: **29-Mar-1989** — Report Date: — Examiner:

Overall Condition: **GOOD**

Remarks: "Good - completely patinated w/ copper oxide; abrasion on bottom of handle (produced in or before 5/86, when director tested for age of attaching elements."

SURVEY INFORMATION — Survey Type: **Subsequent Condition**

Survey Date: **31-Jan-2013** — Report Date: — Examiner: **Mary LaGue**

Overall Condition: **GOOD OVERALL**

Remarks

---

scratches overall to patina, not previously noted but on historic images. old painted accession number at 10:00 o'clock position on rim. Passive bronze disease is noted on accompanying photograph. Handle is firmly attached. Brown accretions overall, seem to be unremoved earth from original archeoligical dig.

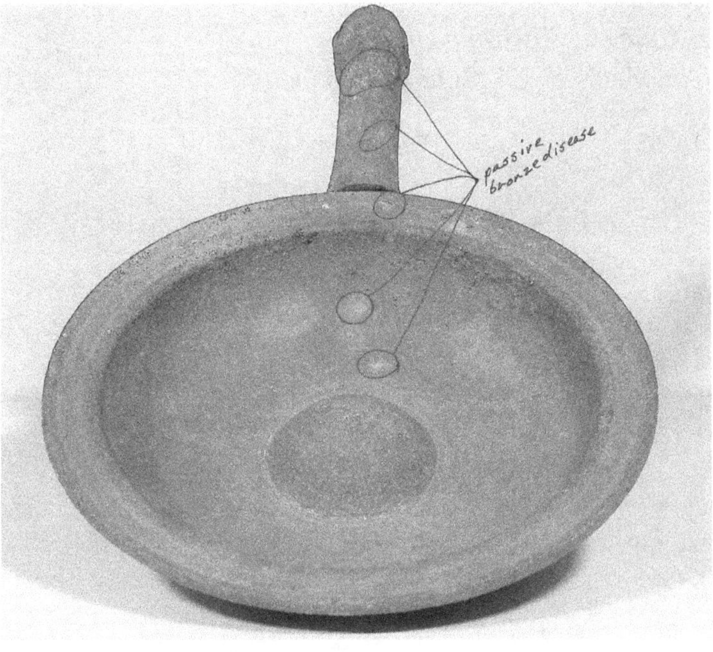

Print Date: 31-Jan-201305:26 PM — Page 1 of 1

Figure 10.1. Metal condition report form.
Source: Mary D. LaGue

Passive: A relatively stable metal surface with low-to-nonexistent corrosion over time.

Patina: An intended layer over a metal surface, often a copper alloy, which may be either naturally occurring or artificially produced.

Pitting: Clusters of very small-textured concavities in a surface, caused by acidic etching or by a casting process.

Scratch: A linear indentation of a surface, caused by abrasion by sharp objects or particles.

Sheen: A highly polished, smooth state. If it was produced in isolated areas of a surface by frequent handling, the term denotes a flaw.

Slag: A semi-glassy compound of impurities refined out while smelting metal.

Tear: A linear separation of sheet material resulting from opposing tension or repeated bending.

NOTES

1. Some of the terms and definitions in the Terminology section are based on *Glossary of Terms* (Houston: National Association of Engineers, February 1988).

2. Barbara Appelbaum, *Guide to Environmental Protection of Collections* (Madison, CT: Sound View Press, 1991), 161.

BIBLIOGRAPHY

Appelbaum, Barbara. *Guide to Environmental Protection of Collections.* Madison, CT: Sound View Press, 1991.

Drayman-Weisser, Terry. "Metal Objects." In *Caring for Your Collections.* New York: Harry N. Abrams, Inc., 1992.

Heller, Don B. "Conserving Metal Objects." *Museum News* 55 (May/June 1977): 25–29.

LaQue Center for Corrosion Technology, Inc. *Corrosion in Action*, 7th ed. Wrightsville, NC: LaQue for Corrosion Technology, Inc., 1985.

National Park Service. "Appendix O: Curatorial Care of Metal Objects." In *Museum Handbook Pt. 1: Museum Collections.* Washington, D.C.: National Park Service, 1990.

Weber, Alicia, and Kathy Erickson, eds. *Care and Maintenance: Recommendations for Artwork in the Fine Arts Collection/U. S. General Services Administration.* Washington, D.C.: U.S. General Services Administration, 2005.

11

Mixed Media and Composite Objects

Robin P. Croskery Howard

> Condition, however, is neither a physical fact nor a direct observation. It is a *conclusion* that comes from a comparison of the object's current state with some other, presumably more desirable, state.
>
> —Barbara Applebaum[1]

In daily life, one encounters objects created using different materials; the computer at work contains plastics, metal, glass, etc.; clothing, vehicles, framed artwork, purses, the shopping cart. All of these are examples of mixed media (or composite) objects, which can be one of the more challenging types of materials on which to provide a condition report. Both mixed media and composite objects require a basic knowledge of most issues that may befall an object of any material typology. For the purposes of this chapter, we will be discussing both mixed media and composite objects, as the nature of, and knowledge needed, to write these condition reports falls at the same level of difficulty.

There are defining characteristics that differentiate mixed media and composite objects from other types of objects that you may encounter. Simply, these objects are made of more than one type of material. *Mixed media* objects can therefore be defined as fine arts objects (paintings, drawings, sculptures, etc.) that are intentionally made using more than one type of material to create a single object (or set of objects) encompassing an artist's vision. *Composite objects* differ in that they are generally everyday or utilitarian objects intentionally made using more than one type of material to create a single object (or set of objects) to fulfill a need, which may or may not be artistic in nature.

Writing a condition report can become a bit trickier when discussing the object typologies within a single object that are different, such as using a cotton-polyester-blend textile with a rayon textile to create a chemise. In general, one should not consider these as mixed media/composite objects as it is wholly one type of object; in the previous example, it is a textile.

Therefore, the characteristics that define these mixed media and composite objects are at least two different material typologies to create a single object, such as a fine arts sculpture that is made of chicken wire, papîer maché, acrylic paint, feathers, etc. From here on out, we will discuss both as mixed media objects, though composite objects should be treated in the same manner.

The difficulty in creating a basic condition report for mixed media objects is to understand the nature of materials that create these objects. It is imperative to use correct terminology for each typology to describe the nature of the object; consistency in terms is key and necessary to maintain between one report and the next. Should the terminology be unfamiliar, be sure to use clear, descriptive words that the next person will understand. If possible, augment these descriptions by using specific material terminology for clarification.

The basics of all mixed media condition reporting is identifying the materials that comprise each object. Investigate each object and determine what materials were used to create it; use databases to become familiar with objects that you regularly encounter. Take note of the material typologies that comprise these objects, so that cursory investigations become easier over time. Learn common failures of objects due to inherent vice, human error, or other agents of deterioration. This level of knowledge is the best way to understand how to create a basic condition report for any mixed media object.

Common material typologies that you may encounter in an object include textiles, paper, photographs, metals, acrylic, oil, and watercolor paints. Other materials include papîer maché (which is technically mixed media itself), leather or hide, wood, and adhesives, both organic and inorganic. This list is not exhaustive by any measure, but it is a good starting point. In understanding the rudimentary nature of deterioration for each of these object typologies, you should be able to provide a basic condition report that will ensure the next person is able to see if any condition changes have occurred. The remainder of the book discusses these typologies in more detail, so it is important to take note of the terminology used to discuss each of the areas of issue that may occur for these typologies.

There is one way that quickly provides detailed information regarding an incoming object: Create a condition report that includes a comprehensive checklist of possible issues with a blank area for details. This list allows one to fill out the intake form quickly and succinctly.

Be sure to maintain positional consistency when describing any issues on an object. Creating a virtual four-quadrant grid over the object provides the simplest descriptions. When working with a three-dimensional, mixed media object, it is important that this grid encompass all aspects of the object. Use the terms *obverse*, *reverse*, *proper right*, *proper left*, *top*, and *base* to describe the general six sides of the object. If not previously delineated, provide a short summary of the shape, color, etc., of the area that has the issues.

It is important to understand structural stability when discussing mixed media objects. Often, different areas and material typologies will fail or deteriorate at different rates due to inherent vice, display and storage, and the interaction of the material typologies with each other. An object may come to the institution as structurally stable, in that one could display it without causing any further damage to the underlying structure, but additional aspects of the object are failing. These non-structural elements are still necessary to consider in the overall delineation of status for the object (poor, fair, good), but it doesn't matter how good of a condition the paint is in if the structure of a sculpture is crumbling.

For instance, a painted metal sculpture made of different types of metals will deteriorate at different rates. On a chemical level, the material of one metal is sacrificed to bolster another metal of a more positive charge. A painted wooden panel piece with ferrous metal fasteners will deteriorate at a faster rate around the areas where the metal touches the painted wood. These examples demonstrate the need for understanding how material typologies interact, even on the most basic level.

Handling an object can bring a more intimate knowledge of an object's condition through simple interaction; understanding the basics of handling provides the best possible starting point for handling mixed media objects. The technique to handling mixed media objects is in knowing the mechanisms in which they function or functioned and the primary materials that comprise the object. For instance, handling a piece of flat mixed media artwork varies greatly from that of a glass-beaded textile. Both require care and consideration as to how to manipulate the objects during both transportation and installation.

As ever, flexible objects should be supported using rigid structures such as a tray or box transported on a cart, dolly, or carefully by hand; and rigid objects should be supported in a similar manner, using soft archival materials to support any areas that are especially vulnerable to damage or loss during transportation. In general, it is best to use the correct personal protective equipment, ensuring protection for yourself from the object, and the object from any harmful things that you may have on your person. Basic suggestions for mixed media objects is to remove all jewelry that may interfere with the object, wear disposable nitrile gloves (or similar), don a close-fitting mid-length apron or lab coat, and opt for framed glasses over contacts if you require corrective lenses.

A note on condition reporting: It takes time, as it should, to properly examine an object, even on a cursory level. Do not feel rushed to come to a conclusion as to what state the object is in immediately. To be sure, immediate recognition of particular individual issues is necessary, but even in basic condition reports, it is good to take the time to look at the object closely a second time; the eye may miss something on the first look.

The following list of definitions is by no means exhaustive and meant as a simple reference guide. These are terms common to most material typologies that encompass the elements of mixed media. Knowledge of these terms provides the reporter with a balance and breadth of knowledge to tackle any basic condition report with confidence. There are online databases of these definitions with clear visual examples; be sure to visit the Australian Institute for the Conservation of Cultural Material's Visual Glossary webpage for a thorough and in-depth working manual.

CONDITION GLOSSARY

Abrasion: Scratching, roughing, or wearing of an object's surface due to friction or contact with other surfaces.

Accretion/Accumulation: The attachment of solid foreign matter to the surface of an object; this can be in a localized area or blanketed across the object (e.g., dust).

Bleeding: Generally seen in works on paper (e.g., documents, books, watercolors); dye, ink, or paint has become partially soluble and leached or wicked into the fibers of the surrounding area, creating a blurry appearance.

Break: A full and complete separation of areas of an object from one another due to unintentional damage; this is often caused by a sudden shock, occurring at weak points of an object.

Corrosion: The interaction of chemical agents (including oxygen) that cause deterioration to a solid object, especially metals. These may provide some protection to the overall stability or further accelerate damage to an object.

Crack: An opening between two parts of a material, but which has not fully separated the pieces from one another. This may or may not be along a grain or manufactured direction.

Crazing/Crizzling: Micro fissures or cracks in the varnish of a painting or the slip of a glazed ceramic. The cracks may widen over time due to fluctuations in environmental conditions.

Delamination: Visible separation of the layers (lamination) of objects, which may result in flaking or losses.

Deterioration: The overall loss in condition of either a specific area or full aspect of an object. This may be due to inherent vice or environmental conditions.

Embrittlement: Overall loss of mobility or flexibility of an object, causing the area to be fragile and brittle; often due to the loss of some sort of moisture or fats to keep the object supple.

Failure: Complete and total loss of function of a specific area of an object, usually due to another condition issue (e.g., adhesive no longer holding an area together).

Foxing: Red-brown discolorations that appear as random spots or dots on older works on paper, such as artwork or documents.

Fraying: The unraveling or worn edges of textiles or other organic objects (e.g., paper), often due to recurring abrasion(s).

Friability: The ability of an object or area on an object to be easily crumbled through simple movement or touch. This is often seen as powder or fine dust along with the loss of stability in the object. It may also be in the nature of the media used to create the object (such as crayon or charcoal) or a product of another type of deterioration.

Glass Disease: Caused by the inherent instability in the chemical nature of the original glass formula, it is the deterioration and failure of the glass from the microscopic to the macroscopic level. Signs of this deterioration include cracking, crizzling, delamination, spalling, and weeping to either side of the glass.

Iridescence: The appearance of multiple colors on the surface of an object that appear to change with the viewing angle. Often seen due to the breakdown of the chemicals in emulsion layers of photographs or the surface of glass.

Light Damage/Fading: The loss of intensity of color, structure, or other chemical nature of an object due to the exposure of sunlight. This is irreversible and cumulative.

Loss: Missing area, element, or piece of an object; may refer solely to the surface of a flat work, or be used to describe a missing element.

Missing Element(s): The complete loss of a particular element (e.g., button from a shirt) that completes the look, stability, and/or function of an object.

Oxidation: The interaction of oxygen with the chemicals of an object that creates a stable patina or leads to corrosion of the object. Most often seen on the surfaces of metal objects and may also be described as tarnish.

Pest Damage: Physical damage done to an object by an insect, rodent, or other pest. This is often seen as long holes or bores in wood or paper, frass by-product, or bite marks from the localized consumption of the object.

Repair/Mend: Previous attempt or successful treatment of an object to stabilize it on a structural, visual, or chemical level. This may be indigenous/contemporaneous to the creation of the object or much later by an amateur or trained professional. Failure of a repair is not uncommon.

Spalling: Small areas of chipping or flaking of a hard surface, such as stone or glass.

Stability: The relative strength of an object, often referring to the structure or chemical nature, that allows an object to securely be handled, examined, researched, and/or exhibited without further damage occurring.

Tear: The separation of areas of an organic element (paper, textile, canvas), often along lines of manufacture or areas of inherent weakness/previous damage. Though it can occur at any point in the object, it most often occurs from an edge and spans inward.

Use-Life Wear/Wear: Any damage that occurred during the normal course of time the object was used for its intended purpose.

Warping/Distortion: Changes from the original dimensions of the object resulting from inherent vice or other agents of deterioration. May also be used to describe a physical misshape of an object through twisting or the rounding of the object. Most often used to describe organics.

NOTE

1. Barbara Appelbaum, *Conservation Treatment Methodology* (Oxford: Butterworth-Heinemann, 2007), 22.

BIBLIOGRAPHY

Appelbaum, Barbara. *Conservation Treatment Methodology.* Oxford: Butterworth-Heinemann, 2007.

Ashley-Smith, Jonathan. *Risk Assessment for Object Conservation.* Oxford: Butterworth-Heinemann, 1999.

Australian Institute for the Conservation of Cultural Material. "Visual Glossary." Accessed

January 20, 2021. https://aiccm.org.au/conservation/visual-glossary.

Buys, Susan, and Victoria Oakley. *The Conservation and Restoration of Ceramics.* Oxford: Butterworth-Heinemann, 1996.

Florian, Mary-Lou E., Dale Paul Kronkright, and Ruth E. Norton. *The Conservation of Artifacts Made from Plant Materials.* Marina del Rey, CA: Getty Conservation Institute, 2002.

Grieve-Rawson, Susanne. Class Lectures, Introduction to Conservation, East Carolina University, Greenville, NC, January–May 2011.

Kite, Marion, and Roy Thomson. *Conservation of Leather and Related Materials.* Oxford: Butterworth-Heinemann, 2006.

Koob, Stephen P. *Conservation and Care of Glass Objects.* New York: Archetype Publications, 2006.

Landry, Gregory J. *The Winterthur Guide to Caring for Your Collection.* Winterthur, DE: Henry Francis du Pont Winterthur Museum, 2009.

MoMA Learning. "Glossary of Art Terms." Accessed January 20, 2021. https://www.moma.org/learn/moma_learning/glossary.

12

Natural History Specimens

Kara J. Hurst

Natural history specimens fall under the broad scientific disciplines of botany, earth sciences, and zoology. These specimens—naturally occurring in nature—are fauna, flora, fossils, minerals, and rocks (including meteorites and moon rocks). Unlike art or other disciplines where an object is unique and one of a kind, it can be beneficial to have multiple specimens of say, a particular bird, collected from the same locality over many years, if not hundreds of years. Although there may be similar specimens in a collection, due to the research value of natural history collections, each specimen is important. Natural history collections shape our understanding of the natural world around us, and importantly, how it is changing due to both natural and human impacts. Museum collections provide baseline data from a point in time to the present.

TYPES OF COLLECTIONS

As natural history collections are comprised of naturally occurring materials, their preservation is a moment suspended in time that halts the natural decay or degradation of the material. Preservation may be deliberate, in the case of scientifically collected fauna and flora, minerals and rocks, or it may be a fortuitous event, such as with fossils or meteorites. A good condition report will provide a record of the specimen prior to an action or event, such as initial acquisition, accession, and cataloging, or movement for an exhibition or research loan.

Collected specimens are prepared, or prepped, in different ways, including dry, wet, mounted, jacketed, pinned, or thin-sectioned, with variations on any of these methods possible.

- Animals may be dry prepped, which consists of separating the skeleton from the skin with possible tissue samples taken. The skin and skeleton may or may not be stored together in the same storage location, while the tissue sample would be frozen.
- Animals also may be wet prepped in a fixative solution (i.e., formalin) then a wash solution before final long-term storage in a fluid solution (i.e., formalin and ethanol). Percentages of the different solutions vary depending on the species.
- Herbarium (or botany) specimens will be field prepped using a plant press, then the dried specimen will be mounted to an acid-free paper support using a pH-neutral adhesive. Loose items, such as seeds, may or may not be stored in direct association with the plant specimen.
- Entomological specimens are preserved by threading a pin through the body of the insect, then the specimen is stored pinned in a cork-bottomed box or case.
- Paleontological specimens may be jacketed in a hard-plaster case, both for transport out

of the field and later for long-term storage in collections, although clamshell fiberglass jackets may also be used for long-term storage. Plaster jackets allow only one side of the fossil to be studied since the plaster and supporting materials are adhered to the fossil, whereas fiberglass clamshell jackets allow for study on both sides of a fossil in succession. Fossils can be large and heavy yet fragile, and consolidants and adhesives are generally used during lab preparation when excess matrix is removed from the often-fractured fossil bone.

- Rocks and minerals need minimal preparation but can present similar problems as fossils in that they may be large, heavy, and fragile, with protruding crystalline features. Some minerals may require storage in darkness or a substrate to preserve the unique qualities of the specimen. For example, when exposed to prolonged light, Realgar, an arsenic crystalline mineral, degrades to Pararealgar, which is unstable and crumbles to a yellow powder.
- Natural history specimens may be thin-sectioned, which is a process where a very narrow cross-section of the specimen may be sliced off the whole—usually from a center portion of the specimen—for microscopic analysis.

HANDLING AND DANGERS

Given the broad array of natural history specimens, it is important to understand how specimens were collected and prepared, as well as the anticipated immediate and long-term uses. In all aspects of museum work, it is imperative to remember that personnel safety takes precedence over any museum object. Although most natural history specimens provide unique challenges and dangers, specimens can be safely handled, condition reported, and utilized through careful handling and minimized exposure.

In general, handle natural history specimens in a similar fashion to art, history, or archaeology objects. Best practices include supporting the heaviest portion broadly using supports, padding delicate portions and protrusions, and following the general rule of not picking up a specimen prior to having an open path of travel and receiving location on which to place the specimen.

Remembering that natural history collections are preserved at a moment in time, with their natural decay or erosion process all but halted, agents of change will affect natural history collections, including: adverse relative humidity, adverse temperature, criminals, dissociation, fire, light and radiation, pests, physical forces, pollutants, and water. Given the purpose for which natural history collections are acquired—namely research—all agents of change incur risk, but of note, dissociation—data loss and data becoming separated from the specimen—is particularly of concern.

Generally, natural history collections have been collected by a researcher who is entrusted with a state or federal agency collecting permit, with permits having stipulations attached thereto. Stipulations may require that the specimens collected must be used for scientific research and educational purposes with results disseminated and acknowledging credit to the permitting agency; non-consumed specimens must be sent to an approved repository (i.e., museum) for storage; and title to the specimens remains with the permitting agency on behalf of the public. Specimens are occasionally offered by an individual as a donation to a museum, but researchers often prefer to use scientifically collected specimens to ensure that data about where, when, and how the specimen was collected is available, as well as making sure collected specimens are legally obtained.

Natural history specimens may be an attractant to pests, including dermestids. Often specimens historically have been treated with pesticides to eradicate infestations and deter future infestations in museums. Application of a pesticide can take many forms, including object immersion, liquid or solid topical application, and gaseous penetration. The U.S. Environmental Protection Agency

(EPA) now rates many chemical agents previously employed, such as arsenic and mercuric compounds, as Group A: human carcinogens. Because pesticides can enter the human body through ingestion, absorption, or inhalation, the use of personal protective equipment (PPE) is essential when handling specimens, especially when the history of specimens is unknown. At a minimum, PPE may include nitrile gloves, a mask, and a lab coat. More robust PPE, such as a respirator, may be necessary given the specimen's documented history, or the physical presence of a possible pesticide on the specimen. Limited handling by a knowledgeable person in a well-ventilated space or under a fume hood is advisable.

Other dangers lurk within natural history collections, such as natural asbestos that can desiccate and become airborne, radioactive mineral and fossil specimens, or ethnobotanical collections with potentially dangerous chemical properties. Additionally, the storage materials utilized, such as plaster jackets over fossils or a formalin solution, can become respiratory irritants. It is important to know the specimen, materials used in conjunction with it, and the appropriate protective and safety measures to employ. It would be prudent not to have potentially dangerous specimens in a collection if they cannot be safely managed by experienced personnel

EXAMINATION

With careful observation, any registrar can adequately examine and condition report a natural history specimen provided one treats the specimen as a general museum object. For a two-dimensional object, such as an herbarium sheet, the condition report will more closely resemble that of a framed artwork. While the plant specimen is the focus of the examination and report, special note should be taken if the paper support has any damage, such as tears, mold, or foxing, that would negatively impact the specimen itself. For a three-dimensional object, such as a taxidermy mount, the condition report will more closely resemble that of a sculpture.

Three-dimensional specimens can be examined in sections to simplify the process. First, view the specimen generally to conceptualize the process, and then apply that process by closely examining the specimen in a thorough, logical fashion, such as top to bottom or in a clockwise rotation. When addressing multi-component specimens, such as separate skin and skeletal components, care should be taken to keep the components in conjunction with each other to prevent dissociation.

As some natural history specimens can be susceptible to dermestid infestations, particular care should be taken during examination of dense areas of feathers, fur, and hair. At joints and around ears, it is advantageous to use simple tools, such as a microspatula or bone folder, and magnifying glass to closely inspect these dense areas from the surface of the fur down to the hide to locate potential dermestids. Remember to use appropriate PPE to mitigate potential hazards, known and unknown.

On items with a calcium carbonate composition, such as malacology and birds' egg specimens, look for powdery residue on the surface that could be an indication of Byne's Disease. This "disease" occurs with improper conditions, such as an acidic enclosure with high humidity, which can cause a reaction that results in a powdery residue on the specimen. Not really a disease, this residue is actually salt that crystallizes on and through the specimen and will eventually consume and destroy the entire specimen. Further damage to the specimens can be halted through improvement of conditions, but damage already done is irreversible.

PHOTOGRAPHY AND DOCUMENTATION

Through advances in digital technology, photographs and condition reports have become quicker, are more streamlined, and can be linked directly to collections databases through the use of tablets and similar digital devices. Although some collections databases now include standard condition report modules, it is best to supplement with additional photos and narrative documentation as warranted for each specimen. There also are separate condition reporting software options available that provide robust reporting templates that can be saved or emailed as PDF reports directly from the tablet device. It is advisable to digitally scan past paper condition reports into one's collection database for ease of reference and retention.

Should digital cameras or tablets be unavailable, grid paper can be useful for sketching the specimen with one developing their own key for any symbols used to delineate damage or areas of concern. Photodocumentation should always be used in conjunction with a standardized form that also allows for narrative documentation.

In general, one should refrain from using specialized terms and instead use plain language, which helps people find what they need, understand what they find, and use what they find to meet their needs. It doesn't require the user to know a specific discipline's nomenclature or jargon. Condition reports should provide a continuum of documentation for a specimen, and by using plain language, these reports can be utilized for the life of a specimen.

Natural history specimens should have at least one catalog number tag and may have multiple tags that document the specimen from field collection to preparation to collections storage. There may be additional tags or labels relating to pesticide or ethnobotanical hazards, whether on the specimen itself or a cabinet door or drawer, and it is important to note these hazards on one's condition report and take all necessary precautions.

Measurements are a necessary aspect of condition reporting and should be listed on the report in a standardized fashion. Given the unique nature of natural history specimens, it is advisable to state the orientation of the specimen on the report since the "top" and "bottom" of a specimen may not always be clear, particularly for fossils or mineral specimens. If measurements will still not be clear even after orientation is stated, a sketch or photograph with measurements labeled can eliminate confusion.

Should the specimen have an attached mount, such as a small log for a taxidermy animal, or metal armature, such as for articulated paleontological specimens, it is advisable to state whether measurements include the mount or armature. Additionally, if the specimen and the mount or armature detaches in a particular way, this should be documented in the condition report so proper handling can be exercised when the specimen is moved in the future. Likewise, if stabilization or conservation have been undertaken or there are damage or weak areas of concern, these should be noted on the condition report.

Given the variety and quantity of natural history field-collected specimens, condition reports are generally not completed when these collections are accessioned. Instead, they are done when a specific need arises, such as a loan and/or exhibition. In many cases, an in-depth condition report need not occur if the natural history specimens are being loaned only for research purposes since the specimen(s) may be modified or partially consumed by the research, as allowed in the loan agreement. However, a general condition assessment should occur and be documented on the loan form. When specimens are loaned for research, the receiving museum or research institution (i.e., university) should be accredited by the American Alliance of Museums (AAM) or recognized in the U.S. Department of Education Office of Post-Secondary Education (OPE) accreditation database. Should the natural history specimen(s) be loaned for exhibition and educational purposes, an in-depth condition report should occur on an object-by-object basis.

Due to the diverse nature of natural history collections, it is difficult to design one form that covers every material type covered by the category.

Please use and modify the basic form at the end of chapter 1 as a basic form for these collections.

CONDITION GLOSSARY

Abrasion: A wearing away of the surface caused by scraping, rubbing, grinding, or friction; often superficial.

Accretion: Any external material deposited on a surface; often results from burial conditions or accidental deposits, such as splashes, drips, fly specks, etc.

Adhesive Residue: May be from glue, paste, or pressure-sensitive tapes.

Articulated: When components of an animal skeleton or fossil are joined together in the relative position of original existence.

Cataloging: Assigning an object to an established classification system with a unique identifying number and having a record containing such things as identification, provenance, accession number, and location of that object in the collection storage area.

Chip: A defect in a surface characterized by the breaking away of material.

Condition Report: An accurate written and photographic description of an object to document its state of preservation at a moment in time and updated each time the object is involved in any activity, such as going on loan or exhibition.

Consolidation: Application of a liquid polymer in a viscous solution that imparts strength to a fragile specimen.

Crack: A surface fracture or fissure across or through a material, either straight-line or branching in form; no loss is implied. A crack may be described as blind when it stops partway, as hairline when it is a tiny fissure, and as open when it is a large fissure.

Delamination: A separation of layers; splitting.

Dent: A defect in the surface caused by a blow; a simple concavity.

Discoloration: A partial or overall change in color caused by aging, light, or chemical agents. Yellowing and darkening can occur, along with bleaching, the lightening of color, and fading, a loss of color or a change in hue.

Disjoin: A partial or complete separation of a joint between two members of an object, as distinguished from a crack, tear, check, or split.

Distortion: A warping or misshaping of the original shape; shrinkage may occur.

Documentation: All paper and other physical records and electronic records of information relating to an object or collection; the term is also used for the process of creating records pertaining to each object in a collection.

Embrittlement: A loss of flexibility causing the material (e.g., paper, parchment, leather) to break or disintegrate when bent or curled.

Fixing: The use of a chemical, often formaldehyde, that reacts with tissue to limit deterioration.

Frass: Insect excrement and shed skins left as waste on specimens; duff.

Hair Loss: Area of loose or missing fur in objects and garments made of pelts; often due to pest activity or improper processing of the hide.

Infills: A gape or hole in a specimen that is filled with a foreign material for structural stability or aesthetic integration.

Loss: Missing area or hole.

Mold: Biological in nature, mold or mildew can be in the form of foxing; of colored, furry, or weblike surface excrescences; and/or of musty odor.

Molding and Casting: Techniques used to make three-dimensional copies, generally of fossil specimens.

Nomenclature: A system of terms used in a particular science or discipline, for example, an international system of standardized New Latin names used in biology for kinds and groups of animals and plants.

Pest Damage: Surface loss, tunneling, holes, fly specks, etc., obviously caused by insects or other pests.

Preparation: The process of readying natural science specimens for storage in a museum collection.

Preventive Conservation: Measures to maintain the collections in stable condition through preventive maintenance, condition surveys, environmental controls, and pest management (as opposed to processes involving physical intervention—e.g., restoration).

Relative Humidity (abbreviation: RH or rh): The amount of moisture vapor (gas) in the air, expressed as a percentage of the maximum possible at that temperature. This is usually expressed as a percentage of the moisture level of saturated air at a given temperature.

Shrinkage: A loss of mass or size that can be in response to dry relative humidity conditions.

Spalling: Shallow losses or flaking from the surface of stone or ceramic materials.

Stain: A color change as a result of soiling, adhesives, pest residue, food, oils, etc. A diffuse stain is without a distinct boundary; a discrete stain has a distinct boundary; a liquid stain has a discrete boundary or tide-line that is darker than the general area of the stain; a centered stain has a darker or more intensely colored center within its general area. In metallic staining, adjacent materials are discolored as a result of metal corrosion.

Tanning: Methods used to change the chemical structure of skin making it resistant to deterioration.

Type Specimen: The specimen used to describe a new species for the first time; type specimens have extremely high scientific value.

Wear: Surface erosion, usually at edges, due to repeated handling.

BIBLIOGRAPHY

"Appendix Q: Curatorial Care of Natural History Collections." In *NPS Museum Handbook, Pt. 1: Museum Collections*. Washington, D.C.: National Park Service, 1999.

"Appendix T: Curatorial Care of Biological Collections." In *NPS Museum Handbook, Pt. 1: Museum Collections*. Washington, D.C.: National Park Service, 2005.

Boylan, P. J., ed. *Running a Museum: A Practical Handbook*. Paris: International Council of Museums (ICOM), 2004.

"Byne's 'Disease': How to Recognize, Handle and Store Affected Shells and Related Collections." *Conserve-O-Gram* 11/15 (2008). National Park Service.

"Database of Accredited Postsecondary Institutions and Programs." U.S. Department of Education Office of Post-Secondary Education. Accessed March 18, 2021. http://ope.ed.gov/accreditation/.

Demeroukas, M. "Condition Reporting." In *Museum Registration Methods*, edited by R. A. Buck and J. A. Gilmore. Washington, D.C.: The AAM Press, 2010.

Douglass, D. L., C. Shing, and G. Wang. "The Light-Induced Alteration of Realgar to Pararealgar." *American Mineralogist* 77 (1992): 1266–74. Accessed March 18, 2021. http://www.minsocam.org/msa/collectors_corner/arc/realgar.htm.

"Health and Safety Issues with Geological Specimens." *Conserve-O-Gram* 11/11 (2006). National Park Service.

Hurst, K. J. "Repositories." In *Museum Registration Methods*, edited by R. A. Buck and J. A. Gilmore. Washington, D.C.: The AAM Press, 2010.

Kubiatowicz, R., and L. Benson. "Oh No! Ethnobotany! The Safe Handling and Storage of Hazardous Ethnobotanical Artifacts." *Collection Forum* 18.1–2 (2003): 59–73.

Makos, K. A. "Hazard Identification and Exposure Assessment Related to Handling and Use of Contaminated Collection Materials and Sacred Objects." *Collection Forum* 77.1–2 (2001): 93–112.

Malaro, M. C., and I. P. DeAngelis. *A Legal Primer on Managing Museum Collections*, 3rd ed. Washington, D.C.: Smithsonian Books, 2012.

"Mineralogy." National Museum Wales. Accessed March 18, 2021. http://museum.wales/curatorial/natural-sciences/mineralogy.

Odegaard, N. "The Issue of Pesticide Contamination." In *Caring for American Indian Objects: A Practical and Cultural Guide*, edited by S. Ogden. Saint Paul, MN: Minnesota Historical Society Press, 2004.

"Pesticides." National Museum of the American Indian, Smithsonian Institution. Accessed March 18, 2021. http://nmai.si.edu/explore/collections/conservation/pesticides/.

"Radioactive Minerals." *National Park Service Conserve-O-Gram* 11/10 (2006). National Park Service.

Rose, Carolyn L., Catharine A. Hawks, and Robert Waller. "A Preventive Conservation Approach to the Storage of Collections." In *Preventive Conservation: Collection Storage*, edited by Lisa Elkin and Christopher A. Norris. Society for the Preservation of Natural History Collections, 2019.

Sirois, P. J., and G. Sansoucy. 2001. "Analysis of Museum Objects for Hazardous Pesticide Residues: A Guide to Techniques." In *Collection Forum* 77.1–2 (2001): 49–66.

"Ten Agents of Deterioration." Canadian Conservation Institute. Accessed March 18, 2021. https://www.canada.ca/en/conservation-institute/services/agents-deterioration.html.

U.S. Environmental Protection Agency. Accessed March 18, 2021. http://www.epa.gov/.

Viscardi, Paolo. 2011. "Natural History Collections: Why Are They Relevant?" *The Guardian.* Accessed March 18, 2021. https://www.theguardian.com/science/punctuated-equilibrium/2011/apr/12/2.

USEFUL WEBSITES

Canadian Conservation Institute Notes: http://www.cci-icc.gc.ca/publications/notes/index-eng.aspx.

National Park Service Museum Management Publications: http://www.nps.gov/history/museum/publications/.

The Society for the Preservation of Natural History Collections (SPNHC): http://www.spnhc.org.

13

Paintings and Frames

Dixie Neilson

Condition reports are generally done on paintings (and other collection objects) for several important reasons: New acquisitions need a report that establishes a baseline against which future examinations can be compared; incoming loans must have a report written upon unpacking, listing any defects in condition as a way to protect your museum from claims of damage or liability upon their return (damage noted should be immediately reported to the lender); your painting is going to or returning from a loan; your work is going to or returning from a multi-venue traveling exhibition; the painting is going on exhibit in your museum or has been recently deinstalled; collections are being prepared for movement due to building renovation; when damage occurs; before and after any conservation work is done; and general assessments done as routine collections care. Your aim in doing the report dictates the makeup of the form, and the length of condition information needed. Paintings being prepared for a lengthy traveling exhibition need a great deal of information, while those done as part of a routine condition check may only need a quick review.

If you are doing a report on a painting that has been in your collection for some time, it is likely that you already have at least one condition report stored in the object's documentary file. In those cases, it is best to review and update the information on the same sheet of paper as the original report. Starting a new report each time the condition is assessed will result in numerous forms that all need to be consulted and compared in order to accurately determine the painting's condition, as well as time wasted rewriting the same information. New notes should be included on the old report with the reporter's initials and the current date. If the report becomes chaotic after numerous additions, a new form should be attached for continued writing. Do not start the report over again.

Painting is generally characterized as the manual application of pigments (either ground or mixed in a medium) to a surface. Components of a painting usually consist of the *support*, the paper, canvas, wood panel, plaster wall, sheet metal, or other material that acts as a base upon which the painting is executed; the *ground*, a preliminary coating (e.g., gesso, sizing, lead white) given to the support to make a more desirable surface for rendering the painting; and the *design layer*, the pencil, chalk, ink, paint, etc., applied to the ground or directly to the support to form the painting. Paintings sometimes suffer from the use of nontraditional materials and techniques that are unusual and incompatible. In these cases, the painting should be considered a work of mixed media, with reporting done on each component using appropriate terms for each material type. Be especially vigilant in the areas where one material is attached to another, making sure the adhesions are secure.

Frames provide protection and stability for painted surfaces, and they often enhance the aesthetic quality of a work of art. Like paintings, frames are made with a composite of materials, usually metal or wood, with gesso, gilding, and hanging hardware. Frame types may include: square beaded back edge, plain back hollow, scrolling foliage top edge, plain front hollow, plain cushioned strip, foliage strip, or chamfered sight edge. Because of the composite nature of paintings and frames, and the fact that much of their makeup is of hygroscopic (water-absorbing) materials, they are extremely susceptible to damage due to fluctuations in the environment. These fluctuations cause each of the various materials to expand and contract at different rates and in different directions. Many other factors affect the physical condition of a painting, including age, light, storage methods, housekeeping practices, and previous restoration techniques.

TERMINOLOGY FOR PAINTINGS

Canvas: Cloth material used as the paint support. Material is commonly cotton, hemp, flax, or sometimes silk.

Enamel: A hard-gloss paint varying somewhat in composition. Generally, the medium consists of heat-treated oil combined with either natural or synthetic resins.

Encaustic: Method of painting with wax that was developed early in the sixteenth century. The process consists of melting or burning wax, mixed with color and resins, into the painting's surface.

Fresco: A painting on damp plaster that uses lime water as a medium. Often finished with egg tempera, also known as *buon fresco.* When painted on dry plaster, it may be called *secco fresco.*

Gesso: Pale, creamy, white priming that provides a ground layer for oil and tempera paintings. The term originally meant a substance composed of burnt gypsum (or plaster of Paris, named for a large gypsum deposit in Paris) mixed with glue, but it has come to have a wider meaning and now includes grounds made from chalk (whiting) or other inert white pigments bound with glue size (usually parchment size, calfskin glue, rabbit skin glue, or isinglass).

Gouache: Synonymous with poster paint, an opaque watercolor thinned with liquid glue. Also known as *distemper.*

Liner/Lining: A fine linen canvas made to adhere to the reverse side of a canvas painting to counteract structural weakness in the original canvas, or to secure cleavage between the paint/ground and canvas layers.

Lining: A new canvas added to the back of an old, deteriorating canvas for additional support.

Medium: Material that holds together pigment particles in paint.

Moisture Barrier: Layer with high water vapor impermeability, such as beeswax, which is often applied as the last stage of conservation treatment to the back of a painting on canvas. Wax-resin lining acts as its own moisture barrier. A moisture barrier may also be applied to the reverse and edges of panel paintings to protect them from changes in atmospheric humidity.

Oil Paints: A paint consisting of pigments pulverized in a drying oil, usually linseed. After drying, oil paintings are often varnished to increase the amount of light reflected by the pigments and to impart a somewhat glossy finish to the painting.

Panel: A stiff first or secondary support of wood, metal, or composition board.

Pastel: Chalk or crayon made from pigments and fillers held together in stick form by a weak gum medium.

Relining: The act of removing and replacing an old canvas lining.

Size: In its broadest sense, any material that is used to seal a porous surface. The term is frequently applied to a glutinous mixture of gelatin, skin glue, starch, resin, or gum in water. Raw canvas is normally "sized" before the application of the ground or priming.

Stretcher: The wood frame to which the canvas is attached.

Surface Coating: Transparent layer or series of layers applied over the surface of a painting for protection and for a uniform reflection and surface texture. Usually consists of natural or artificial resins, waxes, or oils.

Polymer: Type of thermoplastic material (i.e., may be softened with heat) that is dissolved in a solvent when used as a medium for mixing with pigments to create synthetic polymer paint. Common synthetic polymers are polyvinyl acetate, polyesters, epoxies, and acrylic resins.

Tempera: Until the fifteenth century, it may have meant all painting media, but the term generally refers to a medium prepared from egg.

Varnish: Transparent surface coating used to protect and enhance the design layer. Varnish contains resinous matter either dissolved hot in drying oil (oil-resin varnish), or cold in a solvent (solvent-type or spirit varnish).

TERMINOLOGY FOR FRAMES

Backing Board: Sheet attached to the back of a frame to protect it from dust, pollutants, and mechanical shock.

Batten Cleat: Strip of wood nailed or glued across parallel boards or across the grain of a panel for reinforcement, flattening, or to prevent warping. Several battens constitute a *cradle*.

Compo (short for *composition*): Any of various combined substances, such as mortar or plaster, formed by mixing ingredients.

Cradle: Wood structure slotted and joined with glue to the back of a panel painting. Designed to prevent warping, the cradle often forces the panel to crack with changes in humidity.

D Rings: Hanging hardware so named because of its shape. Available in various sizes, a D ring is screwed into the proper right and proper left sides of the frame's reverse so the painting may hang safely from two hooks.

Glazing: Transparent glass or acrylic sheeting that sometimes covers the surface of a painting. Some glazing materials have added ultraviolet (UV) protection to absorb short-wave UV energy, thus reducing fading from light exposure.

Gilding: Goldleaf or paint containing or simulating gold, usually applied in very thin layers.

Keys, Stretcher Keys: Thin triangular pieces of wood that, when tapped into the corner of a stretcher, cause the stretcher members to be forced apart, thus tightening the canvas. Paintings should contain eight keys, two in each corner. Loose keys may fall out and migrate during handling, becoming wedged behind other areas of the frame. If not located and removed, they may damage the painting's surface.

Mending Plate: A hardware device with screw holes used to secure the painting and the frame together.

Miter, Miter Joint: The corner where two perpendicular sides of a frame meet. Made by cutting the edges of two frame pieces at a 45-degree angle and fitting them together to form a 90-degree corner.

Rabbet: Groove cut in the edge of the frame to hold the painting.

Stretcher: Wood frame, often with jointed corners, over which canvas paintings are stretched. May be expanded and the canvas tightened by driving in keys or various kinds of springs.

HANDLING

Never carry more than one painting at a time. For a large panel or canvas, ask two or more art handlers to assist you. It is much better to wait for help than to risk damaging a work of art because you attempted to move an unwieldy piece alone. If the painting is heavy or you need to move several paintings at once, use a trolley or side cart. The cart should have a padded floor with a lip along the front and back. Be sure to arrange paintings evenly on each side of the cart to prevent tipping.

When working with unframed works, wear thin gloves to protect painted surfaces from dirt, oils, and fingerprints. Firmly, but gently, grasp the painting at its edges. Before touching a framed painting, examine it carefully. Ensure that the work is secure in the frame and that the frame hardware is sound. Hanging wires are discouraged, as they become brittle and may snap as your painting hangs on the wall. Use D rings in their place. Wooden frames usually have keys, small triangular pieces of wood or plastic, used as wedges to tighten the canvas. Each frame should have eight keys, two in each corner that fit into slots in the frame. If any are missing, check the frame edges carefully to see if the key has become detached and migrated across the canvas back. They may become lodged between the frame and the canvas, and if not removed, will eventually cause damage to the painting. If you have concerns about the condition of the frame or the painting, consult a conservator. Once you are confident of the condition, gently lift the painting with both hands. Lift larger paintings with one hand placed on each side of the frame at a point where it is solid. Larger paintings may be carried with one hand on the side and one underneath. Never lift or carry a framed painting by the top of the frame or by the stretcher bar. It may not truly be secure, and you will be left with a piece of the frame in hand and the painting on the floor.

Stacking paintings in storerooms is inherently risky and should be avoided if possible. If stacking is unavoidable, it should be done on a short-term basis. Stack like-sized paintings together upright, front to front and back to back, in as short a stack as possible. Make sure no frame edges rest on the face of the painting behind it. Only the frames should touch each other. Never lay paintings flat (unless the painting is flaking and awaiting conservation). Ideally, paintings should be hung from D rings on a painting screen or in bins separated by acid-free padding, such as pieces of polyethylene foam, mat board, or paper bolsters.

Before starting your review, check to see if there is an existing condition report in the object's documentary file. If so, review it carefully. Check any areas that had been noted as concerns to see if the amount of damage has stabilized or worsened. Information from your new exam should be added to the original report to ensure that all information is passed along. Having several pages of reports for the same object can become confusing, and some information is bound to be missed. Make sure to initial and date any new information that is added.

EXAMINATION

Choose a clean, well-lit, and secure area in which to conduct your examination. Allow enough time to give the objects a careful review and write concise but informative reports. Gather and lay your tools out in advance to avoid having the object unnecessarily exposed to light while you look for your implements. The table on which the paintings are to be examined should be clean and well padded. In order to avoid placing the painted surface directly on the table, place it on padded blocks when examining the back (verso). If the frame is particularly ornate or fragile, you may prefer to have someone hold it in an upright position while you examine the back.

Use two adjustable lights for general illumination and cross lighting. Portable gooseneck lamps with dichroic halogen lights that prevent overheating are ideal. In addition, you should have a flashlight, a head-fitting jeweler's loupe and/or magnifying glass, gloves, a digital camera, soft pencils, examination forms, and a metal measuring tape. Cloth measuring tapes quickly stretch out and will not give you accurate dimensions, but care should be taken not to touch the painting or frame with those made of metal. You may also need pliers and a screwdriver for removing frames and hardware, if necessary.

It is often easier and less time-consuming to have a two-person team work on the condition reports. One person conducts the exam verbally, while the other person writes the information. This way the examiner does not have to constantly take his or her eyes off the work and stop to write the information.

PAINTINGS

Begin the examination with a visual once-over to assess the basic nature and condition of the piece. Note any large or obvious areas of concern, then begin a systematic review of every square inch of the painting under well-lighted conditions. It is important to view the painting using several different angles of light, as certain defects will appear only under specific lighting angles. A one-directional light is not adequate to the task. The light source should not be directed at any one area for too long, nor should the light be too close to the work in order to protect the painting from overheating or overexposure to light. Remember to turn off the lights whenever you are not actively using them to limit the time of any light exposure.

SOURCES OF ILLUMINATION

Sources of illumination include:

45-Degree Oblique Angle: Use to conduct the initial, overall exam with a light source at a 45-degree angle. This reveals obvious surface defects and allows the examiner to scan the painting in general before moving on to a detailed inspection.

Specular Reflection: When the light source is placed at a 30-degree angle, the examiner is better able to spot uneven gloss or matte areas.

Raking Light: This type of light, positioned horizontally along the top or bottom edge of the painting that is lying flat on a worktable, fully illuminates the surface and often obscures the details of the composition. It is useful for locating small losses of paint and ground, and identifying various types of crack formations.

Transmitted Light: When the light is shone from the reverse of the painting, through the support, it emphasizes surface irregularities such as small holes, as well as cupping and cleaving paint and ground.

Ultraviolet Light: Use sparingly and in a darkened room. An ultraviolet light will help detect past conservation efforts and any residue on the painting, including resins or adhesives.

Measure and note the extent of each defect. For example, a tear may be listed as "a diagonal tear, one inch in length, five inches from the bottom and three inches from the left," thus enabling a future examiner to quickly locate the spot you described and determine whether the defect has changed. Describe all defects with the following standardized degrees of severity: *negligible*, *slight*, *moderate*, *marked*, and *extreme*.

LOCATION

It is helpful to make a sketch, no matter how rough, to indicate the placement and nature of the flaw. The condition report form should have a blank space large enough to accommodate a drawing of this nature. Be sure to record any information on any labels or any existing inscriptions, and take a photograph of the entire front and back of the piece, as well as detailed shots of areas of concern. Print a digital image on regular copy paper to add notes or drawings to help clarify areas of concern.

Note on the condition report whether the examination was done while the painting was framed or unframed. Describing a painting's condition while it is in the frame presumes a certain imprecision in measurement and condition. Remember to turn the painting over and report on the condition of its back (verso). A great deal of condition information can be learned by looking at the reverse side of the painting. What often looks acceptable from the front is not an accurate representation of the whole piece. Any labels found on the back of the painting should be left in place unless they are causing damage. Provenance can often be traced through those labels. However, do not attach any new labels, such as exhibition information, without the owner's permission.

WHAT TO LOOK FOR IN PAINTINGS

Paint Layer

Using the light methods described above, start your examination in one area and move methodically over the entire work. Look for any defect in the ground or the paint layers and distinguish between obviously older (historic) damage and that which has recently occurred. Describe any evidence of older repairs. Inherent flaws, such as a paintbrush hair embedded in the paint layers, may be described at the reporter's discretion. Check to see if there are obvious cracks. If so, describe their depth. Do they only go through the surface layer or all the way through the paint and ground layers? Are there signs of paint lifting or losses? Do the losses expose the ground layer, the support, or another layer of paint? Has the color noticeably changed, faded, or been stained? Some paintings that have been subjected to cigarette or cigar smoke may be yellowed. Is the painting a different color or shade in the area where the frame has been?

Surface Layer

Many paintings have been varnished following their creation. Others may have a wax surface. Is the coating visible? Is it evenly covering the entire surface, or has it worn off in certain spots? Is the gloss evenly applied? Is it clear, or has it turned yellow and milky, or does it have another appearance? Is the surface chalky or powdery? Can you see any cracks in the surface material? Is there dirt or grime in the cracks?

Ground Layer

Is the ground layer clean or dirty and dusty? It is secure, or is it crumbling or brittle? Is there evidence of cupping or cracking? Is it well adhered to the support, or are there any losses?

Once the front has been examined, turn the painting over and look at the reverse of both the support and the frame. Unframed paintings may be placed facedown on a lightly padded, glassine-covered surface only if the pigment layer appears stable. Otherwise, one person should gently hold the painting in an upright position on a table while the examiner looks at the reverse.

Support

Examine the back of the painting. Often, damage that is not visible from the front is evident by looking at the reverse, or verso. Information on the support may best be discovered by looking at the back of the painting. If the paint is obviously flaking, do not lay the painting on its face, as this is likely to cause further damage. Looking at the back is also a way to see the true edges of a framed painting that may have been obscured by the frame. Use this opportunity to obtain correct dimensions of the painting.

Is the support rigid or flexible? Is there a backing board attached? What is the material? Is there cardboard attached? If it is possible to remove a cardboard backing, do so. This will prevent the highly acidic cardboard from "burning" acid marks onto the painting. Is the support worn or deteriorating? If the support is made from more than one piece, are they still firmly joined? Are the corners intact? Is the backing flat or misshapen?

If there is a stretcher bar, can you identify the wood? Is the canvas attached to the stretcher with nails or tacks? Are they all there? Look at the edges of the canvas. Is it firmly attached to the stretcher bar? Is the back dirty and dusty? Is there any evidence of pest infestation? Is there any evidence of water damage on the back of the painting?

Insect Damage

Inspect the surface of the painting for "fly specks" or "spider marks," which are deposits left behind by insects. The former look like tiny round dots, and the latter are teardrop-shaped specks. Both of these deposits are highly corrosive and should be removed by a conservator.[1] Shed insect skins may become lodged in the painting edges just inside the frame. In some cases, it is enough to push the canvas out of shape so they can be removed.

When you see paint losses, try to determine if they have come about as a result of a chip or crack, or if the paint or canvas has been eaten by some kind of insect. The two causes have different features. Paint losses from damage often look as though a piece has broken off, and there may be a distinct edge line, like a missing puzzle piece. Insect damage is more subtle, but often entails a larger area. Paint eaten away may look like some of the color has been erased, with indistinct edges. If you are familiar with a sweater hole made by a moth, you will recognize the same characteristic in canvas, another of their targets. Also, look for sawdust type material and tiny pinholes indicating pests have bored into the work. If active infestation is suspected, paintings may be fumigated, but this should only be done by experienced pest control specialists on the advice of a painting conservator.

FRAMES

A frame's ornamentation may be carved solid wood, metal, or a composite molded material. Some frames are themselves works of art, have historic value, or are creations designed by the artist and meant specifically to complete and complement the work. If the frame is important to the painting, that information should be noted in the object's documentary file and on the condition report form. If a frame is removed from its painting, note its location in your database or object records so that it, and the painting, may be rejoined at a future date. Frames created by the artist should be considered as part of the work of art. In such cases, exhibiting the painting without the frame that the artist intended is a misrepresentation of his or her work, and may be a violation of the Visual Artists Rights Act (VARA). Keep in mind that VARA applies to living artists only. One obvious exception is in cases where the frame has been damaged and/or has become a physical threat to the painting. In these instances, the frame should be removed by a conservator, and the artist or estate notified for instructions. When storing a frame that has been removed from a painting in the museum's collection, identify it with a tag that says "Frame for: (accession number)."

Examine the frame using the same methodical approach as with the painting. Start in one corner and look at the entire frame carefully. In highly ornamental frames, problems may be more difficult to spot due to the intricate surface. A jeweler's loupe and/or a magnifying glass will help you to identify problem areas.

WHAT TO LOOK FOR IN FRAMES

What is the material used to make the frame? Is there decoration? If so, is it all intact? Is there a decorative finish such as gilding? Look at the security of the painting within the frame. It should be firmly and properly inserted and held in tightly. Is the frame strong enough to hold the painting? Check the miters to ensure they are tight and that the frame is not coming apart at its joints. Measure scratches, abrasions, and cracks, and include their dimensions on the report in order to track any changes over time.

Examine the frame-hanging apparatus. Remove wire along with its eyelet attached to the frame. Paintings should be hung by D rings that are securely screwed to the frame, or other hardware recommended by a conservator.

Look for small holes shedding sawdust, which may indicate an active insect infestation. Consult a conservator prior to extermination of frame pests such as wood borers, as some fumigation techniques may be harmful to the frame finish. A conservator can help determine whether insects have traveled from the frame to the stretcher, and can also recommend an appropriate treatment.

DOCUMENTATION

While brevity is important on the condition report form, so is clarity. A condition report becomes a permanent part of the object's documentation and may be read a hundred years from now, presumably when the reporter is not there to explain what he/she meant. Keeping in mind that it is likely that someone else will be reading the report, make sure to use commonly known terms and write as legibly as possible. Always sign and date the report. When updating an old form, date and initial new entries.

Make every attempt to describe the three attributes of any defect: its nature, its location, and its extent. The nature of the defect refers to the actual flaw, which may be noted as an inherent condition (aka "historic" or "original"), or actual damage. Location can be described in a number of ways; the zone and matrix systems being the most common (see chapter 1 in this volume). Additional information, such as "above the man's head," may be added for clarity.

When discussing the left and right side of a painting, it is preferable to use the terms *proper left* and *proper right* for clarity. To recall the correct orientation, imagine that the painting had a left arm that would be described as the proper left side. In other words, right or left from the object's point of view.

CONDITION GLOSSARY FOR PAINTINGS AND FRAMES

Basic terms such as *discoloration*, *soil*, *mold*, and *insect damage* have not been added to this glossary list. Only terms specific to paintings and frames are included. Review other chapters in this handbook for general definitions.

Abrasion: Damaged area of upper paint layers or frame surface, resulting from scraping, rubbing, or grinding away.

Accretion: Accidental surface deposit of known or unknown origin (e.g., fly specks, spatters).

Blister: Bulge in the paint surface indicating cleavage of paint or ground layers either from each other or from the support.

Bloom: Hazy, bluish-white cloudiness that appears on all or part of the surface of some varnish. Results from the breakdown of the consistency of the coating by moisture or other pollutants.

Buckling: Appearance of waves or bulges in a canvas that has slackened on its stretcher.

Chalking: Loss of pigment in a paint layer by powdering off. Results from either an insufficient quantity of binding medium in the paint when originally applied, or the loss of the binding medium as a result of damage or deteriorating conditions.

Check: Rupture in wood running along the grain from the edge of a board or panel for a part of its length.

Cleavage: Separation between paint layers, paint and ground layers, or ground and support. Occurs where adhesion between layers has deteriorated.

Crackle, *Craquelure*: Network of fine cracks that develop in the ground, paint layer, or surface coating of a painting as the materials age or dry or as the result of a blow. *Age cracks* usually penetrate both the paint layer and ground. They are caused by strain from movement of the support. *Drying cracks* or *youth cracks* are caused by the failure of the film to withstand its own

Condition Report Form
Paintings and Frames

Accession Number:________________________ Artist:__________________________________

Title: ____

Description:

____

____

____

Media:

____

Dimensions:________________________________ Frame: ________________________________

Examiner: _________________________________ Examination Date: _______________________

Please record any problems below. Include the type of problem, size/extent, and location.

I. SUPPORT

( ) Slack

____

( ) Buckling

____

( ) Puncture/Tear ____

( ) Breaks/Splits ____

( ) Warp ____

( ) Draw

____

( ) Keys Missing

____

( ) Other

____

____

II. GROUND & PAINT LAYERS/SURFACE COATING

( ) Abrasion

____

( ) Accretion

____

( ) Blister

____

( ) Bloom

____

( ) Chalking

____

Figure 13.1. Paintings and frames condition report form.
Source: Dixie Neilsen

( ) Cleavage

____

( ) Crackle

____

( ) Cracks

____

( ) Cupping

____

( ) Dent

____

( ) Discoloration

____

( ) Flaking

____

( ) Stretcher Crease ____

( ) Other ____

III. LINER

( ) Soiled

____

( ) Tear ____

( ) Losses

____

( ) Disjointed Miters

____

( ) Other

____

____

IV. FRAME

( ) Miters Loose ____

( ) Wires & Screws Attached ____

( ) Chipped

____

( ) Cracked ____

( ) Loose Pieces

____

( ) Losses

____

( ) Gesso or Finish Flaking

____

( ) Other

____

____

Figure 13.1. ***(continued)***
Source: Dixie Neilsen

contraction during drying. They usually do not penetrate the whole structure from support to surface. *Mechanical cracks*, although similar in appearance and character to age cracks, are often caused by external local pressure and frequently appear in a "bull's-eye" pattern of concentric circles.

Cupping: Consists of islands of paint with upward curving edges bounded by cracks. A weak canvas is often drawn upward with the curving edges.

Dent, Dig, Gouge: Defect in the surface caused by a blow. A *dent* is a simple depression in the surface. A *dig* implies that some material has been displaced. A *gouge* indicates that material has been scooped out.

Draw: System of wrinkles radiating from a corner of a stretched fabric, or parallel wrinkles emanating from an edge of a stretched fabric.

Dry Rot: Decay of seasoned timber caused by fungi that consume the cellulose of wood, leaving a soft skeleton that is readily reduced to powder. Can occur in frames, stretchers, keys, and wood supports.

Efflorescence: Powdery surface crust that is formed when substances in plaster or varnish migrate to the surface and crystallize upon contact with air.

Flaking: Breaking away or detachment of one or all painting layers in either small particles or larger areas. See *blister*, *buckling*, *cleavage*, and *crackle*, of which flaking is an extreme stage.

Foxing: Brown or reddish-brown spots caused by mold or the oxidation of iron particles in a paper support, mount, or backing.

Impasto: Thick, often opaque area of paint that protrudes above the surface to which it has been applied.

Inpainting: Introduction of new paint material into areas of loss in an original construction.

Loss: Missing flake of paint or ground from the surface of the painting.

Overpainting: An addition that wholly or partially covers original paint. Paint added by artists or restorers wishing to "improve" a painting was more commonly practiced in the past. Overpainting to change the appearance of another artist's work is today considered an unethical violation of the artist's rights.

Pentimento: Phenomenon in which the translucency of upper paint layers allows for the emergence of tones beneath. As more light penetrates the paint layer, the drawing and underpaint, once concealed, show through. Literally translated from Italian, "repentance" is related to an artist's decision to change his original design when adding the paint layer.

Split: Rupture in wood running along the grain from end to end of a panel or board causing complete separation.

Stretcher Crease: An impression in the form of the stretcher bar, appearing on the paint surface. Although the impression is not always marked by a cracked or cupped surface, the edge of the stretcher sometimes causes parallel straight cracks on the surface. Stretcher creases are common in a painting whose surface exhibits crackle.

Tenting: Lifting up of paint from a canvas into a small tent shape. If untreated, it may become a small crack.

Wear: Surface erosion, usually at the edges, resulting from repeated handling.

NOTE

1. Rustin Levenson, Florida Conservation Associates, Miami, FL, in Condition Report segment, *From Here to There: Museum Standards for Object Handling*, HD DVD Video, 2012.

BIBLIOGRAPHY

Buck, Rebecca A., and Jean A. Gilmore, eds. *Museum Registration Methods*, 5th edition. Washington, D.C.: American Association of Museums, 2010.

Canadian Conservation Institute, Technical Bulletins, www.cci-icc.gc.ca. Retrieved from: http://www.cci-icc.gc.ca/cci-icc/about-apropos/index-eng.aspx.

Caple, Chris, ed. *Preventative Conservation in Museums*. New York: Routledge, Taylor and Francis Group, 2011.

Condition Reports. Museums and Galleries, Woolloomooloo, 2011. Retrieved from: http://mgnsw.org.au/uploaded/ConditionReports.pdf.

Leisher, William R. 1992. "Paintings." In *Caring for Your Collections*, edited by Harriet Whelchel. New York: Harry N. Abrams, Inc.

National Park Service. *The Museum Handbook: Museum Collections*. Washington, D.C.: Museum Management Program. Retrieved from: http://www.nps.gov/history/museum/publications/handbook.html.

National Park Service. "Storage Screens for Paintings." *Conserve-O-Gram* 12/1, July 1993.

Neilson, Dixie. *From Here to There: Museum Standards for Object Handling*. HD DVD Video, 2012. www.artcare.biz.

Shelly, Marjorie. *The Care and Handling of Art Objects: Practices in the Metropolitan Museum of Art*. New York: Harry N. Abrams, 1987.

Stolow, Nathan. *Conservation and Exhibitions*. London: Butterworths, 1987.

14

Paper

LaToya Devezin

Paper, invented by the Chinese official Cai (sometimes written Tsai) Lun[1] around the second century BCE, provides a method to record our historical narrative, communicate, examine collective memory, and preserve our legacy for future generations. The secrecy of its construction was well guarded until the eighth century, when the first papermill was established in Samarkand by the Arabs following an invasion of China. It traveled through the Middle East and expanded swiftly into the Western world, where the use of the innovation soon became a universal practice with the inventions of moveable type, the printing press, and the arrival of the Industrial Revolution. The etymology of the word *paper* derives from the word *papyrus*, a plant that was also used as a medium for writing in the ancient world, much like its contemporary *parchment*, which was made from untanned animal skins.[2] Paper is a sheet(s) primarily made from extracting interwoven cellulose plant fibers, which is pressed through matting or felting, dried, then sized, and finished. The process of papermaking can vary based on the location, and it can be made with a variety of materials, including cotton and silk.[3] The quality and manufacturing of paper changed in the nineteenth century with the introduction of wood pulp paper (both chemical and untreated groundwood), which is still used in modern papermaking. Ironically, wood, which served as one of the catalysts for the invention of paper due to the difficulty of writing on and transporting it, is now what most paper is made from.[4]

Paper's "metaphysical power of transmitting the meaning of the mark it carries" also corresponds with its use as a medium for the creation of works on paper.[5] Works on paper are mostly two-dimensional prints, drawings, paintings, pastels, watercolors, mixed media collages, manuscripts, maps, bound volumes, and photographs. Contemporary works can also include three-dimensional and digital printing. Though works on paper can vary in materials used in their creation, they require similar methods for their handling, examination, and documentation. During evaluation and completion of condition reporting, consideration should be given to the risk assessment, reference checklist, and their subsequent preservation and conservation needs.

HANDLING

When handling works on paper, consider the object's inherent vice and valuation. Hands should be clean to avoid the transferring of oils and dirt to works on paper. The use of gloves can be controversial because they protect the works from handling, but they can also provide an obstacle for extremely delicate items. When gloves are not the best option, try to focus on handling the piece from the edges. Pay close attention to fingernails and do not use any lotions or oils on your hands. Be mindful of jewelry, especially bracelets and rings, which can snag or tear the works.

When preparing to examine a work on paper, make sure that the area is a large, flat, well-lit, and clean surface. Cover the area with acid-free paper or support board to make sure that the object is not coming into contact directly with the table's surface or any products that were used to clean the surface. Be sure that the area is free from food, liquids, or any other items that could damage the work on paper.

Once the examination area is prepared, consider whether the work on paper is mounted, unmounted, or two- or three-dimensional prior to transporting it to the work area. Carts made for specific items, such as a *U*-shaped cart for an architectural drawing, microspatulas, acid-free folders, boards, light boxes, and interleaving paper or tissue are all excellent items to have on hand to aid in handling works on paper. For delicate unmounted works, such as drawings, documents, or prints, transport the items in acid-free folders and use pencil or graphite for making necessary marks. Acid-free folders prevent the works from damage due to their fragility.

Mounted, matted, or framed works on paper can also be moved in a similar manner to unmounted objects if they are smaller in size. Larger matted works should be kept flat if possible, and framed and mounted works usually have a hinge that should be checked for security prior to transporting them. If stacking framed items, stack them with the like sides touching, for example, back to back.[6] Avoid grabbing works mounted on canvas by their frames, as these can be fragile. When transporting larger works, use a cart and another staff person when possible to alleviate pressure on the item since these tend to be heavier. When not working on an object, place a protective acid-free covering, such as a board or paper, on it with a note to alert others who may enter the workspace to prevent damage. Handling occurs before, during, and after the examination phase. The same guidelines apply when transporting three-dimensional works on paper, except for the placement of an acid-free covering when not examining the object.

EXAMINATION

Ideally, examination occurs when an object is accessioned, though it can occur at any time while an object is in a collection. Newly acquired works on paper should be examined for preexisting condition issues in order to "eliminate, if possible, their causes, and to stabilize or repair any existing damage to the extent necessary to safely catalog and prepare the work for rehousing and storage."[7] Prior to examining and handling items, a collection assessment by survey can be conducted "to establish physical and intellectual control over collections, which results in a clearer idea of the scope and needs of the materials."[8] Not all cultural heritage institutions have time to conduct a collection survey because the process can be time-consuming; but, "As the first step to increase access, many institutions have used collections surveys to assess all types of materials within their care to better understand the needs of the backlogged materials and to plan and prioritize projects that will uncover these collections."[9] Examination of works on paper involves an item-level notation of the physical characteristics, chemical structure, the intrinsic value of a work, the item's provenance, and its preservation and conservation needs. An example would include examining the papermaking technique used, checking for the presence of watermarking under a light source, and closely looking for signs of major damage to works on paper, such as "photo-oxidation, acid-migration, biodeterioration, mechanical injury, and improper framing and storage."[10]

After the survey and examination, the condition of the work on paper is recorded on the condition report. To accommodate both paper and digital condition reports, photographs are normally taken or graphic diagrams are used of a work on paper during the examination period to capture the physical characteristics of an object. Examination should be usable on both paper and digital condition reporting, which can vary per institution. The date and the person conducting the examination should be recorded. The documentation for the condition report occurs after the examination of an object.

DOCUMENTATION

Condition reports can be a detailed checklist, a narrative, or a combination. A report "written by a registrar, curator, or collection manager is not the same as a condition report written by a conservator [the former aids in collection management and the latter aids in the planning and conserving of objects]."[11] Condition reports can vary depending on the object, which is highlighted in the sample digital condition report samples following this essay. Digital condition reporting usually occurs within a collections management system where high resolution, detailed photographs of collection items can be uploaded to place all information in a searchable, comprehensive format.

A detailed condition report should include the following: the date of the record's creation, the name of the reporter, the accession number, the type of item, the title of the item (e.g., a painting or book), the number of pieces or parts for the items (e.g., set of framed prints includes multiple pieces), creator name (e.g., author or artist), location and date of origin, provenance, physical characteristics of the item, fitting, frame, mount, damage and cause if known (e.g., brittleness and yellowing for works on paper due to light exposure), conservation needs and level (e.g., tempera paint flaking on a Renaissance-era painting), the dimensions of the work, and photographs or graphics if available. A graphic report usually includes an overlay that can include additional notes about damage or conservation needs for an item or to point out important details. The graphic and photograph can be overlaid together on a paper report, and a digital report can include detailed photos highlighting the same notes. Whether paper or digital, the condition report serves as an integral part of the collections management process. It informs the creation of the collections management policy and ongoing preservation and conservation plans.

GLOSSARY OF COMMON TERMS[12]

Abrasion: Deterioration that is caused by friction or rubbing against the surface of a work on paper, such as a scratched area.

Accretion: A material attached to a paper support, such as mold.

Accession: Refers to the act of acquiring a new item in a collection; an acquisition, or the act of establishing physical and intellectual control over an item.

Acid-Free: The state of having a neutral or alkaline pH level.

Acid Migration: Structural and color damage due to contact with acid or reactive materials such as wood pulp, adhesives, rubber bands, certain pigments that contain or emit harmful acids, or chemicals that are aggressive.[13]

Acidity: The state of having a pH chemical state lower than a 7; can cause brittleness due to moisture in a work on paper.

Biodeterioration: Damage caused by mold growth or insects as a result of high temperature and relative humidity, and a lack of air circulation or cleanliness.[14]

Bloom: A cloudy, white appearance on lacquer or varnish that could be attributed to moisture.

Carbon Ink: A chemically stable ink made with carbon particles carried in glue or gum.

Cockling: A condition that affects paper characterized by concave and convex distortions or ripples, often in parallel ridges.

Crack: A separation or break within one or more layers of material.

Crease: A mark or delineation caused by folding paper.

Deckle Edge: The uneven edges of a paper sheet caused by an uneven set of plant fibers.

Dimpling: The indentation in a paper support.

Discoloration: A chemical reaction that causes a change from the original color—e.g., the yellowing of paper.

Dogear: A crease or fold applied to the corners of paper or a paper support.

Embrittlement: The tendency of paper to break when folded or handled, usually occurs due to environmental factors, such as heat, light, or chemicals used in papermaking.

Encapsulate: The process of using two pieces of a transparent film (usually mylar) to create a sealed enclosure around a piece of paper.

Fading: A process that occurs due to a shift in light or change in pH levels that results in a change in pigments used in a work on paper.

Flaking, Flaked Loss: When an object has undergone physical stress, it can lose binding, which results in the detachment of pigment and binder; often seen with paint.

Foxing: Reddish-brown spots that appear on paper.

Gouge: A concave distortion that occurs as the result of physical damage to a paper support.

Inherent Vice: A material's ability to deteriorate due to instability in its chemical makeup.

Insect Damage: Accretions, losses, or damage due to insects, such as a loss in paper support due to cockroaches eating the glue, or fly speck.

Intrinsic Value: The significance of a work ascribed to its physical qualities or those of its creator; it can sometimes be a combination of both.

Lignin: A polymer that serves as a binder for cellulose molecules in plants; acidic.

Loss: The area of a support that is semi-detached or removed.

Manuscript: A handwritten document.

Mat Burn: Also referred to as a mat stain; a browning or staining of the mat board that occurs when acidic components make up its composition.

Mold, Mildew: A surface growth of fungus that occurs due to damp and humid conditions.

Mount: An additional support affixed to a primary support.

Newsprint: A highly unstable, lightweight paper made from wood pulp with a high amount of lignin; acidic and subject to yellowing.

Papyrus: A predecessor to paper; sheets of writing material made by weaving strips of pith taken from the plant.

Parchment: Writing material made from sheepskin or goatskin.

Photooxidation: Structural and color damage caused by excessive or prolonged exposure to high levels of illumination—including daylight and fluorescent light (both contain ultraviolet radiation).[15]

Powdering: A defect in printing that results in ink rubbing off due to not being fixed on the surface of paper; also referred to as chalking.

Provenance: Information involving the origin of a work.

Recto: Right-hand side of a book opening or the front of a sheet of paper.

Red Rot: The deterioration of leather that results in an orange or reddish powder; often seen on leather used on a bound volume.

Silking: An application technique formerly used to protect paper that included adding a layer of silk with paste to the recto or verso of a paper artifact; fell out of popularity because silk deteriorates rapidly, which damaged the work it was meant to protect.

Soil: A discoloration that lies within the fibers of a support.

Support: (1) Primary support—directly bears the image or work on paper; (2) secondary support—additional paper or fabric adhered to the primary support; (3) auxiliary support—a material affixed to lend additional structure to a primary support, such as a mat or stretcher.

Tear: Physical damage that causes separation of a piece of work into one or more pieces.

Vellum: Writing material made from calfskin.

Verso: Left-hand side of a book opening or the back of a sheet of paper.

Watermarks: A marker that can help identify the provenance of paper; a design created within paper during the papermaking process that makes a distinctive impression.

Wood Pulp: (1) Chemical wood pulp—a paper pulp made from trees by cooking the wood with an alkaline solution to neutralize naturally occurring acids and to remove lignin, which is highly acidic; (2) mechanical wood pulp—a paper pulp made by physically grinding wood without separating the cellulose fibers from impurities such as lignin, making it more acidic and less stable.

Wove Paper: Paper with an even appearance manufactured on mesh either by hand or by machine.

PHOTOGRAPHS

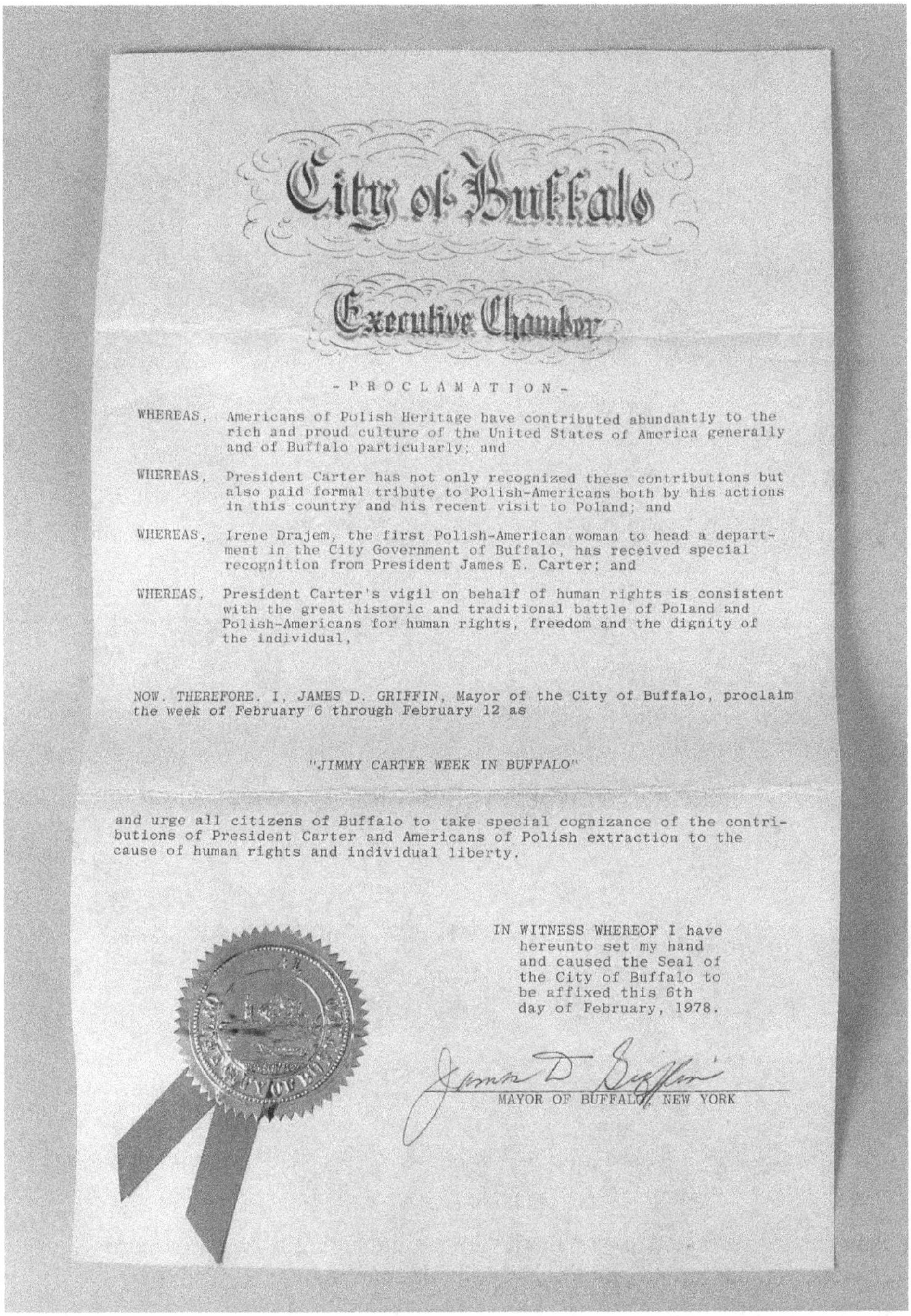

City of Buffalo

Executive Chamber

-PROCLAMATION-

WHEREAS, Americans of Polish Heritage have contributed abundantly to the rich and proud culture of the United States of America generally and of Buffalo particularly; and

WHEREAS, President Carter has not only recognized these contributions but also paid formal tribute to Polish-Americans both by his actions in this country and his recent visit to Poland; and

WHEREAS, Irene Drajem, the first Polish-American woman to head a department in the City Government of Buffalo, has received special recognition from President James E. Carter; and

WHEREAS, President Carter's vigil on behalf of human rights is consistent with the great historic and traditional battle of Poland and Polish-Americans for human rights, freedom and the dignity of the individual,

NOW, THEREFORE, I, JAMES D. GRIFFIN, Mayor of the City of Buffalo, proclaim the week of February 6 through February 12 as

"JIMMY CARTER WEEK IN BUFFALO"

and urge all citizens of Buffalo to take special cognizance of the contributions of President Carter and Americans of Polish extraction to the cause of human rights and individual liberty.

IN WITNESS WHEREOF I have hereunto set my hand and caused the Seal of the City of Buffalo to be affixed this 6th day of February, 1978.

James D. Griffin

MAYOR OF BUFFALO, NEW YORK

Figure 14.1. This figure includes an example of a paper document from a museum collection. Note the discoloration, yellowing, fading, and creasing on the paper. The seal is adhered with an adhesive, and there is colored ribbon. Eventually, the adhesive will eat through the paper. This item is stored in temperature-controlled storage.

Source LaToya Devezin

Figure 14.2. There are several examples of works on paper in this image, including a bound volume, framed and matted works, rolled posters, an unmounted painting, scrapbooks, and maps.
Source: LaToya Devezin

Figure 14.3. A closeup photo of collections storage taken during a collection survey to assess preservation needs for the collection. Note the rolled posters and framed prints. The drawing in the middle had adhesive on it at one point from a previous mat that demonstrates a loss.
Source: LaToya Devezin

Figure 14.4. This is the image that corresponds with the digital condition report shown in Figure 14.5. Note the description and its correlation with this image.
Source: LaToya Devezin

SAMPLE CONDITION REPORT

See attachments of digital condition report of works on paper from the Jimmy Carter Presidential Library and Museum using TMS (The Museum System) software.

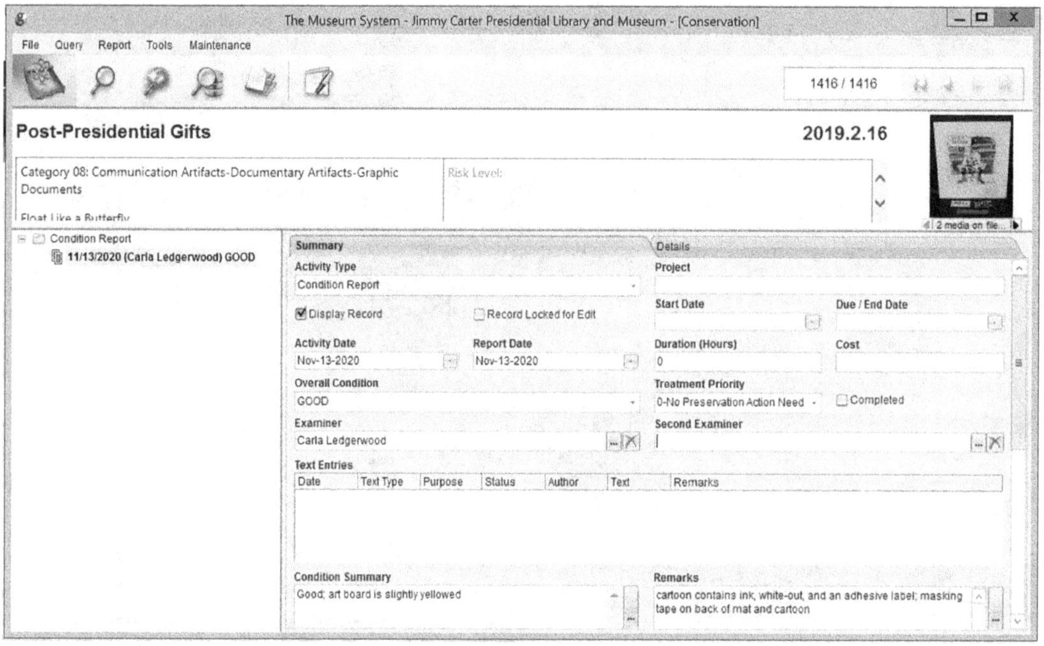

Figure 14.5. This is a digital condition report that corresponds with the image of the work on paper, a matted and framed political cartoon, in Figure 14.4. The report was generated in The Museum System (TMS).
Source: LaToya Devezin

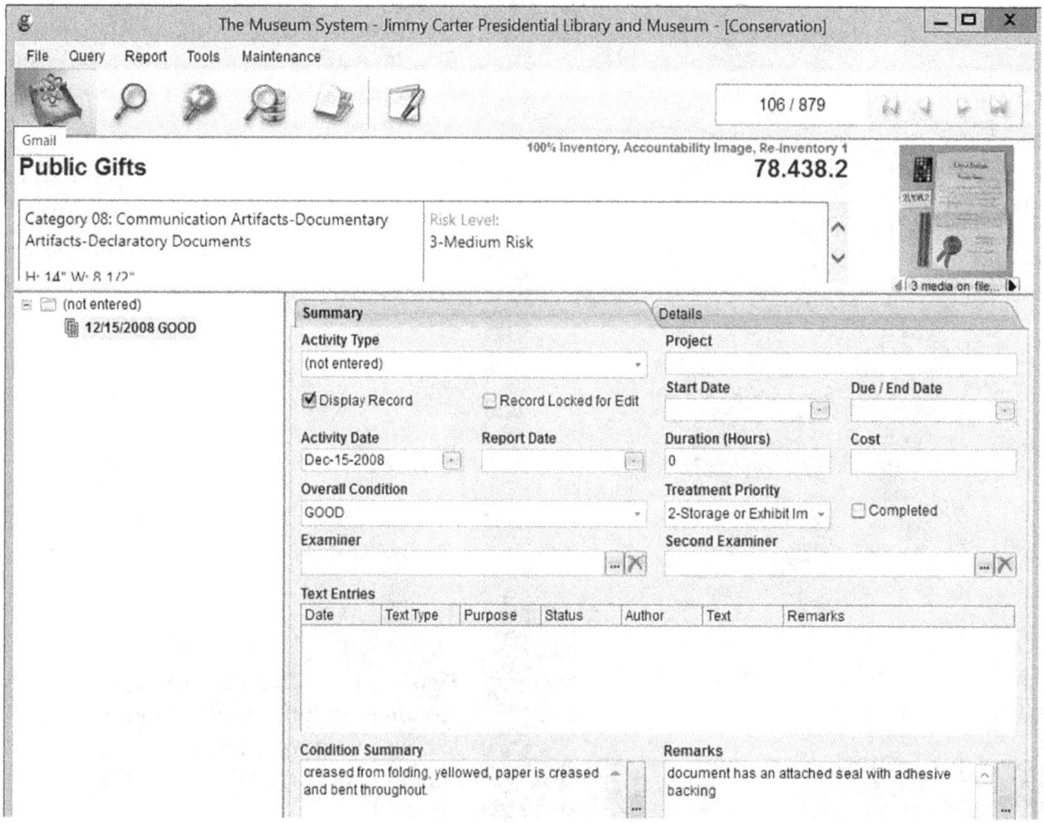

Figure 14.6. This is the digital condition report that corresponds with the document featured in Figure 14.1. The report is generated in The Museum System (TMS).
Source: LaToya Devezin

NOTES

1. Basbanes, Nicholas A. *On Paper: The Everything of Its Two-Thousand-Year History* (New York: Random House, 2014), 7.

2. Ellis, Margaret Holben. *The Care of Prints and Drawings*, 2nd edition (Lanham: Rowman & Littlefield, 2017), 12.

3. Society of American Archivists. *Dictionary of Archives Terminology, Paper*, accessed February 25, 2021, https://dictionary.archivists.org/entry/paper.html.

4. Hunter, Dard. *Papermaking: The History and Technique of an Ancient Craft* (New York: Dover, 1987), 48.

5. Ellis, *Care of Prints and Drawings*, 20.

6. Powell, Brent. *Collection Care: An Illustrated Handbook for the Care and Handling of Cultural Objects* (Lanham: Rowman & Littlefield, 2017), 87.

7. Ellis, *Care of Prints and Drawings*, 201.

8. Pflug, Wendy. "Assessing Archival Collections through Surveys." *The Reading Room*, Fall 2016: 69.

9. Ibid., 78.

10. Bachmann, Kostanze. *Conservation Concerns: A Guide for Collectors and Curators* (Washington, D.C.: Smithsonian Books, 2012), 35.

11. Powell, *Collection Care*, 250.

12. Definitions are from the Society of American Archivists, *Dictionary of Archives Terminology*, accessed February 25, 2021, https://dictionary.archivists.org/, and the American Institute for Conservators' *Glossary of Terms*, accessed February 25, 2021, https://www.conservation-wiki.com/wiki/BPG_Glossary_of_Terms#A.

13. Bachmann, *Conservation Concerns*, 36.

14. Ibid.

15. Ibid.

BIBLIOGRAPHY

American Institute for Conservation. n.d. *Glossary of Terms*. https://www.conservation-wiki.com/wiki/BPG_Glossary_of_Terms#A.

Bachmann, Konstanze. 2012. *Conservation Concerns: A Guide for Collectors and Curators*. Washington, D.C.: Smithsonian Books.

Basbanes, Nicholas A. 2014. *On Paper: The Everything of Its Two-Thousand-Year History*. New York: Random House.

Ellis, Margaret Holben. 2017. *The Care of Prints and Drawings*, 2nd edition. Lanham: Rowman & Littlefield.

Hunter, Dard. 1987. *Papermaking: The History and Technique of an Ancient Craft*. New York: Dover.

Pflug, Wendy. 2016. "Assessing Archival Collections through Surveys." *The Reading Room*, Fall 2016: 64–82. https://kb.osu.edu/bitstream/handle/1811/90845/1/Pflug_ReadingRoom_2016.pdf.

Powell, Brent A. 2016. *Collection Care: An Illustrated Handbook for the Care and Handling of Cultural Objects*. Lanham: Rowman & Littlefield.

Society of American Archivists. n.d. *Dictionary of Archives Terminology*. https://dictionary.archivists.org/.

15

Photographs

Stephanie Gaub Antequino

A photograph can take the form of one of many processes in which light-sensitive materials are used to create a visible image. Because a photograph can take on a myriad of forms, the examiner may be called upon to describe a wide variety of defects particular to the specific material from which each photograph is made. It is important to remember that despite the prevalence of photographs, they are potentially fragile artifacts that can be easily damaged from improper handling or storage as well as exposure to light and fluctuations in temperature and humidity.

To write an accurate and useful condition report, the examiner does not have to know the exact technique used to create the image, but they should have basic knowledge of the various components that make up the structure of a photograph. A basic understanding of the technique used to create the photograph will aid in the description of the condition. For example, an ambrotype, popular in the mid-nineteenth century, consists of a negative image on a glass support that has a black backing, which makes the image appear to the viewer as a positive. Without the background, the image appears to be a translucent ghost image that could be mistaken as a hopelessly faded photograph to an uninformed examiner.

All photographs consist of three basic components: the base or support, the binder or emulsion, and the light-sensitive materials that bear the photographic image. Common photo bases include copper sheet, iron sheet, glass plate, paper, and plastics such as nitrate, acetate, and polyester. Each base has its own inherent flaws: tintypes may corrode, acetate may develop blisters, and unmounted albumen prints will curl due to their lightweight paper base. The binder or emulsion is the material that holds the light-sensitive chemicals to the base and will most likely be collodion, albumen, gelatin, or gum arabic. Inherent vices for these binders include yellowing of albumen prints and the sticking together of gelatin prints that have been exposed to excessive humidity. The light-sensitive materials used to create the image are normally comprised of compounds of silver, iron, or platinum, and color-processing dyes. Silver particles eventually break down and cause silvering, while platinum can cause amber-colored stains on paper stored in contact with the face of the print. All color photographic processes will inevitably fade within a relatively short span of time. Understanding these materials and their inherent vices will aid in identification, description, and condition reporting of the photograph.

Another type of image that may be encountered is a negative or positive transparency on a plastic base, such as motion picture film. Film negatives were made of highly flammable cellulose nitrate until the 1950s. Due to its instability, large collections of nitrate negatives must be considered a hazard. Cellulose acetate film, more commonly referred to as safety film, replaced nitrate film, but has its own set of concerns. As the film degrades, it releases acetic acid, which gives off a distinct vinegar smell that is known as vinegar syndrome.

TERMINOLOGY

Albumen Print: Print consisting of a paper base, a binder of egg whites and salt, and a light-sensitive coating of silver nitrate; produces a purplish brown (sepia tone) or black image that is very susceptible to oxidation. Often mounted on a cardboard secondary support. Popular from its introduction in 1850 through the 1890s.

Ambrotype: Underexposed and developed collodion negative on a glass base. Whitish in tone and backed with or placed against an opaque coating to create the appearance of a positive image. Used from its introduction in 1854 into the 1880s.

Base, Support: Material on which the emulsion lies; common bases include copper sheet, iron sheet, glass plate, paper, and plastics such as cellulose nitrate, cellulose acetate, and polyester. Not to be confused with secondary supports.

Binder, Emulsion: Transparent layer of gelatin, albumen, collodion, or gum arabic that suspends and protects the light-sensitive materials, holding them to the surface of the base.

Cabinet Card: Decorative cardboard secondary support measuring 4.25" x 6.5" and used with albumen prints. Introduced in 1866 and reached peak popularity in the 1880s.

Carte-de-Visite: Decorative cardboard secondary support measuring 2.5" x 4.5" and used with albumen prints. Patented in France in 1854 and remained popular into the early twentieth century with the advent of Kodak's Brownie camera.

Cellulose Acetate: Film created in response to the flammability and chemical instability of cellulose nitrate film and the need for a stable recording medium. Cellulose acetate shrinks over time and emits acetic acid as a byproduct of deterioration.

Cellulose Nitrate: Family of transparent, light, flexible, and easy-to-handle film supports used for motion picture film and photographic negatives. Cellulose nitrate self-destructs over time and gives off acidic byproducts and is highly flammable. Extreme care should be used with these collections. It reached its popularity from 1910 to 1950.

Collodion: Type of binder that is a mixture of cellulose, nitric and sulfuric acid, and potassium iodide. Used for paper prints as well as ambrotypes and tintypes. Introduced in 1851.

Crayon Portrait: Life-sized portrait photographic print finished with pastels or charcoal. Popular from the 1860s to the turn of the twentieth century.

Cyanotype: "Blueprint" process resulting in a distinctive blue photograph. Created infrequently from the 1840s to the 1890s; fairly popular from the 1890s until 1910.

Daguerreotype: Positive image produced on a thin copper-plate base with a mirror-like coating of silver. Occasionally hand-colored and often placed in an elaborate case with a protective piece of cover glass. Invented in 1839 and popular through the 1850s.

Developing-Out Paper: Paper that must be developed chemically to reveal the latent image.

Light-Sensitive Materials: Component of the photograph that actually bears the photographic image; these materials absorb and scatter light to produce the image. Light-sensitive materials include silver halide, iron, gold, platinum, and color-processing dyes.

Platinotype, Platinum Print: Matte print on a paper base; steely gray, black, or slightly bluish-black in color. Used from 1880 to the 1930s; widely used for commercial portraiture after the turn of the twentieth century.

Printing-Out Paper: Paper that must be exposed to light to reveal the latent image. Toning increases image permanence.

Silver-Gelatin Print: Print consisting of a paper base and a gelatin binder that contains silver bromide and/or silver chloride particles. Gelatin printing-out paper was popular from the late 1880s through 1905. Gelatin developing-out paper was popular from the late 1890s through 1960.

Tintype, *Ferrotype*: Print consisting of a base of a thin sheet of iron coated with black or brown enamel, a binder of collodion, and a light-sensitive coating of silver salts. The plate bears the negative image made to look positive by the opaque enamel. First patented in the United States in 1856 and used until the 1930s.

HANDLING

It is important to have handling-and-use policies in place and to ensure that everyone who has contact with photographic collections abides by these policies. Make sure that the workspace is free of clutter and prohibit eating, drinking, and smoking in areas where photographic materials will be examined. Clean nitrile gloves should be worn and handled by their edges to avoid marring the emulsion. If the examiner chooses not to wear gloves, hands should be washed frequently using a cream-free soap and dried thoroughly. Handle photographs one at a time, using both hands, and place a rigid acid-free support, such as corrugated board, under images before lifting or moving.

Some photographic processes require additional precautions when handling.

Cased Images (Ambrotypes, Daguerreotypes, Tintypes)

Be sure that the surface is padded with inert foam such as Ethafoam or Volara Foam to help protect the fragile nature of these images. Never use the case's metal clasps to close it, as this may cause additional damage to the case. Never disassemble a cased image, and do not force the hinges all the way open or tightly closed. Never force a warped case closed, and never remove or clean the cover glass without a conservator.

Images Mounted on Cardstock (Cartes-de-Visite, Cabinet Cards, and Stereographs)

Do not flatten stereographs, as the curve is often an inherent characteristic. Instead of removing mounted images from their acidic backing, place a sheet of buffered board between the image and the backing if possible.

Glass Plate Negatives and Transparencies

Examine these types of images on a surface padded with Ethafoam or Volara Foam. Support glass plates by holding them on diagonally opposite corners with both hands and return it immediately to its storage box after examination. Never touch two plates together.

Oversize Photographs

Do not rifle through photos or *bend* them back to see other materials in the box or map case. Instead, remove photographs from their containers one at a time. Use two people to move oversize images using a flat stiff board or book truck. Never carry oversize photographs in a rolled, folded, or bent manner.

Cellulose Nitrate

Maintain a log of those who work with these collections and document any problems, including odors, discomfort, or ill effects. Work on a surface that is easily washable or use layers of clean non-printed newsprint that can be discarded at the end of the day. In addition to nitrile gloves, wear a long-sleeved washable smock that is washed weekly with a mild soap and water. If you notice any odor or experience any irritation, wear a fitted breathing apparatus and goggles. Discontinue work with nitrate if you experience any breathing, skin, or eye problems. Never touch your eyes, hair, or skin with a contaminated glove. Do not wear contacts when working with nitrate, as gases may build up under the lenses and cause eye injuries.

EXAMINATION

When possible, be familiar with the type of photograph under examination, as this will help you to understand if its current condition has been influenced by the environment, chemical instability of materials, or improper processing during manufacture. Other factors that may affect the condition include adhesives, mats, and wooden frame backs, all of which will leave marks behind.

Never physically alter an object (i.e., uncurl an albumen print or remove a daguerreotype from its case) in an attempt to examine it, as this may cause further damage. If you are unsure how to handle a situation, contact a conservator for advice before proceeding.

When examining a photograph, start with the general condition and then move into specifics. Begin with general statements. Is it yellowed overall? Is the surface silvered? Are there scratches overall? Next, working in a grid pattern, describe specific defects. Is there a paper clip dent at the top left edge? Are the corners dogeared?

DOCUMENTATION

When documenting the condition of a photograph, be sure to have the following tools available: soft lead pencils, condition report form, cloth measuring tape, nitrile gloves, acid-free board, flatbed dolly for oversize photos, and a jeweler's loupe.

Photographs should be described individually on a condition report. Record the most general conditions first, and then record the unique defects. It is easiest to work in a clockwise motion using a grid or matrix system (see the sample Photographic Condition Report form) to note the shape and placement of each. Be sure to note the size and/or length of the defects. When recording the documentation, complete the condition of the obverse, then record that of the reverse. If you are unsure of the cause of damage, use terms such as *possibly*, *could be*, or *may be* to convey what you think is happening without being definite.

CONDITION GLOSSARY

Abrasion: Mechanical wearing away of the surface caused by scraping, rubbing, grinding, or friction; often superficial.

Accretion: Deposit of any external material such as fly specks, paint drops, etc., on a surface. Can occur generally or locally.

Adhesive Residue: Residue remaining on a surface from glue, paste, or pressure-sensitive tape.

Blistering: Small bubbles usually found on cellulose nitrate and acetate film. Also referred to as "bubbling."

Buckling: Soft, concave/convex random distortion.

Cockling: Soft, concave/convex distortion characterized by either horizontal or vertical parallel, repeated ripples.

Crack: Surface fracture or fissure across or through a material, either straight-line or branching in form; no loss is implied. Described as *blind* when it stops partway, as *hairline* when it is a small fissure, and as *open* when it is a large fissure.

Crease: Line of crushed or broken fibers, usually made by folding. A *dog-ear* is a diagonal crease that occurs at the corner.

Figure 15.1. This photo shows signs of creasing in the corners. Source: Stephanie Gaub Antequino

Dent: Simple concavity in the surface caused by a blow.

Discoloration: Partial or overall color change caused by aging, light, or chemical agents. Can be described as *yellowing*, *darkening*, *bleaching* (the lightening of color), and *fading* (loss of color or a change in hue).

Figure 15.2. This photo shows signs of discoloration and scratching. Source: Stephanie Gaub Antequino

Distortion: Warping or misshaping of the original shape.

Embrittlement: Loss of flexibility causing the material to break or disintegrate when bent or curled.

Ferrotyping: Glossy patches on the surface of a photograph that are the result of long-term contact with a smooth surface such as glass or polyester.

Fold: Turning over of a surface so that it is in contact with itself.

Figure 15.3. This photo shows signs of folding and creasing. Source: Stephanie Gaub Antequino

Former Treatment: Any prior treatment that is visible. Can be from conservation or restoration work.

Foxing: Yellow, brown, or reddish-brown spots caused by either mold or the oxidation of iron particles in the paper.

Figure 15.4. This photo shows areas of foxing. Source: Stephanie Gaub Antequino

Frilling: Separation and lifting of the photographic emulsion from the edges of the support.

General Condition: *Good*: object shows minor modification due to age or wear; *Fair*: object shows substantial modification due to age or wear; *Poor*: object shows major modification due to age or wear.

Inclusion: Particle accidentally bonded to the surface during manufacture.

Loss: Missing area or hole.

Figure 15.5. This photo shows areas of loss along the crease lines. Source: Stephanie Gaub Antequino

Mold: Small fungi that may cause foxing, a musty odor, or colored, furry, web-like outgrowths.

Odor: The smell of vinegar or other scent caused by the deterioration of cellulose nitrate or acetate. Stronger odors indicate more severe degradation.

Pest Damage: Surface loss, tunneling, holes, fly specks, etc., caused by pests or insects.

Pitting: Small, irregular, shallow pinhole-sized losses scattered over the surface of metal and caused by acid.

Red Spot, Redox Blemishes: Rust-colored spots of oxidation found on microfilm.

Scratch: Linear surface loss due to abrasion with a sharp point.

Silvering: Shiny or mirror-like discoloration in the shadow areas of black-and-white photographs.

Soil: Any material that dirties an object that is either distributed loosely (*dust*) or firmly ingrained in the surface (*grime*), such as a *smear* or *fingerprint*.

Stain: Color change as the result of soiling, adhesives, pest residue, food, oils, etc. A *diffuse stain* has no distinct boundary; a *discrete stain* has a distinctive boundary; a *liquid stain* has a discrete boundary or *tide-line* that is darker than the main area of the stain; a *centered stain* has a darker center (cf. foxing).

Sweating: Clear or yellow oily liquid found on the surface of deteriorated cellulose nitrate or acetate.

Tarnish: Dulling or blackening of a bright metal surface.

Tear: A break resulting from tension or twisting.

Vinegar Syndrome: Exudation of acetic acid by degrading cellulose acetate film that smells like vinegar.

Wear: Surface erosion, usually at edges, due to repeated handling.

Wrinkling: Angular, crushed distortion.

BIBLIOGRAPHY

Buck, Rebecca A., Jean Allman Gilmore, and American Association of Museums. 2001. *The New Museum Registration Methods*. Washington, D.C.: American Association of Museums.

"Fundamentals of the Conservation of Photographs." n.d. Accessed May 1, 2021. https://

XYZ Museum of Photographic History

Photographic Materials Condition Report

Object ID: Reported By: Date:

Type of Photographic Material: Title:

Dimensions: _________ H x _________ W x _________ D

image: _________ H x _________W x _________D

support:_________ H x _________ W x _________ D

mat: _____ Loose _____ Mounted _____ Matted _____ Framed _____ Other

---

Description:

Overall Condition (check one): Good Fair Poor

Detailed Condition (Damage location recorded on corresponding grid):

Abrasion	Inclusion
Accretion	Loss
Adhesive Residue	Mold
Blistering	Pest Damage
Buckling	Pitting
Cockling	Red Spot, Redox Blemishes
Crack	Scratch
Crease	Silvering
Dent	Soil
Discoloration	Stain
Distortion	Sweating
Embrittlement	Tarnish

Figure 15.6. Photograph condition report form. Source: Stephanie Gaub Antequino

Ferrotyping

Fold

Foxing

Frilling

Tear

Vinegar Syndrome

Wear

Wrinkling

Additional Condition Notes:

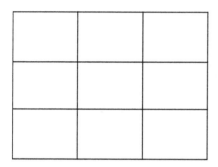

Figure 15.6. ***(continued)***

www.getty.edu/conservation/publications_resources/teaching/photo_so_mf_intro_surveys.pdf.

Institute, Canadian Conservation. 2017. "Condition Reporting—Paintings. Part I: Introduction—Canadian Conservation Institute (CCI) Notes 10/6." September 14, 2017. Accessed May 1, 2021. https://www.canada.ca/en/conservation-institute/services/conservation-preservation-publications/canadian-conservation-institute-notes/condition-reporting-paintings-introduction.html.

Institute, Canadian Conservation. 2017. "Care of Encased Photographic Images—Canadian Conservation Institute (CCI) Notes 16/1." September 14, 2017. Accessed May 1, 2021. https://www.canada.ca/en/conservation-institute/services/conservation-preservation-publications/canadian-conservation-institute-notes/care-encased-photographic-images.html.

Institute, Canadian Conservation. 2017. "Care of Black-and-White Photographic Glass Plate Negatives—Canadian Conservation Institute (CCI) Notes 16/2." September 14, 2017. Accessed May 1, 2021. https://www.canada.ca/en/conservation-institute/services/conservation-preservation-publications/canadian-conservation-institute-notes/care-black-white-photographic-negatives-glass-plate.html.

"Museums and Galleries of NSW | Condition Reports -the Essentials the Essentials." n.d. Accessed May 1, 2021. https://mgnsw.org.au/sector/resources/online-resources/collection-care/condition-reports-essentials/

Public, Sherman-Dunedin, and Art Gallery. n.d. "Condition Reporting He Rauemi Resource Guide 26 Care of Collections and Taonga." Accessed May 1, 2021. https://www.tepapa.govt.nz/sites/default/files/26-condition-reporting.pdf.

Ritzenthaler, Mary Lynn, and Diane Vogt-O'Connor. 2010. *Photographs: Archival Care and Management*. Chicago, Il: Society of American Archivists.

Taylor, Maureen Alice. 2001. *Preserving Your Family Photographs: How to Organize, Present, and Restore Your Precious Family Images*. Cincinnati, OH: Betterway Books.

Williams, Don, and Louisa Jaggar. 2005. *Saving Stuff: How to Care for and Preserve Your Collectibles, Heirlooms, and Other Prized Possessions*. New York: Fireside.

16

Plastics

Mary Coughlin

In a condition report, it may not be enough to just say that an object or a component is made of "plastic" since there are many types of plastics, some of which can pose serious threats to collections. The generic term *plastic* encompasses a wide range of semi-synthetic and synthetic materials that vary in appearance, aging properties, periods of manufacture, and use. Plastics can take the form of three-dimensional objects, flat sheets, films, foams, or textiles, and can be found in any museum collection. It is important to remember that plastics are not always used alone and may be part of a composite object.

It can be difficult to determine the exact plastic present without scientific analysis, but an effort should be made to include descriptions of the plastic, such as appearance, structural quality (rigid, flexible, foam, or elastomer), time period when the artifact was made or used, and signs of manufacture, such as mold lines, makers' marks, or trade names.[1] When combined, this information can provide clues to the type of plastic present.[2]

Certain types of plastics are sometimes referred to as "malignant." These plastics are known to have a propensity for degradation, and the components they release negatively affect other materials nearby. The five plastics frequently found in collections that are considered malignant are:[3]

1. Cellulose nitrate (CN)
2. Cellulose acetate (CA)
3. Vulcanized rubber or hard rubber
4. Polyurethane (PU)
5. Poly(vinyl chloride) (PVC)

If it is suspected that any of these plastics are present, efforts should be made to determine their current condition, whether they are off-gassing acids (refer to *Conserve-O-Gram 8/5*), whether they need to be segregated from other collections, and, finally, whether they need to be deaccessioned. Figure 16.1 outlines some typical signs of degradation for malignant plastics. For these plastics, it is generally recommended to store them in archival corrugated boxes, such as blueboard, and allow for a degree of ventilation to prevent the buildup of acidic vapor and oxidants that may be released, though there are exceptions.

With plastics such as these, there may be a risk of "cross-infection" with the ambient environment.[4] In the past, scavengers like zeolites and activated charcoal/carbon were broadly used to trap degradation products emitted from plastics. However, zeolites are too indiscriminate to be safely used since they can scavenge components like plasticizers, weakening the plastic.[5] For CA and CN that are actively off-gassing, there may be a role for activated charcoal/carbon to play in adsorbing acidic vapor, however, for newer CA and CN, it can actively pull out plasticizers.[6] So, the use of activated charcoal/carbon to manage acids emitted from plastic collections should be decided in consultation with a conservator familiar with plastics.

Another potential exception is PVC, which can be either rigid (not plasticized) or flexible (plasticized). The plasticizers in flexible PVC migrate out and try to reach equilibrium with the surrounding environment; the smaller that environment, the less plasticizer is lost so these plastics can benefit from storage in a sealed inert container, such as a glass jar. Never put PVC in polyethylene bags or rigid polyethylene containers since these can actively leach out plasticizers from the PVC.[7] If the type of plastic is unknown, storage in archival corrugated board is the best default.

Plastic	Names or Form	Typical Deterioration
Cellulose Nitrate (CN)	"Celluloid" "Parkesine" "Xylonite" French Ivory Nitrocellulose	Blistering, brittle, chalking, cracks, crazing, distortion, fogging, shrinkage, warping, weeping May release acidic and/or camphor odor May form acid that can corrode metal and be adsorbed by organics
Cellulose Acetate (CA)	"Lumarith" "Tenite" "Celanese" "Safety Film"	Bloom, blistering, brittle, chalking, cracks, crazing, distortion, fogging, shrinkage, warping, weeping May release acidic odor (vinegar smell) May form acid that can corrode metal and be adsorbed by organics
Vulcanized Rubber	Hard Rubber "Vulcanite" "Ebonite"	Discolors to brown, grey, dark green over time May form acid that can corrode metal and be adsorbed by organics
Poly(vinyl chloride) (PVC)	[especially plasticized PVC]	Bloom, brittle, chalking, discoloration, distortion, odor, tacky, warping, weeping May form acid that can corrode metal and be adsorbed by organics
Polyurethane (PU)	[foam]	Crumbling, discoloration, deformation, loss of elasticity Can release volatile organic compounds (VOC)

Figure 16.1. Typical signs of deterioration for malignant plastics.
Source: Mary Coughlin

Even when a plastic appears to be in good condition, it is best to regard it as a fragile material. Plastics are sensitive to improper handling, light (visible, ultraviolet, and infrared), and fluctuations and extremes in temperature and relative humidity. It is important to remember that each type of plastic contains a variety of components. For example, a synthetic plastic contains the polymer that forms the building block of the plastic (typically what a synthetic plastic is named for, such as polyethylene) that is combined with additives to achieve a desired appearance and workability. These additives can include plasticizers, colorants, fire retardants, UV stabilizers, and fillers. All of these ingredients create a unique formulation that will impact how a specific plastic ages. In other words, two objects made of the same type of plastic may age differently as a result of the additives in each object. This disparity can be further amplified by the environments the plastics were exposed to while in use or in the museum.

TERMINOLOGY

Additive, Modifier: Substance added to a plastic to achieve or retain desired properties (e.g., plasticizers, light stabilizers, antioxidants, and flame retardants).

Elastomer: Material with elastic properties that resumes its original shape when deforming force is removed.

Filler: Material added to a plastic to modify its qualities or to lower costs.

Flash: Excess plastic along the separating line of a molded plastic; looks like a seam.

Flow Mark: Imperfection from uneven flow during casting or molding; looks like wavy lines.

Natural Plastics: Derived from plants, insects, and animals and can be modified into new shapes with heat and moisture (e.g., tortoiseshell, horn, hooves).

Parting Line: Seam on a casted plastic where molds were joined together during manufacture. Excess plastic along the seam is called *flash*.

Plasticizer: A substance added to increase workability, flexibility, or softness of a plastic.

Polymer: A substance formed by the reaction of small molecules (monomers) into repeating units that create a large molecule (polymer). May be natural or synthetic.

Sprue: Circular marking left when excess plastic from molding process is broken off; often from injection molding.

Stabilizer: A substance added to plastics during manufacture to help it retain its properties during manufacture and use. Examples include antioxidants and UV stabilizers.

Semi-synthetic: Natural polymers treated with chemicals to alter their properties (e.g., cellulose nitrate, cellulose acetate, casein formaldehyde).

Synthetic: Human-made polymers; name usually starts with "poly" (e.g., poly[vinyl chloride], polyethylene, polyester).

Thermoplastic: Softens when heated and hardens when cooled. Can be remelted and reshaped. Most plastics.

Thermoset: Permanently hard and rigid. Cannot be remelted and reshaped.

Vulcanization: Chemical alteration, typically of rubber, into more durable materials by the addition of sulfur.

HANDLING

When handling plastics, it is important to always wear nitrile gloves. Nitrile gloves will protect the wearer from potentially harmful materials that may be leaching out of the plastic, while also protecting the plastic from the oils and salts that can be transferred from your hands. Even if the telltale signs of degradation (see Condition Glossary and Figure 16.1) are not present, nitrile gloves should still be worn. Nitrile gloves should be disposed of immediately after handling degrading plastics and not reused for handling other objects. Cotton gloves should *not* be worn when handling plastics. Their porous nature can allow the transmission of materials between the plastic and the wearer and vice versa. Also, since cotton gloves are often used several times between washing, they can lead to cross-contamination.

Take care when handling plastics. Some plastics may look intact, but they can actually be quite fragile, such as a flexible PVC object that has lost its plasticizers and is now rigid and brittle, and it may shatter when handled. Always fully support the plastic object by its body and base, and never lift by a handle or protruding area. If there are detachable elements like a lid, remove before handling or moving. Thin sheets of plastics or film may be quite brittle and prone to fracturing if improperly handled, so make sure to avoid picking them up by the corners or sides. Determine if it is appropriate to use a microspatula to lift it up or slip a supporting material like thin blueboard or Mylar under the sheet so that it will be fully supported. If using Mylar, be careful since it can have a static electric charge that can attract and dislodge fine fragments and may result in loss of material on fragile surfaces. Whenever in doubt about handling a plastic object, contact a conservator for guidance.

When moving a plastic object, the use of a cart or padded box is recommended. If needed to prevent jostling while in transit, acid-free tissue paper can be bunched up and used to keep the plastic object in place and to absorb some of the shock from transit. If the plastic that is being transported is degrading (see Condition Glossary and Figure 16.1), it is a good idea to use a Mylar barrier between the plastic and the cart, box, or basket in order to prevent off-gassing acids or leaching components from contaminating the surfaces. In these cases, Mylar and any acid-free tissue that may have been used should be discarded rather than reused to prevent contaminating other objects.

EXAMINATION

When examining the condition of plastics, it is important to wear nitrile gloves for the reasons outlined in the Handling section. Start by assessing the object's overall condition, looking from top to bottom, and around all exterior surfaces and accessible interior areas. Do not force open any components of the object for sake of examination.

Note any signs of manufacture such as parting lines. Certain manufacturing methods can only be used with certain plastics, so identifying these methods can help in the identification of a specific plastic. Examination with ultraviolet light may help identify previous repairs that may fluoresce differently and may also reveal areas of degradation. Take a look at areas that were likely handled the most during use, such as a handle, or could be points of stress, such as the sprue, a join, or the area marked with the catalog number, as these areas often show the first visual signs of degradation (for example, crazing or discoloration).

During examination, make sure to look for signs of degradation. This could appear in the plastic itself (see Condition Glossary and Figure 16.1) or, in the case of composite objects, in non-plastic materials. Acidic off-gassing that can emanate from some degrading plastics can corrode metals or cause paper and other nearby organics to yellow, even if they are not part of the object itself. It is a good idea to look around at the materials kept near plastics in storage cabinets and display cases, including handles and hinges, as signs of corrosion or deterioration could indicate the plastic is off-gassing. Odors emanating from a plastic likely mean it is either deteriorating or, if relatively new, still curing. If this is the case, the plastic should be separated from other collections and ventilation increased or, possibly, activated charcoal/carbon utilized. The decision of whether to deaccession a deteriorating plastic should be made following museum protocols.

If a plastic is suspected of off-gassing acids, the presence of acidic vapor can be verified with the use of Acid-Detecting (A-D) strips. These indicator strips turn from dark blue through shades of green to yellow if acids are present; the greater the color shift to yellow, the more acid present. Refer to the Image Permanence Institute's *User's Guide for A-D Strips Film Base Deterioration Monitors* for more details on using A-D strips. *Conserve-O-Gram* 8/5 outlines monitoring plastics using both A-D strips and silver, lead, and copper coupons.

DOCUMENTATION

Record in photographs and written reports the overall condition as well as any signs of deterioration (see Condition Glossary and Figure 16.1). Documentation is essential for plastics because once degradation starts, it can be rapid. In some cases when a plastic artifact starts to degrade, it may have to be deaccessioned, and all that can safely remain in the collections is its documentation. Documentation can also be used in the future to determine if plastic degradation has begun or has progressed. To ensure accurate future comparison, include the catalog number and date on all documentation, and a color bar in overall images since yellowing, darkening, or color shifting can be signs of degradation.

Documenting plastics is similar to other artifacts in that you need to determine what will be considered the "front" and start from that reference point. Include in the documentation all key identifiable features that make this specific artifact different from others, such as a maker's mark and decorative elements. It is helpful to note color and if it is bright, vibrant, or pale, and if areas are transparent, translucent, or shiny. These features can help narrow down the possible type of plastic (for help in identification, refer to websites: "Plastic Identification Tool" and "A Curator's Guide"). Changes to appearance can denote degradation.

If the date of manufacture or the period of use is known, include that in the documentation as it can help give clues to the identity of the plastic. To help narrow down plastic options based on time period of manufacture or use, it may be helpful to refer to the timeline in Figure 16.2 or to the more extensive timeline available online from the Museum of Design in Plastics. Of course, if the type of plastic is known through scientific analysis, labeling by the manufacturer, or because of an imprinted recycling code, then that should be recorded.

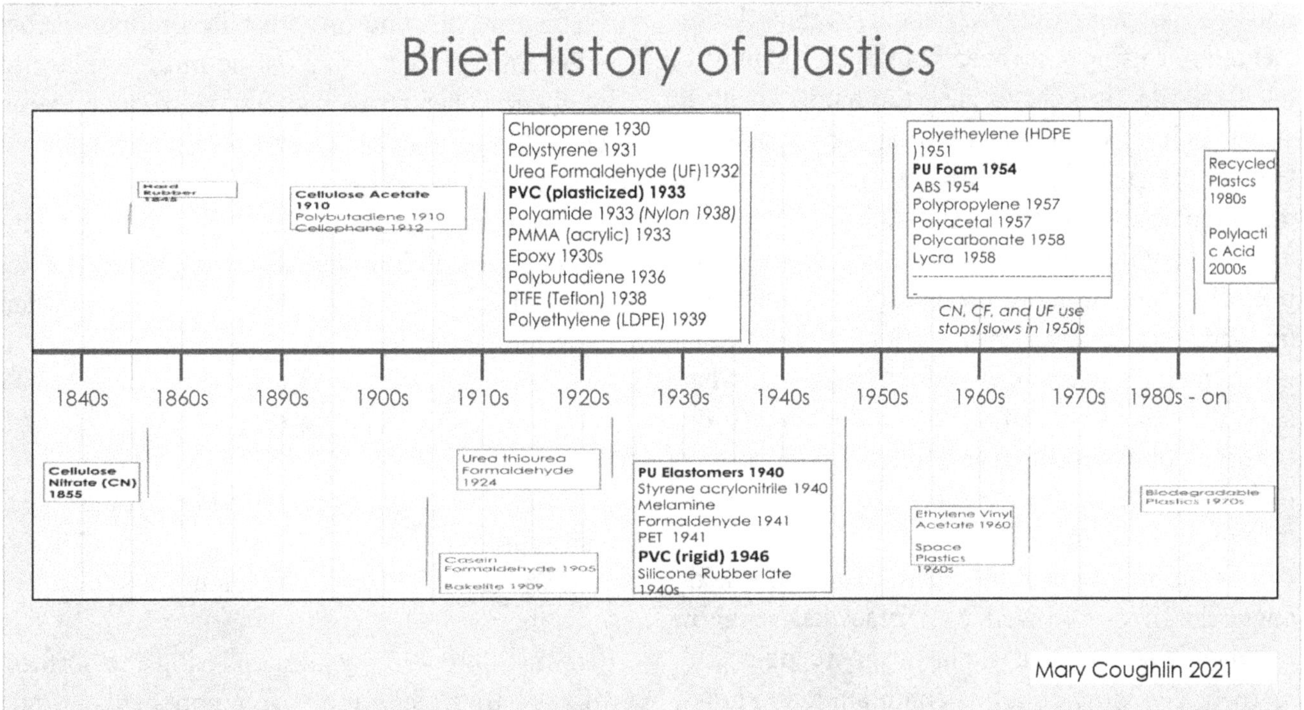

Figure 16.2. A brief history of plastics timeline.
Source: Mary Coughlin

Despite efforts for identification, the exact type of plastic may remain unknown. In those cases, it can be helpful to assign a broad structural category so that people referencing the documentation report will know how the plastic was intended to behave. For instance, as some flexible plastics age, they will lose their plasticizers and become rigid. It is helpful to know that it was originally flexible. Four recommended structural categories are:

1. Rigid Plastic
2. Flexible Plastic
3. Foam
4. Elastomer

Note whether the object has been labeled with the accession or catalog number. Common labeling methods used in museums, such as using adhesive labels or applying a barrier coat and ink, can stress the plastic through interaction with the solvents and cause blistering, crazing, cracking, deformation, and/or discoloration (see Fig. 16.3). If a museum-applied number is present and seems to be causing damage, consult a conservator. If no museum number is present, it is better to add one by tying on an inert tag, labeling a non-plastic element, or using a soft pencil to mark the plastic itself (taking care not to push too hard). Using a soft pencil will not be an option for all plastics since some surfaces will be too slick to write on or, in the case of foams, impossible.

The documentation report should include an overall statement about the condition of the plastic. Broad categories like *unstable*, *poor*, *fair*, *good*, and *excellent* can quickly indicate what state the object was in when the documentation occurred (make sure to include the date on the report) and can help assess any changes that may take place over time.

It is helpful to outline chemical and physical concerns first, followed by surface issues. For instance, the fact that a plastic is weeping and warped tells more about its condition than knowing that it is dusty.

Conservation Priority and Curatorial Priority are sections that can help direct future efforts. If an object is flagged as both high conservation and curatorial priorities, then perhaps time, money, and effort should be channeled to its care, rather than to an artifact that may be in need of conservation but that is of low curatorial importance.

Because the environment, storage, and display materials can affect how plastics age, it is a good idea to include what materials are being used to store or display the plastic as well as current conditions, if known, for temperature (T), relative humidity (RH), and light (visible and UV). If data is not known, it is still helpful to state whether the current conditions seem to be poor, fair, or good. For planning, it is helpful to make recommendations for improvements to the materials used and the environment since those can impact preservation.

Handling and transportation guidelines should be included in the report, as well as whether limitations should be placed on loaning or exhibiting the object because of its condition. In some cases, it could be argued that a plastic that is starting to degrade should be allowed to go on display since it is nearing the end of its usable lifetime. If that is the case, protections must be put into place to safeguard other art or artifacts from degradation products that may be emitted from the plastic.

It may be a good idea to leave room for notes since no matter how much effort you put into making a condition checklist comprehensive yet streamlined, there will always be times when something more needs to be recorded.

CONDITION GLOSSARY

Abrasion: Scratches or scuffs on the surface, possibly from use.

Bleeding or *Blurring*: Becoming less clear or distinct.

Bloom: White or gray film covering the surface, likely from migration of components to the surface.

Blistering: Raised pockets or bubbles on a laminated surface.

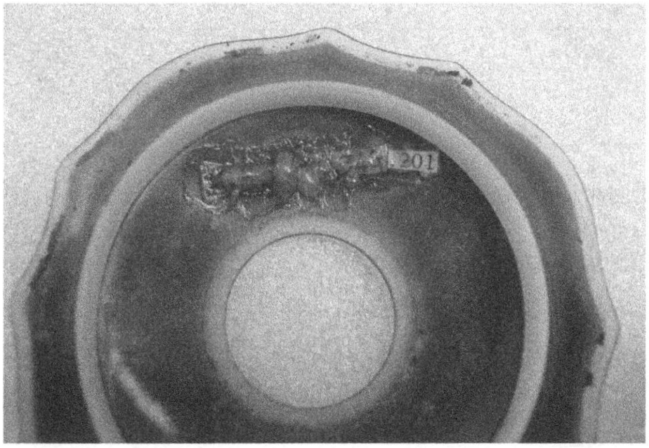

Figure 16.3. Blistering.
Source: Mary Coughlin

Break: Physical separation of an object into two or more parts.

Brittle: Hard and is easily broken, even if lightly touched; sometimes the result of plasticizer loss.

Figure 16.4. Brittle plastic.
Source: Mary Coughlin

Chalking: A dry, chalky, white powder on the surface of a plastic, usually caused by degradation and/or migration of an ingredient.

Chip: A missing piece, usually small.

Corrosion of Nearby Metals: Caused by interaction with components off-gassing or leaching out of degrading plastics.

Crack: A break or split that does not penetrate through.

Crazing: Fine network of cracks; may also be called *crizzling*.

Figure 16.5. Crazing and crizzling.
Source: Mary Coughlin

Crumbling: Loss of material that causes powdering.

Deformation or Distortion: Change from the original shape; may be the result of losing components from weeping or off-gassing, or caused by improper support.

Delamination: Splitting or separating into layers.

Discoloration: Change in color from original; may be the result of light damage or chemical changes.

Fogging: Loss of transparency.

Fume Fading: Loss of dye color in fabrics caused by gaseous pollutants.

Loss: Missing element.

Odor: Smell emitting from plastic; usually a sign of degradation or, in recently made plastics, may indicate that it is still curing.

Off-gassing: Evaporation of volatile chemicals, usually from degrading plastics.

Opacifying: Becoming opaque.

Pitting: Small pits on the surface not caused by physical damage.

Scratch: Slight surface mark caused by something sharp or rough.

Shrinkage: Deformation as material loses mass, often through weeping.

Condition Report Form for Plastic Objects

Object Name	**Department**
Accession #	**Examiner**
Catalog #	**Date of Report**

Description: ____

Museum number applied by: __Tie-on tag __Adhesive label __Barrier coat & ink __Ink

__Barcode __Non-plastic part __Other:______________

Reason for Examination:
__Exhibition __Loan __Damage __ Survey __Inventory __Accession __Other:_____

Dimensions: H__________ L__________ W__________ (*note unit of measure*)

Structural Category: __Rigid __Flexible __Foam __Elastomer

Known Plastic(s) Present?: __Yes __No __Some

Plastic(s) Present:

	Acrylonitrile-butadiene-styrene (ABS)		Polyethylene (High Density)
	Casein Formaldehyde		Polyethylene (Low Density)
	Cellophane		Polyethylene Terephthalate [PET]
	Cellulose Acetate		Polylactic Acid
	Cellulose Nitrate		Poly(methyl methacrylate) [Acrylic]
	Chloroprene [Neoprene]		Polypropylene
	Ethylene Vinyl Acetate		Polystyrene
	Epoxy		Polytetrafluoroethylene [Teflon]
	Hard Rubber		Polyvinyl acetate
	Melamine Formaldehyde		Polyurethane
	Phenol Formaldehyde [phenolic resin] [Bakelite]		Poly(vinyl chloride) [PVC]
	Polyamide [Nylon]		Rubber
	Polybutadiene		Styrene acrylonitrile
	Polyacetal		Silicone
	Polycarbonate		Urea Formaldehyde
	Polydimethyl siloxane [silicone rubber]		Urea Thiourea Formaldehyde
	Polyester		Rubber

	Other Plastic(s):

Other Materials Present: ______________________________________

Plastic Identification Determined By:

Analysis: __Spot Test __FTIR __Raman __SEM-EDS __GC-MS __XRF __Other:_______

Clues: __Marker's mark __Recycling symbol __Imprinted date

Figure 16.6. Plastics condition report form. Source: Mary Coughlin

__Object records __Date of manufacture __Date of use

__Physical characteristics __Type of deterioration __Other:________________

Confidence in Plastic Identification: __High __Medium __Low

Condition: Structure: __Unstable __Stable

Surface: __Poor __Fair __Good __Excellent

Odor: __No __Yes: __Vinegar __Acidic __Camphor __Rubber __Paraffin __Other:_____

Structural Issues

	Blistering		Crazing		Hardening		Scratch
	Break		Crumbling		Loss		Shrinkage
	Brittle		Deformation		Odor		Spalling
	Chip		Distortion		Off-gassing		Warping
	Crack		Delamination		Pitting		Other:

Surface Issues

	Abrasion		Darkening		Loss of gloss		Sticky
	Bleeding or Blurring		Discoloration		Opacifying		Weeping
	Bloom		Fading		Soiling		Yellowing
	Chalking		Fogging		Stain		Other:

Current Storage or Display Conditions: __Poor __Fair __Good

Storage or Display Recommendations: __Improve support __Replace materials __Isolate

__Improve environment __Increase ventilation __Monitor __Other:____________________

Environment: *if known*: T range _________ RH range __________ Light levels ___________

__Monitor T and RH __T and RH need adjustment

__Monitor light levels __Light levels need adjustment

Handling: __Nitrile gloves __Too fragile to handle __Need assistance __Need support

Transport: __Too fragile to transport __Can safely travel

Exhibition or Loans: __Recommended __NOT Recommended

Conservation Priority: __Low __Medium __High

Curatorial Priority: __Low __Medium __High

Deaccession: __Recommended __NOT Recommended

Photos Taken? __Yes __No

Notes:

Figure 16.6. *(continued)*

Soiling: Dirty material on surface; may be loose dust or ingrained grime.

Spalling: Chunks or fragments separating from the whole.

Stain: Discolored mark transferred to the surface.

Tacky: Sticky surface.

Warping: Deformed from original shape often into a wave-like appearance; may be the result of losing components from weeping or off-gassing.

Weeping: Liquid migrating to the surface.

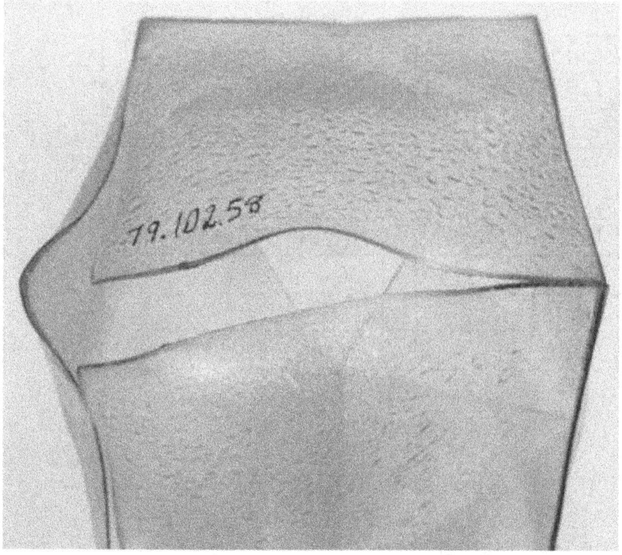

Figure 16.7. Weeping and warping.
Source: Mary Coughlin

Yellowing: Formation of yellow coloration as some plastics degrade.

NOTES

1. Listing of trade names can be found on the Plastics Historical Society website.

2. For example, cellulose nitrate is an early semi-synthetic plastic that was commonly used to imitate natural materials such as ivory and tortoiseshell, principally from the 1850s to about 1950. It was often sold under the trade names Celluloid, Parkesine, and Xylonite and was sometimes referred to as French Ivory. Even during its period of use, the film form of cellulose nitrate was known to be unstable and flammable, leading to the development of cellulose acetate Safety Film. As cellulose nitrate ages, it can start to off-gas acidic vapor that can corrode nearby metals and be adsorbed by porous materials in the vicinity. Cellulose nitrate may also lose its plasticizers, which is characterized as weeping droplets. As plasticizer is lost, the plastic will start to craze, crack, and become brittle and rigid. In a condition report, by noting the appearance, time period of use, trade name or maker's mark, plus the current condition, there should be enough clues to point to the plastic in question as possibly being cellulose nitrate. Once this is indicated, the object should be rehoused in blueboard, documented, and flagged for periodic inspection. Pay attention to the materials surrounding it; if they start to corrode or discolor it could be the result of acidic off-gassing from the plastic. If the plastic object is already deteriorating, it should be isolated, documented, and possibly deaccessioned.

3. R. Scott Williams, "Care of Plastics: Malignant Plastics," *WAAC Newsletter* 24/1 (Western Association for Art Conservation, 2002).

4. Katherine Curran, Alenka Možir, Mark Underhill, Lorraine Gibson, Tom Fearn, Matija Strlič, "Cross-infection Effect of Polymers of Historic and Heritage Significance on the Degradation of a Cellulose Reference Test Material," *Polymer Degradation and Stability*, Volume 107 (Oxford: Elsevier Ltd., 2014).

5. Yvonne Shashoua, Michael Schilling, Joy Mazurek, "The Effectiveness of Conservation Adsorbents at Inhibiting Degradation of Cellulose Acetate." In *ICOM-CC Triennial Conference Melbourne Preprints* (Paris: The International Council of Museums, 2014).

6. Ibid.

7. Yvonne Shashoua, *Conservation of Plastics: Materials Science, Degradation and Preservation* (Oxford: Elsevier Ltd., 2008).

BIBLIOGRAPHY

Chalifoux Zephir, Marianne. "Care and Identification of Objects Made from Plastic." In *Conserve-O-Gram* 8/4. Washington, D.C.: National Park Service, 2010.

Coughlin, Mary. "Monitoring Acidic Off-Gassing of Plastics." In *Conserve-O-Gram* 8/5. Washington, D.C.: National Park Service, 2011.

Coughlin, Mary. "Storage at a Glance: Plastics." In *Preventive Conservation: Collection Storage.* Society for the Preservation of Natural History Collections; American Institute for Conservation of Historic and Artistic Works; Smithsonian Institution; The George Washington University Museum Studies Program. 2019.

Curran, Katherine, Alenka Možir, Mark Underhill, Lorraine Gibson, Tom Fearn, Matija Strlič. "Cross-infection Effect of Polymers of Historic and Heritage Significance on the Degradation of a Cellulose Reference Test Material." *Polymer Degradation and Stability* vol. 107, 294–306. 2014.

Grattan, David W., ed. *Saving the Twentieth Century: The Conservation of Modern Materials. Proceedings of a Conference in Ottawa. Sept. 15–20, 1991.* Ottawa: Canadian Conservation Institute, 1993.

Image Permanence Institute. *User's Guide for A-D Strips Film Base Deterioration Monitors.* 2001.

Keneghan, Brenda, and Louise Egan, eds. *Plastics—Looking at the Future and Learning from the Past.* London: Archetype Books, 2007.

Lockshin, Nora Sharon. "Marking Collections." In *Preventive Conservation: Collection Storage.* Society for the Preservation of Natural History Collections; American Institute for Conservation of Historic and Artistic Works; Smithsonian Institution; The George Washington University Museum Studies Program. 2019.

National Park Service. "Appendix J: Marking, Section E." In *Museum Handbook, Part II.* Washington, D.C.: National Park Service, 2000.

Quye, Anita, and Colin Williamson, eds. *Plastics: Collecting and Conserving.* Edinburgh: NMS Publishing Limited, 1999.

Shashoua, Yvonne. *Conservation of Plastics: Materials Science, Degradation and Preservation.* Oxford: Elsevier Ltd., 2008.

Shashoua, Yvonne, Michael Schilling, Joy Mazurek. "The Effectiveness of Conservation Adsorbents at Inhibiting Degradation of Cellulose Acetate." In *ICOM-CC Triennial Conference Melbourne Preprints.* Paris: The International Council of Museums, 2014.

Williams, R. Scott. "Care of Objects Made from Rubber and Plastic." CCI Note 15/1. Ottawa: Canadian Conservation Institute, 1997.

Williams, R. Scott. "Care of Plastics: Malignant Plastics." *WAAC Newsletter* 24/1. Western Association for Art Conservation, 2002.

Williams, R. Scott. "Plastics Storage Products." In *Preventive Conservation: Collection Storage.* Society for the Preservation of Natural History Collections; American Institute for Conservation of Historic and Artistic Works; Smithsonian Institution; The George Washington University Museum Studies Program. 2019.

WEBSITES

Cultural Heritage Agency (Netherlands). "Plastic Identification Tool." https://plastic-en.tool.cultureelerfgoed.nl/.

Museum of Design in Plastics. "A Curator's Guide." https://www.modip.ac.uk/projects/curators-guide.

Museum of Design in Plastics. "Timeline." https://www.modip.ac.uk/projects/curators-guide/plastics-timeline.

Plastics Historical Society. "Trade Names." http://plastiquarian.com/?page_id=14316.

POPART: Preservation of Plastic ARTefacts http://popart.mnhn.fr/.

Syracuse University Library. "The Plastic Collection." http://plastics.syr.edu/.

Images: Courtesy of the Smithsonian Institution, National Museum of American History/.

Use of images in Glossary was previously granted by Ann Seeger, Former Deputy Chair and Curator, Division of Medicine and Science, Smithsonian's National Museum of American History.

17

Sculpture

Kyle Bryner

Let's do a quick thought experiment. I'm not asking much. Say the word *sculpture* to yourself. Think about it for a few seconds. When you think of sculpture, what comes to mind? Is a sculpture small or large? Is a sculpture indoors or outside? Is it made of metal, stone, ceramic, wood, or something else entirely? Is the Statue of Liberty a sculpture? How about a Japanese netsuke, Michelangelo's *David*, a Moai head, the *Venus of Willendorf*, or a Chinese terracotta warrior? Would you be surprised to learn that all these examples are sculptures?

Sculpture spans a wide array of styles, materials, sizes, and time periods. Sculpture comes in countless media. It can be a carving of any material, a cast object born from a mold, a built-up ceramic, a compound object, or an assemblage of materials. The one aspect all sculpture has in common is it occupies a three-dimensional space. A viewer can move around a sculpture, seeing it from multiple angles and sides. The sculpture exists in the same space as the viewer.

CONDITION REPORTING TIPS

The ability to move around a sculpture can make the process of condition reporting more comprehensive. However, the three-dimensional nature of sculpture can also pose many challenges when completing a condition report. How does one describe location on a sculpture? You must always orient the reader of a sculpture condition report. You need to clearly define and describe the areas referred to on the sculpture in the condition report. If the sculpture is of a human or animal, has a regular shape, or is set in its location with clear cardinal directions, then orienting the reader will be simple. You can use descriptors such as "top of head," "back of statue's proper left hand," or "north side of the monument." For irregular and hard-to-describe objects, you can create a grid system to let readers know where condition issues occur. Define for the reader what the front is and what the back is of the sculpture. Separate the areas of the sculpture into clear designations such as proper right, proper left, front, back, top, and bottom.

Condition reports of sculptures are most beneficial when any barriers to the reader's understanding are eliminated. Whenever you can, use annotated photographs or sketches that point directly to the places of concern. If you can, take advantage of the digital tools available to you. Take pictures or video on your phone, tablet, or digital camera. Use a voice-to-text app on your phone or other device if you want to navigate around a sculpture but not hold a laptop or paper to take notes while doing the examination. Digital images can easily be integrated into a Word document, PDF, or a preset form. If you have a collections management system, check to see if it has the ability to create condition reports for specific objects for you. This can save you time when trying to create a form from scratch.

Methodologies and best practices for handling sculptures are as varied as the types and materials of sculptures. Handling and moving instructions should be tailored for each individual sculpture based upon its size, weight, and condition.

Numerous sculptures across the country that are located in public spaces have been the focus of cultural changes and protests. Special consideration should be taken when condition reporting a sculpture after protest activity may have changed its condition. One should not place judgment upon the condition changes, only document the changes in condition. A prime example is graffiti on Confederate statues. Document the condition to create a complete record of the changes to the object. If the sculpture is slated to be removed or cleaned, fully document the complexity and extent of the changes. The condition report content may be examined as a record of American cultural history in the future.

GLOSSARY OF TERMS

Abrasion: Changes to the surface caused by scraping, rubbing, or scratching.

Accretion: Any foreign matter deposited on the surface of the object. For outdoor sculptures, an example would be bird feces.

Ceramic: A ceramic is any of the various hard, brittle, heat-resistant, and corrosion-resistant materials made by shaping and then firing a nonmetallic mineral, such as clay, at a high temperature.

Chip: A broken piece of the object that can be partially or fully separated.

Clay: Sculpture can be created by shaping, casting, or carving of this moldable material.

Corrosion: Loss caused by a chemical reaction from a foreign agent.

Crack: A fault in a surface where material is pulling apart. Often horizontal or vertical.

Crevice: A narrow opening or fissure in the surface of an object.

Dent: Any lossless concave distortion of the object.

Discoloration: Any change from original color.

Erosion: Any loss of material due to abrasion or outside elements.

Fiberglass: Common type of fiber-reinforced plastic using glass fiber.

Grime: Foreign matter buildup that sticks to an oily medium on the surface. For example, if people touch a sculpture often, oil and dirt from hands will leave a surface prime for accumulating grime.

Intrusion: Common with outdoor sculpture, animals and plants have taken up residence in cracks, crevices, or the base of the object. Intrusion is important to note not just for integrated pest management planning, but also if someone who will work with the object has allergies to the intruders, for example, bees.

Ivory: A hard, creamy-white substance composing the main part of the tusks of an elephant, walrus, or narwhal, often (especially formerly) used to make ornaments and other articles.

Manufacturing Marks: Can sometimes be mistaken for damage in the surface of an object.

Marble: Granular limestone or dolomite (i.e., rock composed of calcium-magnesium carbonate) that has been recrystallized under the influence of heat, pressure, aqueous solutions. Commercially, it includes all decorative calcium-rich rocks that can be polished.

Patina: A green or brown film on the surface of bronze or similar metals, produced by oxidation over a long period.

Plastic: Wide range of synthetic or semi-synthetic materials that use polymers as a main ingredient. Their plasticity makes it possible for plastics to be molded, extruded, or pressed into solid objects of various shapes.

Terracotta: A type of earthenware, clay-based unglazed or glazed ceramic, where the fired body is porous.

EXAMPLES OF SCULPTURES

Figure 17.1. Yayoi Kusama, *Pumpkin*, 2016, at the Hirshhorn Museum and Sculpture Garden.
Source: Kyle Bryner

Figure 17.2. Yayoi Kusama, *Pumpkin*, 2016, at the Hirshhorn Museum and Sculpture Garden.
Source: Kyle Bryner

Figure 17.3. Terracotta Dragon, Museum of the Shenandoah Valley.
Source: Kyle Bryner

Figure 17.4. Carved walrus ivory chess pieces, Viking Ship Museum, Roskilde, Denmark.
Source: Kyle Bryner

Figure 17.5. Example of human and sculpture interaction, Palace of Versailles, Paris, France.
Source: Kyle Bryner

Figure 17.6. Day of the Dead Statue, Compound Object Statue, Museum of Anthropology at Wake Forest University, Winston-Salem, NC.
Source: Kyle Bryner

Figure 17.7. Extremely eroded sculpture of Mayan god Chac, Chichen Itza, Mexico.
Source: Kyle Bryner

Figure 17.8. *The Bedford Boys*, 116th Regimental Combat Team Monument, Omaha Beach, Normandy, France. Excellent example of patina on a bronze statue.
Source: Kyle Bryner

Figure 17.9. Sir Anish Kapoor, *Cloud Gate*, Millennium Park, Chicago. Example of steel sculpture.
Source: Kyle Bryner

Sculpture Condition Report

Examiner: **Date examined:** **Location:**

Object:

Object #:

Artist:

Measurements (HxWxD) in inches: x x

Material:

<u>Metal</u>

- o Copper/copper alloy
- o Bronze
- o Iron
- o Lead
- o Steel
- o Tin
- o Other

<u>Non-Metal</u>

- o Ceramic
- o Clay

Figure 17.10. Sculpture condition report form.

- o Marble
- o Terracotta
- o Plaster
- o Stone composite
- o Other

<u>Synthetic</u>

- o Rubber
- o Plastic
- o Other

Condition Narrative:

Object Sketch or Insert Images:

Figure 17.10. *(continued)*

Recommendations:

- o Further examination by a conservator
- o Immediate attention
- o Repair
- o Stabilization
- o Surface Cleaning
- o Other

OVERALL CONDITION:

- o Abrasion
- o Accretion
- o Break

Figure 17.10. *(continued)*

- Chip
- Cleavage
- Corrosion
- Cracks
- Dent
- Dirt/Grime
- Discoloration
- Insect Activity/Damage/Intrusion
- Loss
- Mold/Mildew
- Pitting
- Scratches
- Tarnish
- Worn
- Old Repairs
- Other:

Additional Comments:

Figure 17.10. *(continued)*

CONDITION REPORT A SCULPTURE

1. Make sure the sculpture is stable! Note if the object is at risk of toppling, moving easily on its base, or shifting position.
2. Determine whether you need a second or even third person to help with the sculpture. Sculptures can be deceptively heavy and awkward. If it cannot easily be moved, don't move it.
3. Look over the sculpture for any obvious damage such as loss, erosion, corrosion, or abrasion.
4. Note any previous repairs and the state of the repairs. Have the previous repairs failed? Has this created a weakness in the object?

BIBLIOGRAPHY

Websites

The America Institute for Conservation of Historic and Artistic Works

Canadian Conservation Institute

- "CCI Notes"
- "Recognizing Metals and Their Corrosion Products"

The Henry Ford Museum

- "Caring for Your Artifacts" Series

National Park Service

- *Conserve-O-Grams*

Publications

Ankersmit, B. *Rust Never Sleeps: Recognizing Metals and Their Corrosion Products*. Parks Canada, 2008.

Hatchfield, P. B. *Pollutants in the Museum Environment*. London: Archetype Publications, Ltd., 2002.

Landrey, G. J., et al. *The Winterthur Guide to Caring for Your Collections*. Winterthur, 2000.

Long, J., et al. *Caring for Your Family Treasures: A Concise Guide to Caring for Your Cherished Belongings*. New York: Heritage Preservation, 2000.

Schultz, A. W., ed. *Caring for Your Collections*. New York: Harry N. Abrams, Inc., 1992.

Simmons, John E., and Toni M. Kiser, eds. *Museum Registration*, 6th edition. American Alliance of Museums, Washington, D.C., 2020.

Warda, Jeffrey, ed., Franziska Frey, Dawn Heller, Dan Kushel, Timothy Vitale, Gawain Weaver. *The AIC Guide to Digital Photography and Conservation Documentation*, 3rd edition. Washington, D.C.: American Institute for Conservation, 2017.

Williams, Don, and Louisa Jaggar. *Saving Stuff: How to Care for and Preserve Your Collectibles, Heirlooms, and Other Prized Possessions*. Washington, D.C.: Smithsonian, 2005.

18

Skin and Leather

Jillian Matthews Bingham

Skin is the largest organ in the body and is made up of three layers: the epidermis, or cuticle, the soft-grain layer that contains the hair follicles, sweat glands, and pigment, and the basic skin, or corium, that contains fiber bundles. When part of a living organism, skin is made up of almost 60 percent water, and therefore, is very flexible. When removed from the animal, or flayed, and left to dry, it becomes very stiff and inflexible. Over the course of centuries, humans have figured out a number of ways to prepare an animal's hide and organs to create functional, decorative, and ceremonial objects, in addition to creating specimens for scientific research.

Skin and leather tend to be a part of a larger composite object, often with other materials such as wood, metal, shells, paint, and glass beads. Additional condition reporting information on those materials can be found in their respective chapters. The various applications of skin and leather include clothing, weaponry, musical instruments, bags and luggage, furniture, and farming equipment, which means that skin and leather objects can be found in a wide variety of museum collection types: history, art, library, natural history, and ethnography.

With different tanning and dressing processes comes a variety of pros and cons to the finished product that can cause a variety of condition issues that a museum professional must deal with. It is beneficial to know the object's provenance, tanning method, species of animal, and any previous conservation to ensure optimal care of the skin or leather. This information will also help ensure that proper safety measures are taken in case the skin was treated with dangerous substances. Certain tanning methods involve applying natural, organic substances to the surface of the skin that should not be touched without gloves due to them being considered unhygienic, such as brain matter, manure, or urine. Meanwhile, other tanning methods may include the application of metals and chemicals to the surface of the skin.

In addition to the tanning process, the skin and leather could have been dressed multiple times in its lifetime. The original owner could have rubbed oil on it to prevent it from drying out while being used or on display. Additionally, previous museum staff could have treated the skin and leather with grease and oils to ensure it did not get dry and brittle. It was common practice in recent past for museum staff to do so, unaware of the long-term damage it could cause. The application of various chemicals to the surface of the skin or leather can actually increase deterioration rates and cause more damage. Good museum registration is key to ensure proper care plans are established for any object subject to more severe damage.

Skin and leather objects are highly susceptible to temperature and relative humidity fluctuations and insect activity. The various tanning methods also provide different storage and exhibition challenges for the materials, and the durability among pieces of leather can be drastically different. Understanding the differences among the different methods is crucial for the long-term care of skin and leather objects.

TERMINOLOGY

Alkali-Tanned Leather: Tanned skin that is processed with a paste-like solution made from laundry soap. The fats in the soap help with softness and flexibility, but the strong alkali content causes quick deterioration; also known as soap-tanned leather.

Alum-Tanned (or Tawed) Leather: Tanned skin that is processed with a mixture of alum and salt, white in color, and is highly susceptible to moisture and shrinking; common to fashion pelts and furs, gloves, and book bindings.

Brain-Tanned Leather, *Buckskin*: A soft, flexible semi-tanned skin, commonly made from deer, that is processed with animal brains and byproducts, white to yellow in color, that is dried then smoked making it resistant to deterioration and stiffening; common to Native American clothing and objects.

Cuir bouilli: Tanned skin that is processed at high temperatures and then molded into shape, often strong and rigid; commonly used as durable wares and containers. Also known as "boiled leather."

Dressing: Further processing the leather to have specific characteristics for its intended use (i.e., applying a laundry soap paste to make the leather soft and more flexible).

Embossing: A raised relief on the surface in the skin to create a design or pattern. Process involves applying heat and pressure to the skin using metal templates or rollers. See Figure 18.1. Compare to "stamping."

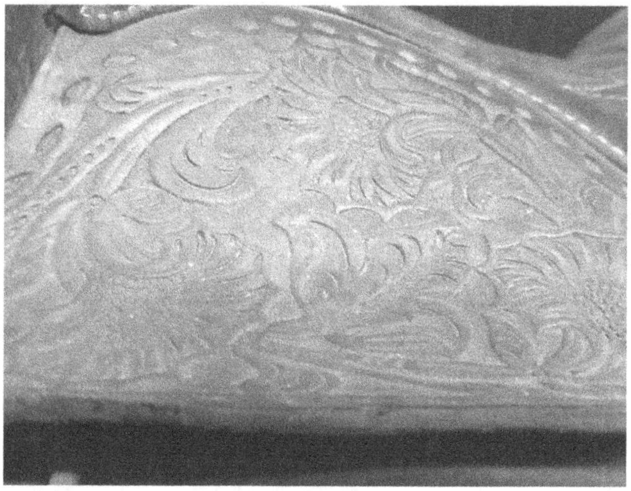

Figure 18.1. Embossed design on a saddle.
Source: Jillian Matthews Bingham

Embroidered: Decorative needlework done by hand or with a machine stitched into the surface of the material, and may include embellishments such as beads. See Figure 18.2.

Figure 18.2. Embroidered design on a Mexican spur.
Source: Image courtesy of The Culture & Heritage Museums of York County, SC (1977.1.93)

Finishing: Decorative changes made to the skin or leather such as embossing, stamping, dying, or staining.

Flesh Side: The side of the skin that was attached to the carcass of the animal, often the back/bottom side of the skin; compare to "grain side." See Figure 18.3.

Fur, *Pelt*: A tanned skin, full or partial, containing the fur of the animal; may be dyed. It is

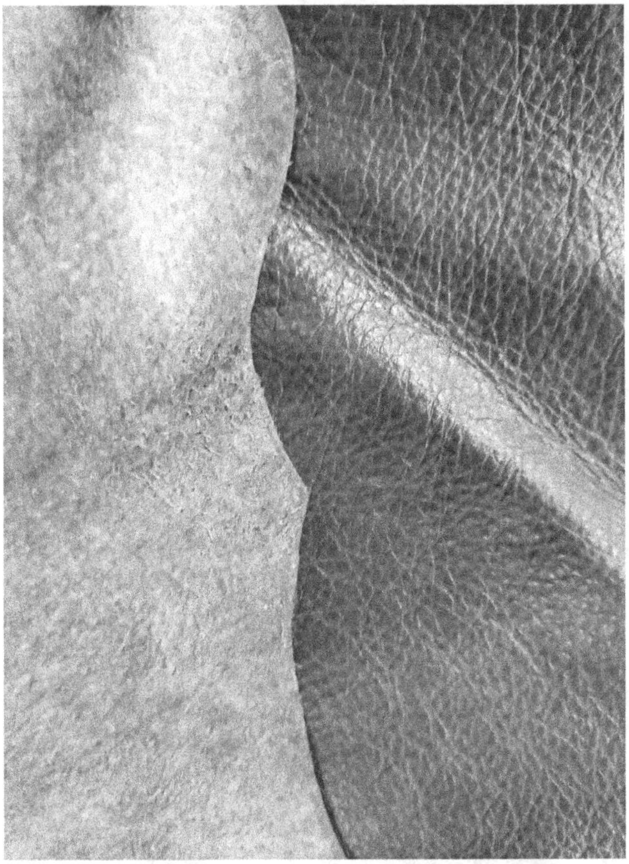

Figure 18.3. Flesh side (left) compared to grain side (right).
Source: Jillian Matthews Bingham

usually flexible enough to be used as a textile for clothing, musical instruments, bags and purses, luggage, furniture, etc. Pelts may also be found in natural history collections as research specimens.[1]

Grain Side: The side of the skin that held the hair. With hair removed, a distinct grain pattern remains created by the hair follicles (e.g., texture of a pigskin football); compare to "flesh side." See Figure 18.3.

Mineral-Tanned Leather: Tanned skin processed with mineral salts such as zinc, iron, or chromium, highly resistant to water though known to lose their shape over time; common to turn of the century clothing, shoes, and gloves.

Parchment: Thin slice of untanned skin, white to yellow in color that was often used as a writing surface, highly susceptible to moisture; often used interchangeably with "vellum."

Patent Leather: Shiny leather covered with an enamel or varnish.[2]

Oil-Tanned Leather, Chamois: Tanned skin treated with oils, fats, and fatty materials (animal brains) and then heated resulting in a strong, flexible, water-resistant leather; common to furs; compare to "brain-tanned leather."

Rawhide: Untanned skin that is commonly removed of all hair then left to dry; it is tough and can withstand dry temperatures, but it is susceptible to moisture; commonly used for musical instruments.[3]

Smoked Leather: Semi-tanned skin spread around a fire burning with green wood, forming a tent-like structure. The chemical reaction between the smoke and the skin makes it stable and water resistant, may have a smoky smell; common to "buckskin."

Staining: Process of purposefully coloring the skin or leather with a dye or pigment stain that may be applied by dipping, spraying, or brushing. Historically stained skins may have been dyed with natural materials; compare to "stained."

Stamping: Counter-relief or pressed design or pattern into the skin using metal templates; compare to "embossing." See Figure 18.4. The term *stamping* also refers to a printing technique that applies ink to the surface with a handheld device.

Figure 18.4. Stamped inscription on the bottom of a nineteenth-century medical bag.
Source: Image courtesy of The Culture & Heritage Museums of York County, SC

Suede: Leather produced by rubbing down the nap of the flesh side of the skin; commonly used for clothing and shoes.

Tanning: Method used to change the chemical and water makeup of skin to make it more durable, flexible, and resistant to water.

Vegetable-Tanned Leather: Tanned skin that is processed with tannins found naturally in trees and other plants; commonly made with skins from the horse and cattle families (Equidae and Bovidae, respectively).

Vellum: Thin, untanned calf skin, white to yellow in color, that was often used as a writing surface, highly susceptible to moisture; often used interchangeably with "parchment."

HANDLING

Before moving any object, it is important to know the route in which the object will travel, and to have a clean workspace prepared prior to moving the object. If the object is housed in an archival box, take the entire box to the examination area before removing the object from it. The same should be done if the fur or pelt is rolled. If the object is too large or heavy to move by oneself, additional staff or equipment (e.g., cart) may be necessary in order to safely relocate the object. Be sure to fully support the skin from the bottom while handling. The examination area should be void of any potential hazards, such as sharp tools or writing utensils, which could damage the leather. Similarly, the examiner should remove all jewelry and accessories that could come in close contact and cause damage.

When handling skin, leather, or fur, the examiner should always wear gloves to prevent human skin oils and sweat from being absorbed into the fur and leather. Gloves also help protect the examiner from potentially hazardous substances that were used during the tanning process. Additional personal protection equipment (PPE) may be required depending on the potential hazards. Staff should consult the object records to review provenance, tanning process, and previous treatment plans to ensure that proper PPE is worn. If the object shows signs or has a history of red rot, mold, bloom, or corroding metal, the examiner should change their gloves before touching another object. These substances are easily transferable.

Objects made from skin and leather may require additional support while in storage or on display to prevent damage. Three-dimensional objects, such as bags, should be filled with unbuffered archival tissue paper to help maintain their original shape. Thin, flexible objects such as whips may require an archival support at all times to prevent breakage in the thin leather cords. Larger, heavier pelts and leathers should be rolled, rather than folded, to prevent creases. Items with fringe may be heavy and require to be laid flat to prevent stretching or tearing. If the object is awkwardly shaped or is unable to support its own weight without causing damage,

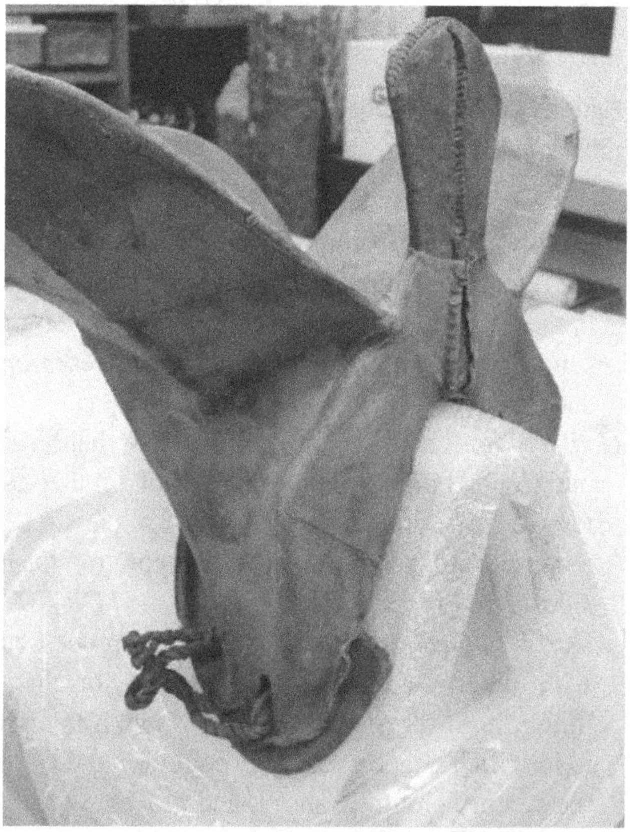

Figure 18.5. A custom wooden base covered with archival foam to support a leather camel saddle made by the Tuareg people from the African Sahara.

Source: Image courtesy of the Culture & Heritage Museums of York County, SC (1984.31.19A)

a custom base may be required, as shown in Figure 18.5. As tempting as it may be, do not play or test the musical instruments. Rawhide and leather surfaces of drums and other instruments could be brittle and break, or sinew strings could snap.

EXAMINATION

The examination of leather and skin products should occur systematically. Pick a starting point and move around the object (inside to outside, front to back, etc.). When referring to the location of condition issues, the examiner should establish a viewpoint, such as "viewer's left (VL)" or "proper right (PR)." The key is to be consistent.

Commonly used objects, such as clothing and shoes, tend to see more wear and damage than decorative and ceremonial objects. Similarly, objects featuring fur, leather, and skin tend to be part of a larger object made from other materials. Examine all parts of the object (seams, stitching, attachments, beading, handles, etc.), paying close attention to areas where different materials are joined together that may be weakened. Some issues may be inherent to the object while other issues may have been caused by the object's own attachments while in storage. When compared to commercially tanned skins, ethnographic furs and leathers tend to experience more hair loss and increased brittleness due to the more natural tanning methods that were used.

Objects featuring furs, skins, and leathers can provide quite the welcoming environment for pests and insects. Thick furs provide warmth for insect eggs and larva. Hair loss may be caused by grazing larva or rodent's use of the fur for nesting materials. A small insect casing or larva may resemble a small piece of dirt. Careful examination is imperative to prevent an infestation. The examiner should use tools such as a spatula, magnifying glass, or bone knife when needed. Any active signs of an insect or pest presence should be treated immediately to prevent a museum-wide issue. If the examiner is unsure if the pest damage is active or inactive, they should consult past condition reports to see if similar damage was previously reported.

If the object is stored on a custom support, examine it while on the support as much as possible before examining the areas blocked by said support to minimize handling of the fragile object. Additional staff may be needed to assist with the examination if the object is too large or awkward to examine alone. An object may need to be examined while on exhibit, but it may be unable to be fully examined due to its installation method. If this is the case, examine as much as possible and document what areas were unable to be assessed so they can be thoroughly examined later.

While visual examination of the specimen is important, it is also important for the examiner to smell the object without getting too close. A musty smell may be the first sign to a relative humidity issue that could lead to mold growth. Some tanning processes use animal byproducts like manure and urine. When stored in poorly ventilated areas or containers, the proteins in the urine break down and cause the object to have a vinegar-like smell to it, similar to vinegar syndrome, which affects film and photographs. This damage is irreversible, but it can be slowed down by storing the affected object in a better ventilated space.

DOCUMENTATION

Every condition report should include some basic information about the object: catalog number, object name, and dimensions. If the tanning method and species of animal skin are known, they should also be documented. It is important to note if there are any important handling issues associated with the object, such as it being heavy, fragile, or potentially treated with hazardous substances (arsenic, poison, animal brain matter, etc.). This information may be on the catalog tag or on the object's storage container. The examiner should also be sure to include their name and the date in which the examination was completed.

A detailed description of each condition issue should be provided and include measurements of cracks, length of tears, and other issues that can help monitor the damage over time. Noting its exact location will help with quick identification. If the cause for the damage is known, such as cracking on a purse flap due to wear and use prior to the museum's acquisition, it should be noted. If the cause of damage is unknown, the examiner should use words such as *possibly* or *could be* to help future staff understand the examiner's observations. If a treatment plan, such as replacing a support component, is recommended or completed due to the examination, the treatment should be noted.

A visual documentation of the condition issues should be made. General condition reports usually include a small area for the examiner to sketch out the object. This is relatively easy to do with flat, two-dimensional objects by utilizing the grid or quadrant system. Sketching three-dimensional objects may be intimidating for those who lack artistic skills, so this should not be required. Photographing the condition issues should be required, though, and fairly easy to do, given the accessibility of cameras today. Take photographs of every condition issue and try to include a small paper ruler to provide reference to scale. Detailed photographs will help monitor the damage over time.

GLOSSARY

Abrasion: Wear on the surface of the skin caused by friction or scraping.

Accretion: Foreign deposit of an external material on the surface of the skin; often the result of drips, splashes, etc.

Adhesive Residue: Could be left behind from glue, paste, or tape.

Bleeding: The spread of ink or other applied color to adjacent materials often caused by water or other liquids.

Bloom: Cloudy substance on surface of skin, similar in appearance to mold; may appear waxy or crystalline in appearance.

Cockling: Wavy appearance to the material, particularly parchment and vellum, due to water damage or fluctuations in relative humidity; compare to "distortion."

Corrosion: A chemical reaction on the surface of metal caused by environmental conditions or chemical agents purposefully applied to the metal's surface. The color of the corrosion varies between different types of metals. Corrosion of metal adornments to skins may cause a reaction on the leather's surface. Certain tanned leathers may show signs of green corrosion due to the deterioration of the chemicals used in the tanning process.

Cracked: A surface fracture or fissure across or through a material; no loss and usually occurs from wear or distortion; commonly found in objects such as belts, straps, purses and other bags, and shoes.

Crease: A line in the material (leather, paper, textile, etc.) as a result of the material being folded or wrinkled; commonly caused by use and/or poor storage.

Delamination: Separation of layers, splitting; common to objects made of layered leather, such as the separation of leather from a leather covered medicine box. See Figure 18.6.

Figure 18.6. Delamination of the leather covering on an 1880s medicine box with fraying along the edges.
Source: Image courtesy of the Culture & Heritage Museums of York County, SC (HB1986.29)

Dirt, Grime: Soil or dust accumulation on the surface of a specimen, could result in a temporary discoloration if thick enough.

Discoloration: Changing of color caused by light, chemical agents, aging, etc.; the degree of discoloration can range from lightening of color, darkening, yellowing, or changing of hue.

Distortion: A warping, twisting, or misshaping from original shape. See Figure 18.7.

Figure 18.7. Distortion of an Ethiopian vellum scroll.
Source: Image courtesy of the Culture & Heritage Museums of York County, SC (1976.13.7)

Embrittlement: Loss of flexibility causing the material (paper, parchment, leather, tanned skin) to break or disintegrate when bent or curled; commonly caused by humidity and temperature fluctuations and/or aging.

Fraying: Worn, fibrous appearance at edge of textile or around a hole; often found along unfinished or damaged seams and hems. See Figure 18.6.

Hair Loss: Area of lost or missing fur caused by overhandling, pest activity, deterioration of the skin, or inadequate tanning; may be active or inactive.

Indentation: Caused by long-term pressure of one object or component against the object's surface.

Infestation: Signs of insect or rodent presence, such as frass (insect excrement), rodent droppings, eggs, insect casings, remains, or nesting materials; may be active or inactive; see also "pest damage."

Inherent: Wear or damage that is permanent, essential, or original to the specimen, such as the scarring that occurred to the animal during its lifetime or the pinholes and seams created during the mounting process.

Loss: Missing area or hole.

Missing or Loose Element: Loss of a key part of a specimen, such as a hoof or ear; may be missing or stored separately.

Mold: Biological in nature often caused by high levels of humidity and/or temperature; can be active or inactive. An inactive infestation would present itself as stains. An active mold infestation would be fuzzy and requires immediate attention to prevent a larger infestation from occurring.

Pest Damage: Asymmetrical holes, surface loss, shortened feathers or fur, gnaw marks, or tunneling, etc., obviously caused by insects or rodents; see also "infestation."

Polish, Sheen: An area of luster or shine different from the rest of the surface created over time, often caused by the object's frequent use or where another object rubbed against the surface.

Odorous: Chemical reaction or deterioration over time, detectable by smell.

Red Rot: Reaction to vegetable-tanned leather caused by a chemical reaction between the acidic leather and environmental conditions, such as high temperatures, relative humidity, and air pollutants, which appears in the form of a red, powdery substance and makes the leather highly susceptible to damage.

Salt: White, crystalline accretion often caused by the transfer of sweat on to utilitarian leather.

Scratched: Linear loss due to contact with a sharp object.

Shrinkage: Loss of mass or size as a result of low relative humidity and a skin drying over time; may cause seam separation.

Stained: Unintentional change in color resulting from soiling, adhesives, pest residue, mold, foods, oils, etc.; compare to "staining."

Torn: A break or tear in the tanned or untanned skin.

Wear: Surface deterioration caused by use or movement over time. See Figure 18.8.

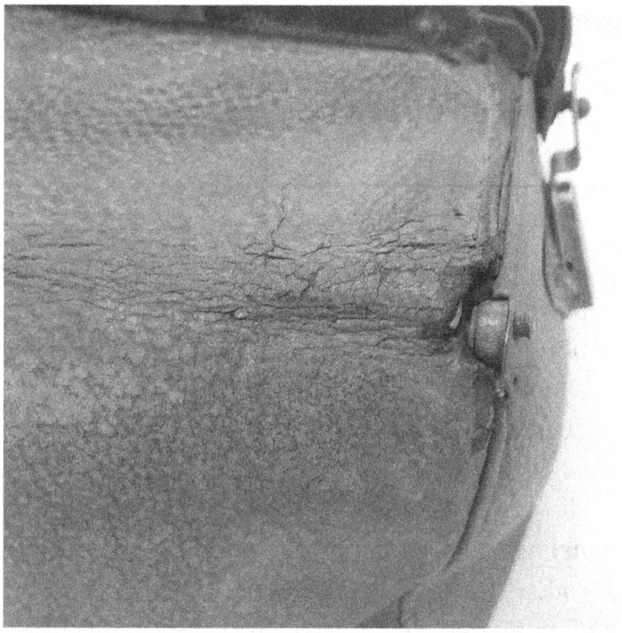

Figure 18.8. A nineteenth-century medical bag with various signs of wear from use by the original owner.
Source: Image courtesy of the Culture & Heritage Museums of York County, SC (1982.26)

NOTES

1. For additional information on prepared animal pelts used for scientific purposes, see the chapter on taxidermy.

2. Historically, patent leather was made from real leather that was covered with layers of lacquer or varnish. Modern patent leather is not actually leather, but rather a synthetic material made to look like real patent leather, and it will need to be preserved and conserved differently.

3. Untanned organs of the animals may also appear like rawhide. The tendons and ligaments (sinews) can be dried and used as bow strings or sewing thread, bladders can be dried and used as containers, and intestinal linings can be used as cordage and musical instrument strings.

BIBLIOGRAPHY

Buck, Rebecca A., and Jean A. Gilmore, eds. *Museum Registration Methods*, 5th edition. Canadian Conservation Institute. "Care of Alum, Vegetable, and Mineral-Tanned Leather." *CCI Notes* 8/2 (1992): 1–4.

Canadian Conservation Institute. "Care of Rawhide and Semi-Tanned Leather." *CCI Notes* 8/4 (1992): 1–3.

Cockerline, Neil, and Melinda Markell. "The Handling and Exhibition of Potentially Hazardous Artifacts in Museum Collections." *History News* 64, no. 4 (Autumn 2009): 1–8.

Dirksen, Vicki. "The Degradation and Conservation of Leather." *Journal of Conservation and Museums Studies* 3 (1997): 6–10. Accessed January 6, 2021. doi: http://doi.org/10.5334/jcms.3972.

Grantz, Gerald. *Home Book of Taxidermy and Tanning.* Mechanicsburg, PA: Stackpole Books, 1969.

Guldbeck, Per E. "Leather: Its Understanding and Care." *History News* 24, no. 4 (April 1969): 75–86.

Howatt-Krahn, Ann. "Conservation; Beadwork." *American Indian Art Magazine* (Autumn 1986): 24–49.

Howatt-Krahn, Ann. "Conservation: Skin and Native-Tanned Leather." *American Indian Art Magazine* (Spring 19867): 44–51.

Landrey, Gregory J., Kate Duffy, Janice Carlson, Lois Olcott Price, Bruno P. Pouliot, Margaret A. Little, Linda Eaton, Debra Hess Norris, John Krill, Betty Fiske, Mark F. Bockrath, Michael S. Podmanicsky, and Mary C. Peterson, eds. *The Winterthur Guide to Caring for Your Collection.* Winterthur, DE: Henry Francis du Pont Winterthur Museums, 2000.

National Park Service. *Museum Handbook: Museum Collections*. Washington, D.C.: National Parks Service, 2007.

Stone, Tom. "Care of Mounted Specimens and Pelts." *CCI Notes* 8/3, edited by Carole Dignard. Ottawa: CCI, 2015.

19

Taxidermy

Fran Ritchie

Taxidermy is a preserved animal skin or hide that has been secured to a manikin, creating a lifelike pose. The taxidermy process has developed over hundreds of years and unlike other art forms, there are no standardized materials and techniques. However, generalities may be made, especially for museum-quality taxidermy. For medium- and large-sized mammals, the preservation technique for the hides is tanning (such as chrome or vegetable tan). For birds, small mammals, fish, reptiles, and amphibians, the skins are too thin to tan, and the preservation typically involves scraping all fats and soft tissue, then applying a desiccant that removes remaining oils. The preserved skins and hides are glued, sewn, and nailed onto manikins that have been sculpted to mimic the species in musculature and pose. The three most typical manikin forms are bound, hollow, or foam (see Terminology). Because it is challenging to effectively clean skulls, and because teeth break over time, skulls are often replaced with similar forms made of dense plastic. Eyes are replaced with glass or plastic replicas, and tongues are replaced with plastic or tinted wax replicas. The specimen is finished by applying paint, tinted wax, and other sculpted materials that compensate for loss of color and suppleness (see "Finishing" in Terminology). Internal wires from the manikin extend outside the taxidermy to provide an anchor of support when securing it onto a display base, inside a diorama, or hanging on a wall. If the taxidermy is posed in an anthropomorphic scene, fabrics and props are added, as well.

Articulated skeletons and skeletal materials, mummified animals, animal study skins, pinned insects, specimens preserved in fluid, and fossils are not taxidermy and should be considered in the chapter on Natural History Specimens.

TERMINOLOGY

Anthropomorphic: Animals depicted in postures and performing activities that are typically human. For example, kittens arranged at a table drinking tea and wearing dresses, or frogs standing on hind legs playing an instrument.

Display or *Habitat Base*: A piece of plain or varnished wood onto which the taxidermy is secured, for the purpose of display. If real or faux vegetal or other habitat materials are present on the display base, it is referred to as a habitat base.

Figure 19.1. Kingfisher taxidermy mount on a wooden display base. Source: Fran Ritchie

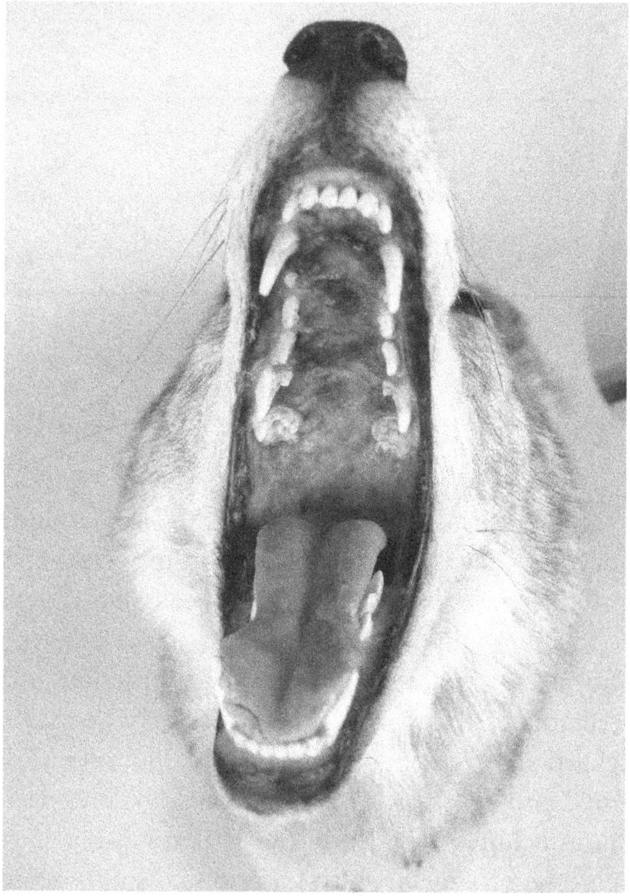

Figure 19.3. Painted wax mouth flesh and tongue on coyote taxidermy mount. Note the broken tip of the tongue. Source: Fran Ritchie

Figure 19.2. Prairie dog and chipmunk on a habitat base. Source: Fran Ritchie

Diorama: A complete scene that includes a background depicting a habitat and a foreground with vegetal materials and taxidermy mounts. If there is no painted or photographic background, but there are vegetal materials, the taxidermy is on a habitat display base, not in a diorama.

Finishing Materials: Final materials added to a specimen to make it appear alive. For example, bird waddles and bird feet lose their color after the animal has died, so those areas are painted to match the original vibrant hues. Mammal noses dry out and shrink over time, so sculpting materials may be added and painted to appear shiny and fleshy.

Hide versus Skin: The skins of most animals are referred to as skins, but for larger mammals like cows and buffalo, the skin is referred to as hide.

Manikin: The internal form of taxidermy that replicates the postures and musculature of a specific animal. The "manikin" or "mannikin" spelling is used to denote scientific accuracy, as opposed to "mannequin" that is a general form. Note that unless the skin or hide of the animal has sustained damage that reveals the internal manikin, the exact type of manikin/materials most likely cannot be determined.

- *Bound manikin*: The form of the animal is created by using thread to bind or wrap into place loose material (wood slivers called wood wool or excelsior) applied over an internal metal frame armature to resemble musculature.
- *Foam manikin*: The form of the animal is sculpted, molded, and then cast out of semi-dense polyurethane foam. These manikins can be lightweight, even if the animal is large.
- *Hollow manikin*: The form of the animal is sculpted, molded, and then cast out of layers of lightweight materials built up inside the mold. The result is a hollow manikin that can be lightweight, even if the animal is large.
- *Solid manikin*: The form of the animal is sculpted out of solid materials, such as wax, plaster, carved wood, or a combination of materials. These manikins can be heavy, even if the animal is relatively small.

Mount: Because the preserved skin or hide is applied or mounted to a manikin, taxidermy is referred to as taxidermy mounts or mounts. The word mount can also refer to the fact that the taxidermy hung on a wall, or mounted to a wall, such as trophy mounts or shoulder mounts.

Shoulder Mount: The animal is mounted at the "shoulders," displaying the neck and head only. This is a popular pose for game animals with antlers and horns, thus, also referred to as trophy mounts. The taxidermy may be attached to a wooden backing board that extends beyond the animal called a panel.

Figure 19.4. Whimsical shoulder mount of a "jackalope" with a wooden panel.
Source: Fran Ritchie

Taxidermied or *Taxidermized*: Referring to the act of turning an animal into a piece of taxidermy. Although the use of these words is not incorrect, it is more common to refer to a specimen as being *mounted* instead of *taxidermied.*

Trophy Mount: See "shoulder mount."

HEALTH AND SAFETY

As mentioned in the chapter on Natural History Specimens, organic materials in these collections have a history of residual pesticide treatment, i.e., pesticides that remain on the specimen and cannot be removed. Although pesticides were initially embraced because of their efficacy at blocking insect pests from destroying taxidermy specimens, use fell out of favor in the 1960s due to the human health hazards.

The presence of residual pesticides does not mean the taxidermy must be feared or neglected. Wear personal protective equipment (PPE) and be mindful of workplace cleanliness. Arsenic-based pesticides were mixed into a paste form called arsenic soap and smeared onto the interior of a preserved skin or hide before it was attached to the manikin. The arsenic is mostly contained inside the mount, but over time, the small particulates may migrate to the surface through seams and around the eyes and mouth. Avoid touching these areas, especially when not wearing gloves. If examining a taxidermy mount on display, wear PPE listed below and handle the specimen as minimally as possible to prevent stirring arsenic particulates that may have become dislodged.

While arsenic soap was applied during the construction of the taxidermy mount, vapor-based pesticides may have been applied by the taxidermist or by museum staff once the mount was acquired. If vapor-based pesticides were applied to the specimens or storage container, such as mercuric chloride, paradichlorobenzene, and naphthalene, open the cabinet doors, then vacate the room for thirty minutes to allow the built-up vapors to dissipate before examining the taxidermy mount.

Analytical instrumentation (such as X-ray Fluorescence, or XRF) can quickly detect the presence of arsenic, but these analyzers are cost-prohibitive to most museums. Home testing kits for arsenic in water can be adapted for taxidermy specimens, but the results could be false negative, and the procedures are time-consuming. It is best to assume that taxidermy mounts pre-1960s were prepared with arsenic soap. When examining a collection of taxidermy in a workroom, the following procedures can help mitigate risk of exposure to residual pesticides:

1. Cover table surfaces with plastic sheeting that will be thrown away after the examination is complete.
2. Wear personal protective equipment (PPE): nitrile or rubber gloves (no cotton), an N-95 mask or respirator, lab coat that can be bagged and washed after work is complete, and/or hazmat suits or sleeves that can be thrown away after work is complete. Do not touch the specimen with exposed skin. Remember to remove gloves after touching contaminated surfaces and before touching skin, hair, face, clothes, etc. If working in a well-ventilated unconfined space, a respirator may not be needed.
3. Handle the specimen as minimally as possible and do not pet it, in order to prevent stirring heavy metal particulates.
4. If working directly into a computer, vacuum the keyboard after work is complete to remove any pesticide particulates that may have transferred.
5. Vacuum the space after work is complete and the plastic sheeting is removed. Use a HEPA vacuum, if available, because they are filtered and self-contained (i.e., they do not exhaust hazardous air).

Be aware that there was a history of museum staff applying residual pesticides not only to taxidermy, but also other collections composed of organic material. For more information on the history of pesticide use on museum collections, see the bibliography at the end of this chapter.

Remember: "Mothballs" are residual pesticides that are harmful to human health and should not be used in collections or at home. Instead, rely on integrated pest management strategies to prevent an infestation.

HANDLING

It can be difficult to determine the manikin material inside a taxidermy mount with visual examination alone. If the manikin is solid plaster or wax, the specimen will be heavier than it appears. A large animal that was mounted over a foam or hollow manikin will be lighter than it appears. When handling the taxidermy, test the lift first so that the weight is not surprising.

Trophy or Shoulder Mount

If there is a panel and the taxidermy is light enough, handle and carry using the panel. If the taxidermy is large and heavy (for example, a moose), enlist help from another person and have each person place a hand on the underside of the neck of the taxidermy specimen, and one hand on the top of the panel. Try to maintain a vertical configuration that mimics the way the taxidermy is hung on the wall. If it needs to be placed on a horizontal surface, place the shoulder mount with nose up to the sky, resting on the flat portion that would typically be against a wall. Avoid placing the taxidermy on its nose, as that skin is thin and vulnerable to damage. The horns on bighorn sheep are heavy and may cause the specimen to tip. Have foam blocks and other padding materials handy to provide additional support where needed. Bighorn sheep, caribou, and other specimens with hollow guard hairs are very susceptible to hair breakage and damage. Touch hair as minimally as possible.

Taxidermy Attached to a Base

Check the security of the taxidermy specimen attachment to the display or habitat base by gently touching the taxidermy. If it seems secure, handle and carry the taxidermy specimen by the base only, avoiding touching the specimen. If the attachment to the base is not secure and the taxidermy wobbles, carry with one hand on the base and one hand gently on the taxidermy specimen to stabilize it.

Taxidermy Attached to a Habitat Component

If the taxidermy specimen is attached to something that does not lie safely on a table surface, such as a bird attached to a branch that was removed from a diorama, assemble a temporary support to pad where necessary, such as pieces of foam, blocks, and soft shapeable materials. Polyethylene foam blocks can be cut and arranged to accommodate for irregularly shaped taxidermy mounts. (See "Support for Small Taxidermy Mounts" by Thomas.)

Full Body with No Display Base

If the taxidermy mount has been removed from its display mount or from a diorama, there typically will be metal wires extending from the feet. These wires can be utilized to insert into a temporary display mount made from a dense polyethylene foam plank or wooden board (wood can be used temporarily). Ensure that the piece of foam or wood is large enough to distribute the weight of the taxidermy mount. The metal wires can be easily inserted into the foam, but holes must be drilled into the wooden board. Handle the taxidermy by the torso or widest and sturdiest part of the body. Do not lift by the legs, tail, or other protruding components. (See "Support for Large Taxidermy Mounts" by Fuller.)

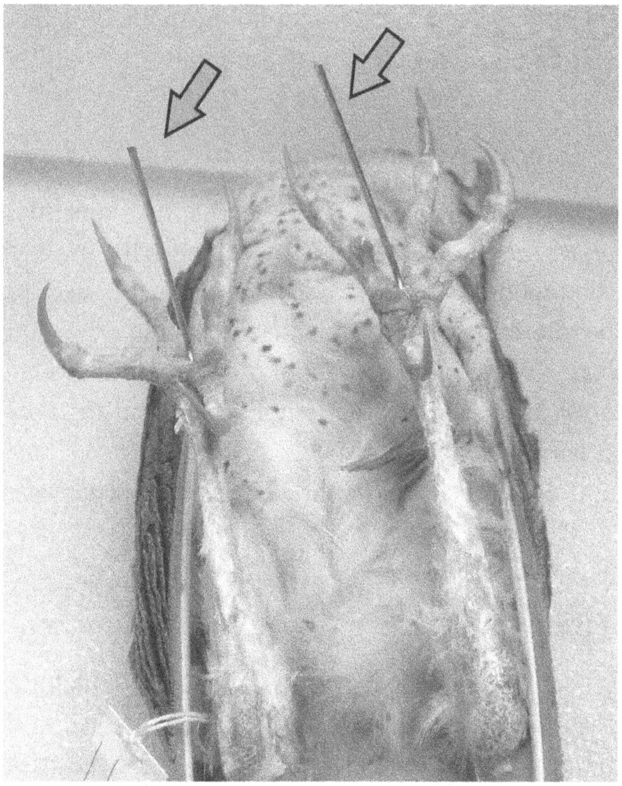

Figure 19.5. Metal internal armature wires extending from the feet of a barn owl.
Source: Fran Ritchie

Figure 19.6. Full-body coyote taxidermy mount temporarily stored on an Ethafoam base.
Source: Fran Ritchie

EXAMINATION

Although the condition of taxidermy mounts varies based on the quality of the skin preservation, stability of the manikin, and storage or display environment, there are areas that are consistently vulnerable on each type of animal.

Mammals

Examine hair for light damage, embrittlement, and loss from pest damage or breakage. Examine the seams for splitting or skin tearing. The thin skin of the ears often tears, and the nose often dries and loses suppleness, resulting in distortion. The toes, tails, and whiskers may have breaks or losses. Check antlers or horns for stability by gently wiggling them. Examine the face for paint and/or wax loss.

Figure 19.7. Broken and bent ear of a ringtail taxidermy mount. Source: Fran Ritchie

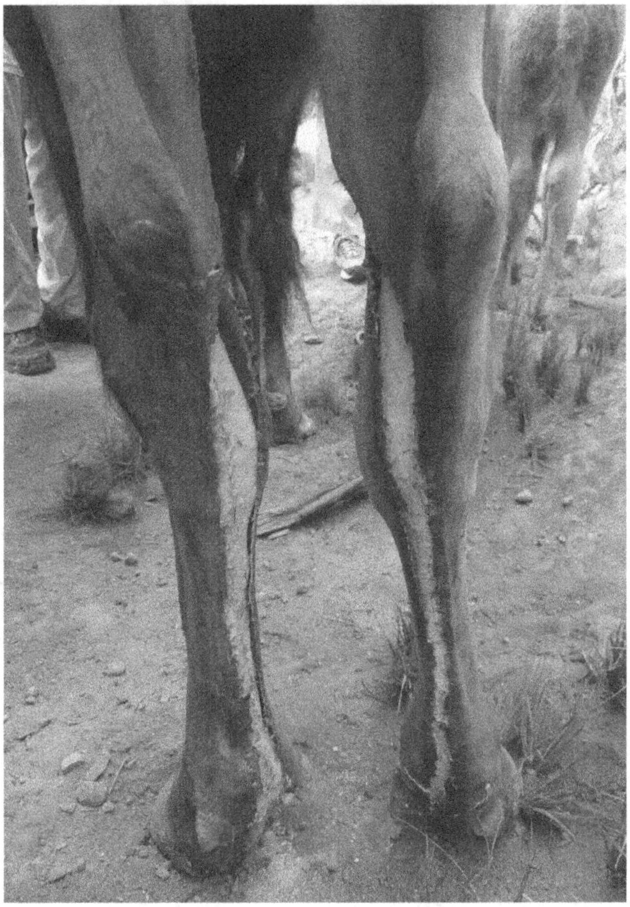

Figure 19.8. Split seams and shrunken hide on the back of the legs of a bison taxidermy mount. Source: Fran Ritchie

Birds

Examine the wings and head for dislocation or detachment. The thin skin around these areas often tears, creating loose wings that are no longer in their correct position and one wing may be unintentionally lower than the other. Examine feathers for loss and discoloration from fat burn. Look for excess oil on the feet of waterfowl and birds that fish, as their feet naturally contain more fats for keeping warm, but are difficult to clean when mounting, resulting in shiny, oily feet that may cause paint to flake. Check the stability of paint around the head and beak.

Figure 19.9. Detached head on a grosbeak taxidermy mount. Source: Fran Ritchie

Fish

Fish mounts may be composed of preserved fish skin over a manikin or, more commonly for newer mounts, painted foam. Examine skin for distortion, tears, and loss. If the fish is painted, examine the paint layer for loss.

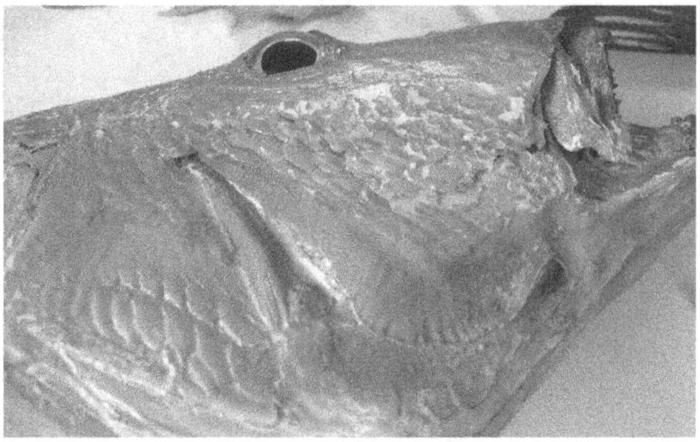

Figure 19.10. Flaking paint and paint loss on fish taxidermy mount. Source: Fran Ritchie

Reptiles and Amphibians

Some species of reptiles and amphibians are difficult to taxidermy, so start by examining the mount to determine if the skin is real, or if it is a replica. Like other taxidermy, examine for skin tears and losses, as well as loss of finishing materials such as paint.

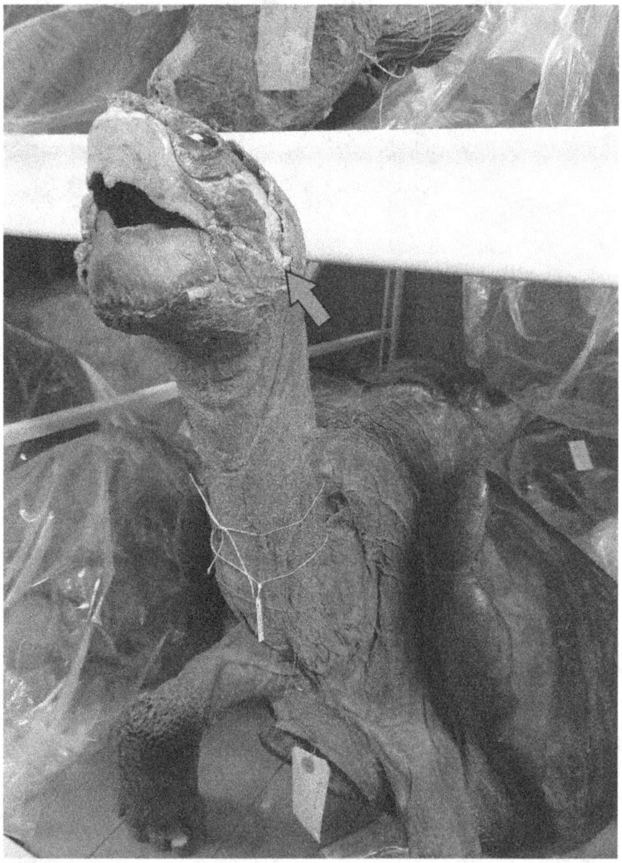

Figure 19.11. Skin tears on head of tortoise taxidermy mount. Source: Fran Ritchie

Figure 19.12. Irregular loss on the tip of a taxidermy rattlesnake rattle, indicating pest damage.
Source: Fran Ritchie

DOCUMENTATION

The General Condition Report Form found in chapter 1 can be adapted for specifically examining taxidermy.

TAXIDERMY CONDITION REPORT FORM

Object ID number:

Evaluation by: (Name/Title) Date:

Object: taxidermy mount of (type of animal, include the common name)

Scientific name: (If known, list the scientific name here, but refer to the taxidermy mount by the common name of the animal throughout the report.)

Description: (Include a description of the pose and what type of taxidermy mount. Shoulder mount on a panel? Full body mount on a display or habitat base, or in a diorama, or with no base?)

Dimensions: (Include measurements of the taxidermy specimen itself, plus separate measurements of the base or panel.)

Provenance:

Hazards: (If known, include any information that indicates use or suspicion of residual pesticides. This could be the age of the taxidermy mount, a known history of pesticide use within the institution, or a chemical smell.)

Previous Treatments or Conservation:

Overall Condition (circle one): Structurally Stable Structurally Unstable
(Instead of subjectively saying a taxidermy mount is in Excellent, Good, or Poor condition, assess the overall structural stability. If the taxidermy is structurally unstable, there are broken components susceptible to loss and the mount requires conservation treatment to prevent further damage.)

Attachment to base (circle one): Stable Unstable N/A (no base)

Condition Notes:
(Further describe the condition of the object in greater detail in one or more paragraphs, moving generally from the structure of the object to its superficial elements, and from damages of greater to lesser significance. Note: damages to the superficial substance of an object, such as losses to fur, are generally considered under Structure, while damages in or on the surface, such as discoloration, scratches, or dust accumulation, are considered under Surface. Include condition of any base/mount/support or label(s) present. Include location and attach photographs or sketches. Annotated digital images are easy to produce and can be much easier to understand than long prose describing location on an object.)

Figure 19.13. Taxidermy condition report form.

CONDITION GLOSSARY

In addition to terms commonly used to describe museum objects, the following terms are added to the lexicon specifically addressing condition issues for taxidermy mounts:

Cloudy Eyes: Plastic and glass replica eyeballs may be cloudy in appearance due to dust accumulation. Glass, however, may also have a condition called "glass disease." Glass disease occurs due to chemical instability of the glass and presents itself as very small white particulates covering the surface, or small networks of cracks called crizzling.

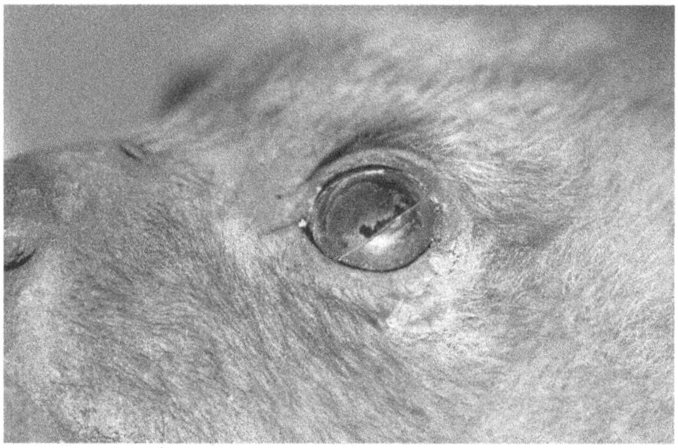

Figure 19.14. Cloudy and cracked glass eye on a mammalian taxidermy mount.
Source: Fran Ritchie

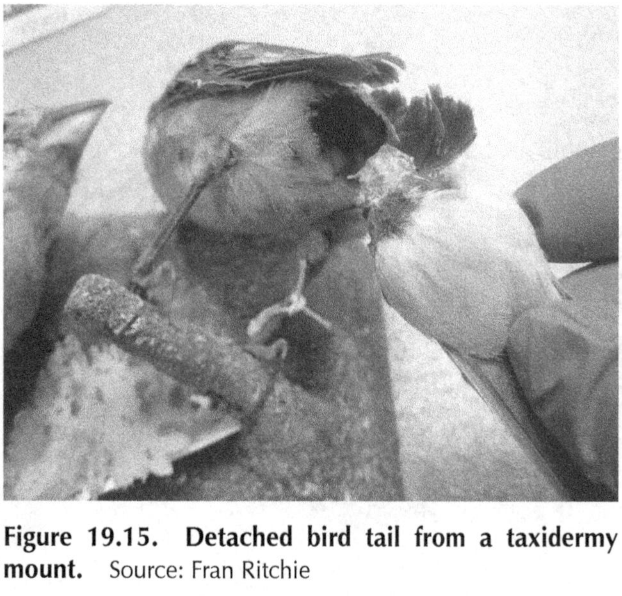

Figure 19.15. Detached bird tail from a taxidermy mount. Source: Fran Ritchie

Desiccation: Extremely dry skin, such as desiccated nose or ear skin that has led to distortion and/or shrinkage.

Detachment: Components of the taxidermy mount that have come off, but that remain extant. Bird tails and wings are especially vulnerable to detachment.

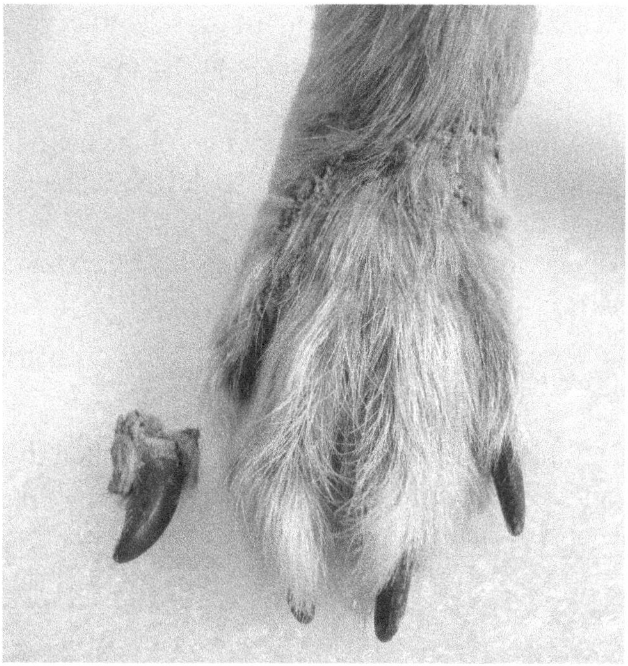

Figure 19.16. Detached claw on a coyote taxidermy mount. Source: Fran Ritchie

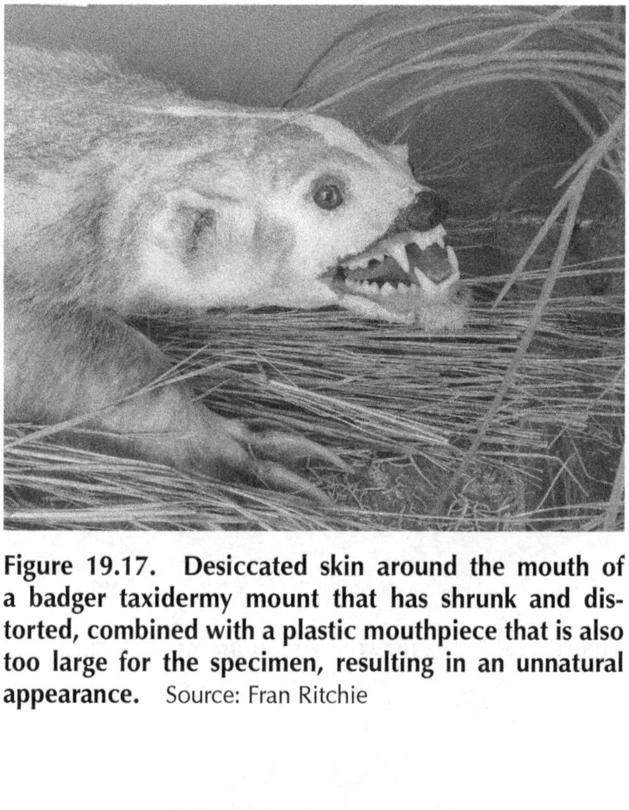

Figure 19.17. Desiccated skin around the mouth of a badger taxidermy mount that has shrunk and distorted, combined with a plastic mouthpiece that is also too large for the specimen, resulting in an unnatural appearance. Source: Fran Ritchie

Distortion: A warp in the skin or misplacement of a component that was not intentional to the original taxidermy mount and now contributes to an unrealistic-looking pose.

Dust Accumulation or Soiling: Taxidermy is often displayed high on walls or in locations that are difficult to clean. When a layer of dust and/or pollutants accumulates on the surface, it obscures the coloration and patterning of the animal, creating a dull appearance.

Fat Burn: Yellow-orange or brown stains especially noticeable on light-colored hair and feathers, caused by inadequate skin/hide preservation techniques during the construction of the mount.

Feather Loss: Bald patches of feathers that can be caused by pest damage (look for signs of frass or casings), and/or improper skin preservation techniques during the construction of the mount.

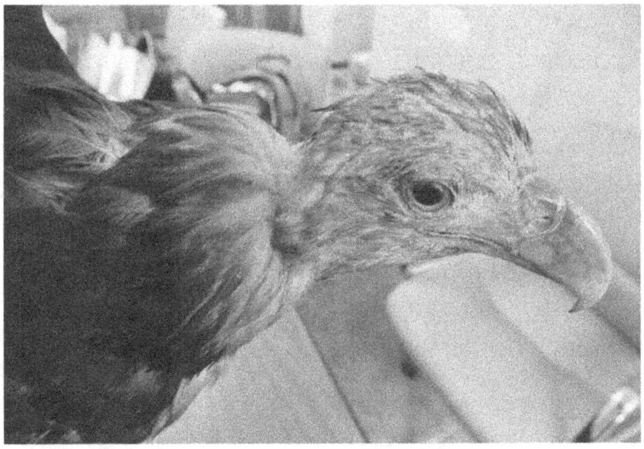

Figure 19.18. Feather loss on the head of a bald eagle taxidermy mount. Source: Fran Ritchie

Fur Loss: Bald patches of fur that can be caused by dermestid or moth pest damage (look for signs of frass or casings), improper skin/hide preservation techniques during the construction of the mount, or inherent issues with the type of hide (such as hollow hairs that were close to molting when the animal was collected).

Figure 19.20. Faded bobcat taxidermy mount on habitat base. Source: Fran Ritchie

Figure 19.19. Hair loss on a ringtail taxidermy mount. Source: Fran Ritchie

Light Damage: Faded or yellowed fur and feathers that are not as vibrant when comparing to a living specimen of that species. Colors tend to fade, while white feathers and hairs will yellow. If unsure, consult reference images of that species.

Oily Skin: Animals endemic to colder climates often have more oils and fats than other species to help keep them warm. These are difficult to remove during the preservation process and over time the oils will leach out, creating a sticky surface. Waterfowl and other birds that prey on fish will often have oily feet that attract dust and cause paint to peel.

Figure 19.21. Translucent, sticky feet of a mallard taxidermy due to excess oils and fats remaining in the specimen after mounting. Source: Fran Ritchie

Pest Damage: Losses due to dermestid beetle larvae (such as odd beetles and carpet beetles) or moth larvae (case-making) eating the hairs,

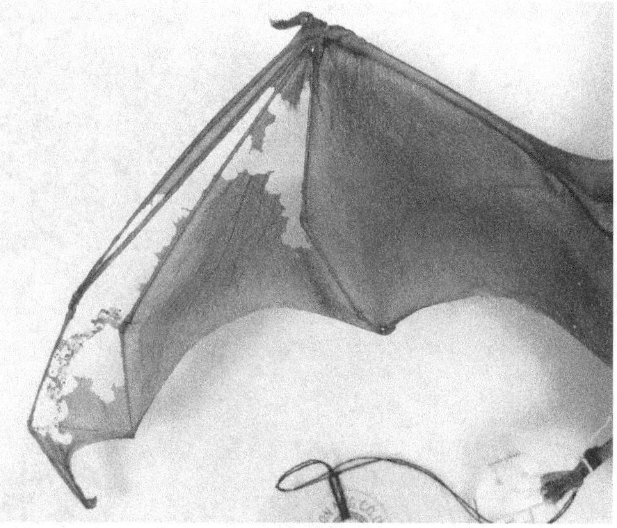

Figure 19.22. Irregular edges on an area of loss on a taxidermy bat wing, including pest damage. Source: Fran Ritchie

Figure 19.23. Dermestic beetle larvae casings on and under a mouse taxidermy mount, indicating pest activity. Source: Fran Ritchie

feathers, and other soft tissues that remain in the taxidermy mount. Rodents like mice or rats may also eat portions of specimens. Look for signs of frass, casings, and teeth marks.

Skin Tear: Skins and hides flex and contract as a response to fluctuations in the environment, pulling against the seams. If the skin shrinks too much, and/or if the manikin is too large for the animal, the skin adjacent to the seam will tear under the tension. Skin can also tear in places

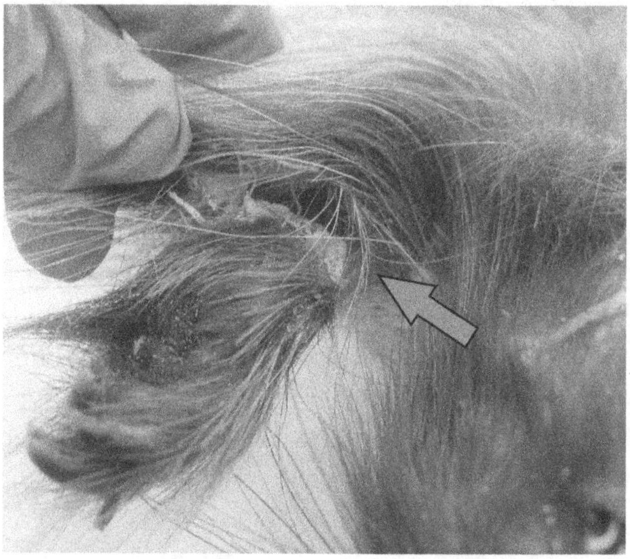

Figure 19.24. Skin tear on a taxidermy porcupine arm, causing deterioration. Source: Fran Ritchie

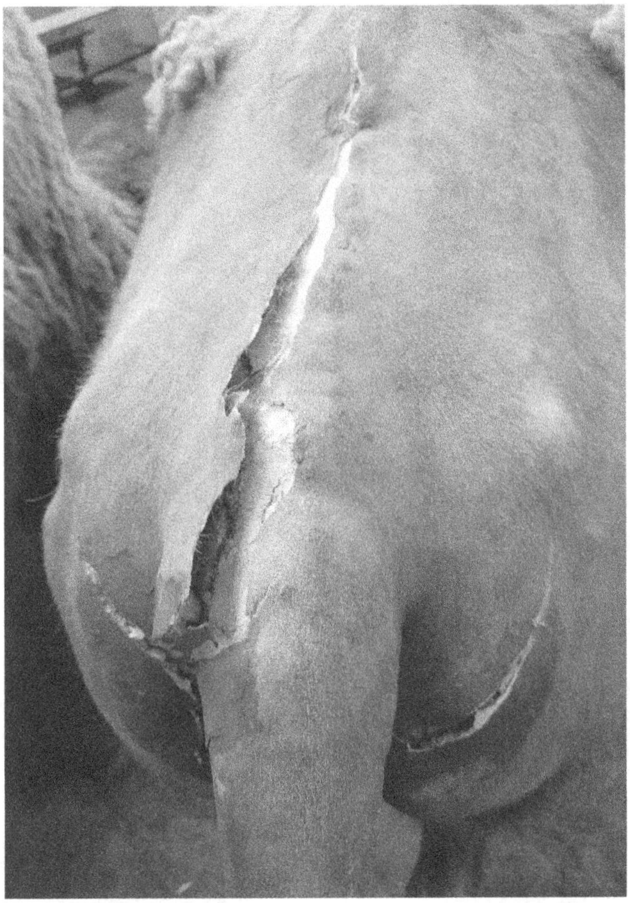

Figure 19.25. Hide tears on a bison taxidermy mount.
Source: Fran Ritchie

that protrude and can be easily disturbed, such as tails and wings.

Splitting Seam: Threads can weaken or loosen over time, causing the seams to open.

Figure 19.26. Split seam on a fish taxidermy mount.
Source: Fran Ritchie

BIBLIOGRAPHY

Dickinson, J. A. "Taxidermy." In *Conservation of Leather and Related Materials* by Marion Kite and Roy Thomson. Butterworth-Heinemann Series in Conservation and Museology. Boston: Elsevier Butterworth-Heinemann, 2006.

Fuller, Tamsen. "Support for Large Taxidermy Mounts | Storage Techniques for Art Science & History Collections." Accessed June 11, 2021. https://stashc.com/the-publication/supports/rigid-supports/support-for-large-taxidermy-mounts/.

Goldberg, Lisa. "A History of Pest Control Measures in the Anthropology Collections, National Museum of Natural History, Smithsonian Institution." *Journal of the American Institute for Conservation* 35, no. 1 (January 1996): 23–43. https://doi.org/10.1179/019713696806124601.

Hawks, Catharine. "Historical Survey of the Sources of Contamination of Ethnographic Materials in Museum Collections." *Collection Forum* 16, no. 1-2 (2001).

Hendry, Dick. "Vertebrates." *Care & Conservation of Natural History Collections* edited by David Carter and Annette K. Walker. Butterworth-Heinemann Series in Conservation and Museology. Oxford: Butterworth-Heinemann, 1999.

In Their True Colors. "Surveying Historic Taxidermy Part 3: Results," May 20, 2016. https://intheirtruecolors.wordpress.com/2016/05/20/surveying-historic-taxidermy-part-3-results/.

In Their True Colors. "What's the Word? A Glossary of Taxidermy Terms," March 14, 2017. https://intheirtruecolors.wordpress.com/2017/03/14/whats-the-word-a-glossary-of-taxidermy-terms/.

Knapp, Anthony M. "Arsenic Health and Safety Update." *Conserve-O-Gram* 2/3. National Park Service, 2000.

Morris, Patrick A. *A History of Taxidermy: Art, Science and Bad Taste*. Ascot: MPM, 2010.

Thomas, Linda L. "Support for Small Taxidermy Mounts | Storage Techniques for Art Science & History Collections." Accessed June

11, 2021. https://stashc.com/the-publication/supports/rigid-supports/support-for-small-taxidermy-mounts/.

20

Textiles

Laura Mina

Textiles are part of collections in museums, historic houses, and archives. Their value may be associated with cultural significance, historical record, and visual appeal. While the term *textile* comes from the Latin word meaning "to weave," it is commonly used to describe a wide variety of fabric structures. In this chapter, *textile* is used with a broad definition to refer to all collection materials that are made of, or include, fabrics. Textiles found in collections in the United States include flags and banners, garments, carpets, quilts, upholstery, needlework, visual and decorative art pieces, and scientific and industrial textiles. For clarity in this chapter, *textile* is used for collection pieces, and *fabric* is used to refer to storage and support materials.

The goal of this chapter is to provide practical information and guidelines relating to the handling, examination, and documentation of collection textiles. It is not possible to include all types of textiles or institutional settings, and there is no formula that can be applied to all situations. Thoughtful decision-making is critical to ensure that specific methods are appropriate for different situations.

This chapter includes terms that are common for many textiles; however, there is no universal vocabulary for textiles. To clarify terminology, there are two glossaries at the end of this chapter. The first includes basic terminology that will apply to many different textile structures. The second includes condition terminology related to textiles. It may be helpful to create an institutional glossary to use with your collection that can be accessed by staff, volunteers, and researchers. This will ensure consistent use of terminology and support visiting researchers and new workers. Additional resources for textile terminology are included in the bibliography at the end of this chapter.

HANDLING

Hands-on contact with textiles is a fundamental part of many collection activities, and handling is necessary to fulfill institutional and research goals. Tactical engagement with textiles can provide valuable information about materials and condition concerns. At the same time, handling should be approached with thoughtfulness and respect to minimize associated physical and chemical risks to textiles. Different textiles have different vulnerabilities, and every piece should be handled as if it is irreplaceable.

- *Look carefully at the textile before touching it or moving it.*

  Check for visual cues that indicate damaged and fragile areas. See Figure 20.1. This will help identify strong areas that can be safely handled. If the textile is being removed from a storage or display support, continue to carefully observe the textile as you move it. The movement may reveal a fragile area that requires additional or different support.

Figure 20.1. Printed textile with areas of loss from deteriorating dyes. Source: William Donnelly

- *Plan ahead before moving a textile.*

  Make sure that there is a planned space to place the textile after it is moved and that there is a clear path to get there. If a textile is large or heavy, it is important to work with partners to minimize risks for people and textiles. For longer moves within a building, it is often helpful to work as a team with one partner who can open doors while other partners focus on moving the textile.

- *Minimize the risk of accidental chemical damage by using clean hands or gloves.*

  Clean, dry hands without lotion are often best for handling textiles since so much information is gained through touch. Sometimes nitrile or cotton gloves can be an appropriate choice. Gloves should be worn:

  - If the textile has metal or plastic components that could be damaged by skin oils.
  - If the textile could be a health risk to a handler (for example, if the textile may have been previously treated with a pesticide).
  - If the handler has a skin condition or wound, or is wearing nail polish, that could pose a risk for the textile.
  - Cotton gloves have the advantage that they can be washed and reused, but their disadvantages include loose fit and shedding fibers.

- *Minimize the risk of accidental physical damage from the handlers' personal clothing and accessories.*

  This includes removing scarves, long necklaces, watches, and jewelry on wrists or fingers. Lariats and ID badges should also be removed. Long hair should be secured away from the face. Smocks, aprons, or lab coats should be worn if the handlers' clothing might pose additional risks due to buttons and other fasteners, or potential shedding fibers.

- *Minimize the risk of accidental physical damage from the textile's own weight and weight distribution.*

  Handlers should use both hands to move textiles; this provides greater stability and weight distribution. See Figure 20.2. Avoid lifting a textile by a corner or crushing a textile by grasping it too tightly. For the safety of the collection and handlers, it is often best to work with partners for textiles that are large, heavy, or fragile.

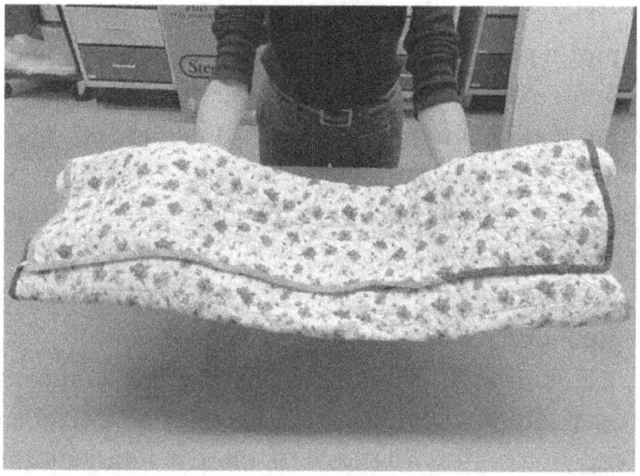

Figure 20.2. Hold textiles with two hands to provide greater stability and weight distribution.
Source: William Donnelly

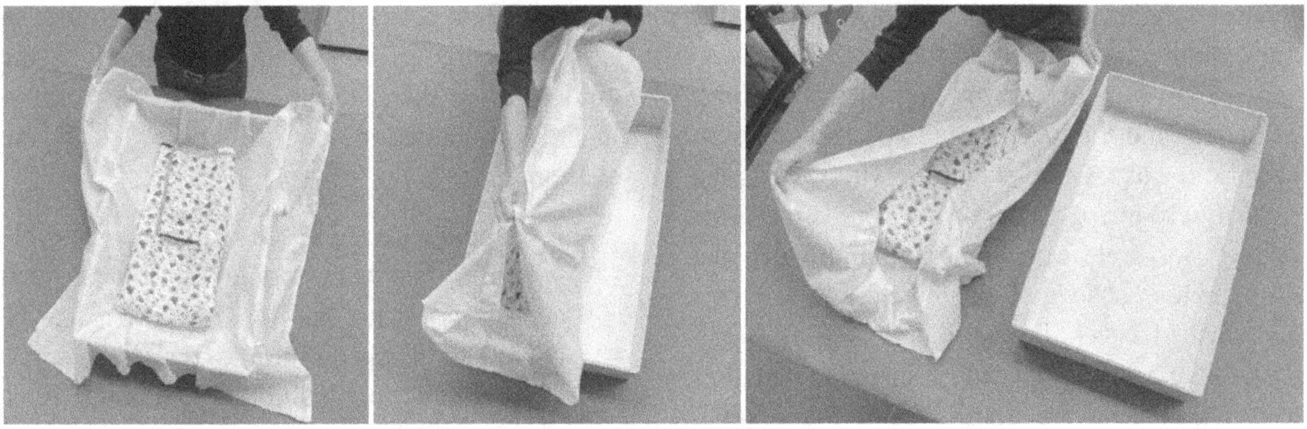

Figure 20.3. A cotton fabric sling provides greater support and control when moving collection textiles into, or out of, storage boxes. Source: William Donnelly

- Place a textile on a piece of archival cardboard or on a fabric sling to provide greater support and control during textile moves. See Figure 20.3.
- When moving a long garment on a hanger, use one hand to hold the hook of the hanger and drape the lower garment over the other forearm to provide additional support and prevent the garment from touching the floor. See Figure 20.4.
- When moving a textile on a mount, hold the mount and not the textile.

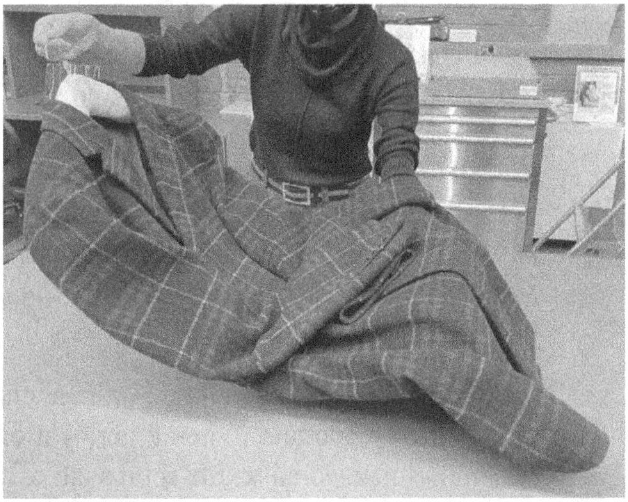

Figure 20.4. To move a garment on a hanger, use one hand to hold the hook of the hanger and the other forearm to support the lower area of the garment.
Source: William Donnelly

- *Use common sense.*
  - Do not smoke, eat, or drink near collection textiles.
  - In most cases, collection textiles should not be used outside of the collection setting, and collection garments should not be worn. Exceptions to this rule include cases where institutions and stakeholders agree to specific cultural, ceremonial, or religious use of collection textiles.

Even with best-practice guidelines, accidents may occur. In such cases, it is important that the event is documented according to institutional policies, such as updating condition reports. While working to reduce the risk of accidents, these events can be valuable learning experiences and lead to improved guidelines and practices.

EXAMINATION

Close examination of textiles can provide valuable information about their materials, structures, and condition concerns. While an examination may prioritize one type of information, most will include all. Similar to the guidelines for moving textiles, it is important to set up a good workspace for examination and to plan ahead.

Most textiles should be placed on tables during examination. Ideally, the table will be large enough to support the textile when it is fully extended, and the table should be cleaned before use. Table covers can be helpful with textiles that are actively losing fibers or are very dirty. Some options for table covers include archival paper, polyethylene sheets, clean undyed cotton fabric, and washed Tyvek. For very large textiles, one of the table cover options can be spread on the floor to provide a clean area for the textile examination.

A few simple tools can aid in textile examination. See Figure 20.5. Good light is essential; however, sunlight should be avoided as it can catalyze and contribute to chemical damage. It may be helpful to have a lamp with an adjustable arm to provide raking light. Soft tape measures are practical for working with flexible textiles, and the metal ends should be removed to prevent snags. Magnifying tools such as linen testers (typically around 10X magnification) and pocket microscopes (typically around 60X magnification) can provide more detailed information about fibers and textile structures. Pencils should be used instead of pens. It is important to keep pencils and eraser crumbs from accidental contact with collection textiles.

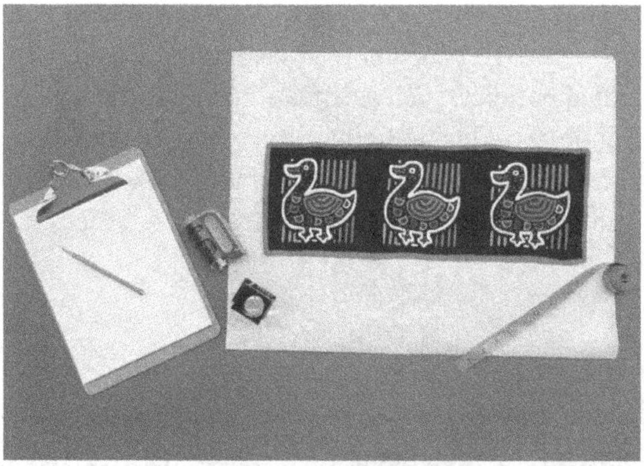

Figure 20.5. This textile is ready for examination. It is on a piece of archival paper to facilitate movement and is surrounded by helpful tools, including soft tape measure, magnification aids, pencil, and paper.
Source: William Donnelly

It is often necessary to handle and move a textile during examination. In addition to the guidelines in the Handling section, the following recommendations can minimize risk during examination.

- Arrange the textile to see as much as possible with minimal contact and movement. Plan ahead so that the textile will not need to be moved and flipped multiple times.
- Place small- to medium-sized textiles on a support (archival paper, board, or fabric) rather than directly on the table. The support can be moved and turned to provide different viewing angles without direct contact to the collection textile.
- Plan ahead when a textile needs to be flipped to examine the other side. There are several strategies that are effective depending on the size, decorations, and fragility of the textile. The goals are to provide holistic support and ensure that the textile experiences as little physical stress as possible. It is helpful to work with a partner for textiles that are large, heavy, or fragile.
    - Sandwich the textile between two archival boards and hold with moderate pressure while flipping. See Figure 20.6. The boards can be padded with polyester felt or batting if the textile would be damaged by pressure between flat boards.
    - Roll the textile onto a tube and then unroll to the other side.
    - Accordion-fold the textile, flip the folded textile, and then unfold to the other side. See Figure 20.7.
- Some garments can be examined on hangers or other support mounts. When a garment or other three-dimensional textile is on a table, it often needs some interior padding to support its intended shape. This padding can also create visual access to the interior of the piece,

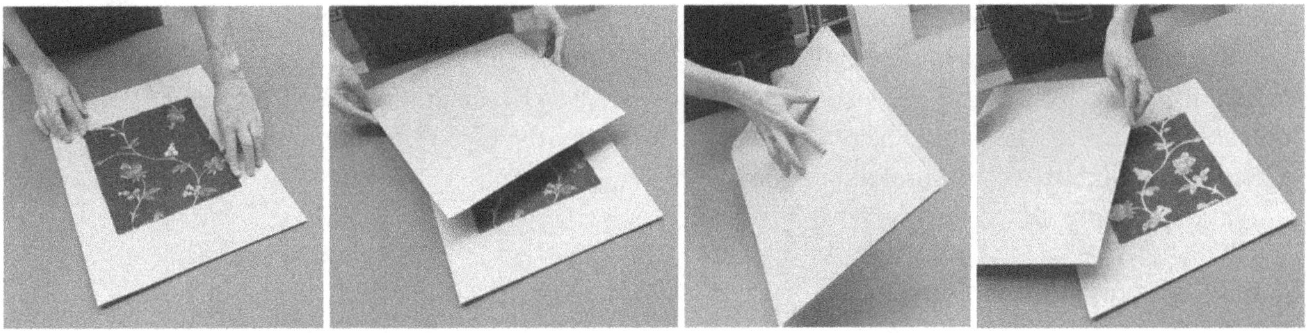

Figure 20.6. Two pieces of archival blue board are used to support a small printed textile as it is flipped to the other side. Source: William Donnelly

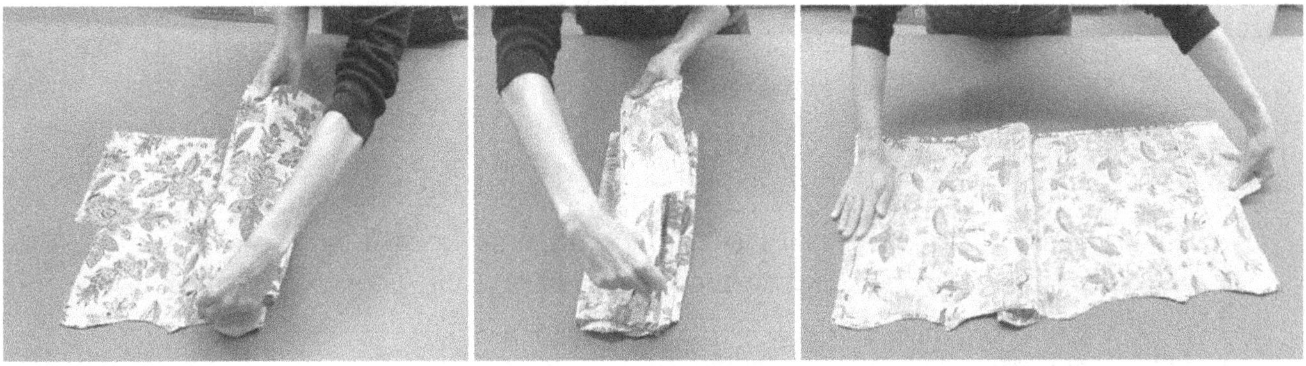

Figure 20.7. A long printed textile is arranged in accordion folds, flipped to the other side, and then unfolded. Source: William Donnelly

and thus, reduce needed handling. In most cases, it is not advised to turn garments inside out. The high risk of damage outweighs the potential advantage for examination. If a garment is determined to be strong enough and there is a compelling reason to turn it inside out (such as looking for mold), it may be helpful to work with a partner to ensure that the garment is manipulated as carefully and minimally as possible.

- Most textiles in frames or pressure mounts should not be removed for examination unless there are plans for the piece to have conservation treatment or be reframed/remounted by an expert. Taking a textile out of a frame or pressure mount often reveals many condition concerns and it can be challenging to safely replace a textile in its frame or pressure mount.

DOCUMENTATION

Documentation is a critical component of collection care that supports preservation and research goals. Documentation can be complicated by the diversity of textile structures and by the time needed for detailed examination and research. It is helpful to use checklists or standardized forms to ensure that consistent information is recorded. In some cases, it is helpful to have different forms for specific types of textiles, for example, rugs and garments.

There are two broad types of documentation, written and pictorial (photographs and drawings). Ideally, both types of documentation are combined to provide detailed information about collection textiles.

Written documentation is often formatted for digital databases, and it can also be recorded with paper and pencil. Typically, written documentation begins with a concise description of the textile, followed by detailed information that is logically organized. The outline below provides a general guideline of what information to include and how it can be organized. The specific information and the level of detail should be determined by institutional and project goals, as well as by the type of textile.

Sample Documentation Form

1. Identification
    a. Collection or accession number
    b. Name or title of textile
    c. Creator, cultural group, location, date of textile (if known)
    d. Name of person doing the documentation
    e. Date of documentation
2. Materials and dimensions
    a. Fiber identification: This should include information about what tool was used to assess the fibers. For example, cotton fiber examined with a linen tester at 10x magnification.
    b. Textile structure or structures: For example, plain weave.
    c. Other components: For example, sequins or metal hooks.
    d. Dimensions: The most typical dimensions are greatest length and greatest width; other dimensions may be helpful for specific pieces such as garments.
3. Description
    a. Start with a one- or two-sentence description that will allow a reader to quickly match a textile with its corresponding documentation report.
    b. Detailed description: The description should begin with general observations and then progress to more detailed information. It may be helpful to use subsections to record detailed information about complex textiles.
        i. The description should begin with the main fabric structure, then decorations and design (such as print or embroidery), then seams, linings, and fastenings (if applicable).
        ii. Organization is typically top down, front to back, interior (if applicable).
        iii. Garments are typically described with "proper left" and "proper right" indicating the side relating to a wearer rather than a viewer.
        iv. Color descriptions should use generally understood terms like *blue* or *pale yellow*, and avoid terms like *chartreuse* or *eggshell blue*.
        v. In some cases, it is helpful to separate decorations like embroidery into their own section for clarity.
        vi. Previous repairs and alterations are often included in the description section, but they may be included in the condition section.

4. Condition

    a. Start with a one- or two-sentence description that will allow a reader to quickly understand the main condition concerns. This type of concise description is sometimes called a BLUF statement. BLUF stands for Bottom Line Up Front, meaning that you are giving the reader the most important information at the top of the report.
    b. If terms like *good* and *poor* are used, there should be a glossary or reference document that clarifies how these terms are defined. This will ensure consistent use of terms.
    c. Organization is often the same as the description, and it is helpful to repeat any subheadings used in the description section.
    d. It can be helpful to make positive statements in addition to recording condition concerns. This provides a record that all potential condition concerns are included in the report. For example, no creases or surface dust.
    e. Some condition issues can be described as affecting the entire textile, but it is often helpful to note specific locations.

        i. Different levels of detail can be used to describe locations. Sometimes it is helpful to use quadrants for flat textiles.
        ii. One strategy is to record the location first, followed by a description of the condition issue. While this does not follow typical grammar, it does make it easy for future readers to locate the areas of concern. For example, proper left sleeve, near shoulder seam: 3" vertical tear.
        iii. For very detailed location information, use measurements to record the distance of the condition issue from fixed points on the textile. For example, a 2" vertical tear with starting point 5" from the top edge and 0.5" from the proper left selvedge.

5. Frame or other associated components

    a. Descriptions and condition notes about frames and other associated components should be included in separate sections of the documentation report.

6. Images

    a. Record photography should include overall images of the front and back sides of the textile. Additional photographs can be taken to show construction or condition details. Ideally, every photograph will include: a color card or grayscale, a scale for measurement, the accession or collection number of the textile, and the date of the photograph. The accession number and date should be written or printed in a size that will be easily legible in the photograph.
    b. Sketches can be helpful tools during research examinations. The process of creating a sketch supports careful and thorough examination.
    c. Annotations on photographs and sketches can clarify construction and condition details. Digital photographs can be annotated with various software programs. Another option is to print a photograph on regular paper in black and white with reduced saturation, and then use colored pencils to indicate relevant details.

7. Recommendations

    a. This can be an opportunity to flag a piece for further research, or to prioritize it for rehousing or treatment.

While condition terms may appear to be objective (the tear is 5" long), our understanding of them is always contextualized. For example, if the tear is on a uniform and tells an important story about the person who wore it, then this tear adds to the specialness of the uniform. It is helpful to indicate context with condition notes to clarify if they support or compromise the significance of a textile. There are two main types of context to consider when making these assessments.

- *Cultural and historical context*: How does the current condition compare to the ideal condition within cultural or historical context? For example, a textile used in a religious context might have stains that contribute to its significance.
- *Collection and exhibition context*: How does the current condition compare to the ideal condition with the collection context? For example, a textile fragment might be in good condition for exhibit and research use even though most of the original textile is gone.

CONCLUSION

Textiles hold special significance within many different types of institutions and collections. Collections care management and procedures strive to slow physical and chemical changes that could create the need for conservation treatment or irreparably compromise the significance of a textile. It is our privilege to interact with cultural heritage textiles and our responsibility to be good caretakers so that these textiles can inspire, inform, and delight future generations.

The information in this chapter is intended to support handling, examination, and documentation of collection textiles, all of which are critical components of preservation activities. While this chapter provides guidelines and suggestions, contextualized decisions should always be sought to ensure that textile care is aligned with institutional and stakeholder goals.

TERMINOLOGY

Fiber and Thread

Natural Fibers: Fibers from plants such as cotton and linen, as well as those from animals such as wool and silk.

Synthetic Fibers: Regenerated natural fibers such as rayon and acetate, as well as fully synthetic fibers such as polyester and nylon.

Twist: The direction a thread or yarn was spun. A clockwise twist is called Z-twist and a counterclockwise twist is called S-twist.

Ply: The number of threads or yarns that are twisted together. For example, many sewing threads are 3-ply.

Thread: Typically reserved to refer to sewing thread.

Yarn: Typically used for thread-like materials used for weaving, knitting, or crochet.

Woven Textiles

Warp: The set of yarns held in tension on a loom. The warp runs with the grain (lengthwise) in a textile.

Weft: The set of yarns drawn over and under the warp yarns. The weft runs crossgrain (crosswise) in a textile.

Selvedge: The "self-edge" of a woven fabric where the weft turns back around the outermost warp yarn.

Bias: The diagonal orientation of a textile and has greater stretch than the grain or crossgrain orientations.

Plain Weave: Woven structure where warps and wefts cross at right angles to form a grid pattern.

Twill Weave: Woven structure characterized by diagonal parallel ribs created by the crossing pattern of warp and weft yarns. Most blue jeans are made with twill weave fabrics.

Satin Weave: Woven structure characterized by one side of the fabric having a high gloss or shine. This is created by warp yarns passing over several wefts. The unbroken vertical surfaces of the warp yarns reflect light. Historically, satin was often woven with silk yarns, but many modern satins are woven with synthetic fibers.

Patterned Weave: Structures that have designs created by warp and weft crossing patterns rather than dyes or prints. In some cases, dyes and prints create additional designs on textiles with woven patterns.

Pile: Made of tufts or loops that stand up from the main textile. Pile can be woven in a velvet or knotted in a carpet.

Non-woven Textiles

Felt: Textile made from unspun, matted fibers.

Braid: Fabric band with all the yarns together at each end and crossing each other in a set pattern.

Net: An open material made with loops and knots that secure the loop spacing.

Knit and *Crochet*: Looping techniques that make stretchy textiles without elastic yarns.

Lace: Decorative, open material that can be made with different tools and designs. Lace can be made with crossed, looped, or knotted yarns. Also, lace can be made by adding embroidery to a net.

Needlework

Embroidery: Made of decorative stitches on a support fabric.

Pulled and *Drawn Work*: Types of embroidery where the support fabric is strategically distorted or removed. It can have a similar appearance to lace.

Beading: Decorative technique for stitching beads on a support fabric.

Color and Pattern

Dye: Used to color fibers, threads, and textiles. Dyes can be made from natural and synthetic sources and can be applied with many different techniques. The dye fully saturates the material.

Print: Specific type of localized dye application done after the textile is completed. Printing can involve many different artistic and industrial techniques, but it is based on either a stamp or a stencil process. Printing does not fully saturate the textile, and one side is often more saturated than the other.

Construction

Seam: Stitched join between two or more textiles.

Lining: Support textile that is added to the back or interior of another textile.

Fastenings: Includes buttons, zippers, snaps, and other materials used to temporarily secure textiles in a specific orientation.

CONDITION GLOSSARY

In this glossary, condition terms are organized into two broad categories: structural and visual. However, these categories are not exclusive, and they overlap in many cases. *Inherent vice* refers to materials that deteriorate due to their own chemical instability and is an example of a condition that can be both structural and visual. For example, this could describe how some plastics will break down in a few years and some dyes will fade relatively quickly.

Physical Condition

- Handling quality
  - *Flexible*: A textile that can bend easily and without being damaged.
  - *Stiff*: A textile that does not bend easily, but is not damaged by the movement.
  - *Brittle*, *shattering*, or *powdering*: Textiles that are damaged when bent or moved.
- Compromised structure—partial
  - *Abrasion*: Physical damage to the surface of a textile. The surface may have a rougher

texture than undamaged areas, or the fabric may appear thinner in the abraded area.
- *Frayed*: A textile where yarns are partially released from their structural pattern. This often occurs along edges of tears and holes.
- *Pilled*: A type of abrasion where fibers are partially released from their original structure and form small, matted pill-shaped bundles on the surface of the textile. This often occurs on knits or textiles made with wool fibers.
- *Grazing from pests*: A type of damage where pests partially eat through the textile creating thinner areas. Grazing is often round or oval-shaped.

• Compromised structure—complete

- *Hole* or *loss*: An area where the textile is completely missing. These can range in size from pinholes to large areas.
- *Tear* or *split*: Linear break in the textile. These can be in any direction, but they are often oriented along either the warp or weft direction.
- *Cut*: Linear break made with a sharp tool. A cut is less likely to have frayed edges than a tear or split.

• Related to use and storage

- *Creases* or *fold lines*: Linear ridges caused by folding and pressure. While some creases are intentional (like creases set into trousers), many creases are caused when stored textiles have unsupported folds. Over time creases can become tears.
- *Distortions*: Areas where textiles are pulled out of their original alignment. While some distortions are intentional (like drawn work embroidery), many distortions are caused when stored textiles have unsupported weight distribution. For example, distortions in a garment's shoulders from storage on a wire hanger.

• Related to stitches and decorations

- *Broken, loose,* or *missing stitches* or *decorations*: Terms that describe changes to stitches and applied decorations.
- *Previous mend*, *repair*, or *alteration*: Terms that describe previous changes intentionally made to the textile.

Visual Condition

• Relating to chemical changes

- *Discolored* or *yellowed*: Terms that describe textiles that have generalized slight color changes from their original appearance. These areas may not have clearly defined edges. These changes could be due to environmental conditions such as air pollution or to chemical changes such as acidic deterioration of plant fibers.
- *Stain*: Discolored area caused by the interaction of a fluid with the textile. Stains often have drip or splatter patterns with clearly defined edges.
- *Soil* or *grime*: Terms that describe discoloration caused by the interaction of particulate dirt with the textile. This type of discoloration rarely has clearly defined edges.
- *Tide line*: Linear stain caused at the wet/dry interface when a textile dries unevenly. Over time, these may become tears.
- *Accretion*: Solid mass that is adhered to a textile. It may be dimensional, or it may be a thin film.
- *Adhesive residue* or *adhesive stain*: An accretion or stain caused by an adhesive.
- *Corrosion*: The result of chemical deterioration of metal components.

• Relating to dyes, prints, and finishes

- *Dye bleed* or *dye migration*: Terms that indicate that a textile was previously wet and the moisture enabled a dye to move to another part of the textile or to an adjacent textile.

- *Dye shift*: When the dye goes through chemical deterioration that causes it to change colors.
- *Dye fading*: When the dye goes through chemical deterioration that causes it to be less saturated.
- *Crocking*: Indicates that dry dye moved to another part of the textile or to an adjacent textile due to pressure or friction.
- *Change in gloss* or *matte surface*: Terms that indicate a change in the surface finish of a textile. For example, a glossy surface on a starched textile might appear dull due to dust accumulation.

• Relating to pests

- *Fly speck*: Small black or dark brown accretion caused by insect excrement.
- *Mold* or *mildew*: Terms that indicate microbial growth on a textile. These discolorations have irregular shapes and can range from brown to green to red.
- *Foxing*: Small irregular brownish discolorations caused by microbial growth and trace metals.

BIBLIOGRAPHY

Resources for Fiber and Textile Identification

Burnham, Dorothy K. *A Textile Terminology: Warp & Weft*. London: Routledge and Kegan Paul, 1981.

"DATS Toolkits." Accessed June 11, 2021. https://www.dressandtextilespecialists.org.uk/dats-toolkits/.

Earnshaw, Pat. *The Identification of Lace*. 3rd rev. ed. Botley, Oxford: Shire Publications, 2009.

Emery, Irene. *The Primary Structures of Fabrics: An Illustrated Classification*. New York: Thames & Hudson, 2009.

"Fiber Reference Image Library—CAMEO." Accessed June 11, 2021. http://cameo.mfa.org/wiki/Fiber_Reference_Image_Library.

Seiler-Baldinger, Annemarie. *Textiles: A Classification of Techniques*. Bathurst, AU: Crawford House, 1994.

The Weavers' Company. "Glossary of Weaving Terms." Accessed June 11, 2021. https://weavers.org.uk/textiles/resources/glossary-of-weaving-terms/.

Tortora, Phyllis G., and Robert S. Merkel, eds. *Fairchild's Dictionary of Textiles*. 7th ed. New York: Fairchild Publications, 2009.

Resources for Collections Care of Textiles

Canadian Conservation Institute. "Caring for Textiles and Costumes—Preventive Conservation Guidelines for Collections," May 11, 2018. https://www.canada.ca/en/conservation-institute/services/preventive-conservation/guidelines-collections/textiles-costumes.html.

Heritage Collections Council. "Caring for Cultural Material 2." Accessed June 10, 2021. https://aiccm.org.au/wp-content/uploads/2020/01/2_caring_for_cultural_material_2.pdf.

Heritage Collections Council. "Handling, Transportation, Storage and Display." Accessed June 10, 2021. https://aiccm.org.au/wp-content/uploads/2020/01/Handling_Storage_transport_Display.pdf.

Heritage Collections Council. *ReCollections: Caring for Collections Across Australia*. Canberra: Commonwealth of Australia, 2000.

"An Illustrated Guide to the Care of Costume and Textile Collections—Collections Trust." Accessed June 11, 2021. https://collectionstrust.org.uk/resource/an-illustrated-guide-to-the-care-of-costume-and-textile-collections/.

Mailand, Harold F., and Dorothy Stites Alig. *Preserving Textiles: A Guide for the Nonspecialist*. Indianapolis, IN: Indianapolis Museum of Art, 1999.

National Parks Service. "Museum Handbook, Part I, Appendix K: Curatorial Care of Textile Objects." Accessed June 10, 2021. https://www.nps.gov/museum/publications/MHI/Appendix%20K.pdf.

National Trust (Great Britain), ed. *The National Trust Manual of Housekeeping: The Care of Collections in Historic Houses Open to the Public*. 1st ed. Amsterdam; Boston: Elsevier, 2006.

Shelley, Marjorie, and Metropolitan Museum of Art (New York, NY). *The Care and Handling of Art Objects: Practices in the Metropolitan Museum of Art*. Metropolitan Museum of Art, 1987. Available online: https://www.metmuseum.org/art/metpublications/the_care_and_handling_of_art_objects_practices_in_the_metropolitan_museum_of_art.

21

Wood

Katherine Steiner

Wood is the hard, fibrous substance that makes up the stems (trunks and branches) of trees and bushes. There are some similarities in behavior and condition issues with other plant fibers, and some of the recommendations here may be useful in working with those materials. By the time wood becomes art or artifact, it is no longer a living thing, though it often behaves as if it were. Wood moves, responding to environmental changes. It absorbs and releases water easily, and rapid humidity changes can do severe damage. It can stain easily and absorb the oils from hands, and it may develop little cracks, called checks, as it dries. Wood is used nearly everywhere. Its strength makes it useful in large construction and yet, because it is easy to cut and shape, it is practical for smaller utilitarian and decorative objects, as well. Museum collections may include any of these objects: structures in the case of historic houses, utilitarian objects like bowls or spoons, farm equipment, art objects, ethnographic materials, furniture, frames, and many other objects both functional and decorative. This chapter will address wood as a medium. More specific information about furniture and frames can be found elsewhere in this publication.

There are hundreds of types of wood, each with its own characteristics. Identifying those types is beyond the scope of this chapter, but images available through the internet have made it simpler to determine when something that might appear to be a flaw can be attributed to the nature of the wood in question. Some types of wood may appear damaged, but they may be quite stable. When unsure, note the appearance so that future reviewers can monitor for changes.

Wood can be defined as hard or soft, and may undergo manufacturing processes like lamination, kiln-drying, or chemical treatment before the final maker begins to work with it. Once the artist or maker begins to work with it, it might be turned, sawn, carved, inlaid, glued, laminated, painted, stained, or other treatments. Each of these things can affect the final object's reaction to stressors.

While it's helpful to know what caused damage to a piece, it's not always necessary. The examiner should describe what is visible. Be cautious identifying specific causes, unless there is certainty. Always be as clear and specific as possible while recognizing that some terms may be foreign to future examiners and may warrant explanation. It may be useful to supply a glossary defining terms.

HANDLING

Wear gloves when handling wood unless gloves pose a risk to the object. If the wood has rough areas, is cracked, or has lifting veneer, use clean bare hands or choose nitrile gloves over cotton. Extremely awkward or heavy objects may be better handled with clean hands as well. Keep in mind that if the wood is bleached or very light in color, oil and dirt from your hands will stain easily.

Before moving the object, make sure you have separated parts from each other, lids from vessels, for example. If the object has moving parts, secure the parts with twill tape, padding the corners with foam. Plan your route and final destination, making sure the path is clear, that you have plenty of space to move, and that you know where you will place the piece when it's time to set it down. Use personnel where appropriate or appropriate equipment like carts, tables, and dollies, padding equipment where it comes into contact with the object. If the object is physically unstable, use fabric "snakes," tissue paper, foam rings, or other appropriate means to stabilize.

Always lift wood objects by supporting thicker areas of wood underneath. Be careful not to put stress on any areas that are thin. Long pieces of wood can break under their own weight, so be sure to have enough people to handle the object. If the object contains multiple pieces of wood that are joined together, be mindful of the joined areas and pick up the object where you can best support the weight.

Objects made of wood should be stored at a stable temperature and humidity if possible. In the case of historic sites, this is sometimes difficult, especially with farm implements and the like. Be aware that some forms of deterioration may occur more rapidly in less ideal conditions. Collections managers may determine that more frequent condition reporting is necessary for objects that are stored or displayed in less ideal conditions.

TYPES OF ISSUES AFFLICTING WOOD OBJECTS

Four Categories of Issues May Affect Wood

- Biological deterioration may be caused by insects, fungi such as mold or mildew, and rodents. In museum settings, consistent humidity and integrated pest management can help mitigate this.
- Chemical deterioration can be caused by the wood itself, or by glues and coatings used in the manufacture of the object. In museum collections, this type of deterioration typically appears as discoloration or embrittlement. Coatings that may have been applied in the past to help preserve the object may contribute to chemical deterioration. This deterioration is exacerbated by high temperature and humidity.
- Physical deterioration is caused by light, rapid changes to humidity, or heat. In museum collections, this is most often seen as discoloration, fading, or distortion of wood fibers leading to cracking or warping.
- Mechanical deterioration refers to most of the damage we can see: cracks, holes, abrasions, etc. It may be the result of one of the other types of deterioration or of poor handling.

COMPLETING CONDITION REPORTS

For non-conservators, it is far more important to be accurate in your description of issues and potential issues than to know what has caused the issue. Make notes understandable for the next examiner. The terms in the glossary below can help with accuracy.

A condition report should be completed when an object comes into or leaves the museum, is exhibited or removed from exhibition, and if the object has been damaged or exposed to potential damage. Even if an object is stationary for long periods of time, it should be checked on a regular basis. This may be difficult given other obligations. Give priority to objects that are at higher risk.

Necessary Tools

- Cloth tape measure

- Pencil. From time to time, it may be helpful to use a pen: to distinguish later notes from the initial evaluation or because a pencil mark isn't visible on a photo. If you use pens, set up a separate work area away from the object and do not let the pen leave that area.
- Good light that can be adjusted to light the object from both above and from the side (raking light). This light can be an examination light, a flashlight, or even the light on a cell phone, as long as the light is bright enough to see fine details.

Helpful Tools

- Calipers (for measuring the diameter of 3-D objects or the width of cracks)
- Magnifying glass or magnifying reading glasses
- Dental mirror or small handheld mirror (to see hidden areas like the inside of vessels)

The simplest way to record condition notes is to take pictures of the object from every angle and record notes directly on the image. These images can be simple cell phone images. If you do this, it is unnecessary to repeat the same information in a separate notes section. Instead, use the notes section for overall comments and note specific issues on the images. Keep in mind that three-dimensional objects have six sides: front, back, left, right, top, and bottom. If the object does not have a clear front side, make sure to identify the orientation of your images. You can do this by referencing a signature, an accession number, or a distinctive characteristic of the object. When completing paper condition reports, notes taken after the initial evaluation should be dated or otherwise distinguished from baseline evaluation. When using digital condition reporting methods, simply choose a color for each subsequent evaluation. If there are specific areas of concern, especially those that might get worse, take additional images of the area in question. Those images can be printed to travel with the condition report, but they should also be maintained digitally so that you can zoom in as needed. Again, most current cell phones will be adequate for most of your needs.

EXAMINATION

Separate all parts, lids from vessels, for example. You will review each part of the object separately. You should examine objects in a consistent pattern that works for you. Jumping from area to area will cause things to be overlooked. Not all objects will have all of the following parts, but make sure you examine the surface, the underlying structure and support elements, joints, hardware, and the interior.

- Begin by looking carefully at the object (or part of the object) as a whole. Are there any obvious vulnerable areas? Are there things that seem to be consistent issues over the entire object like flaking paint, cracks in varnish, stains, etc.?
- If the object consists of pieces of wood joined together, are there loose or open joints? Glue can become soft or brittle depending on environmental conditions, and you should note this if applicable.
- Are there cracks or weak spots in areas that might have experienced stress?
- Do you see splitting or cracking anywhere? It can be helpful to measure both the length and width of cracks to be sure that they do not worsen over time.
- Is there wear on handles or bodies of utilitarian pieces?
- Does anything seem warped or misshapen?
- If the piece is veneered or made of multiple layers of wood (or if wood is layered with other materials), do those layers show any signs of separating or lifting?
- Is the finish stained or discolored?

- Does the object appear to have been bleached by light exposure? (Sometimes wood is bleached as part of the creation process.)
- Is there water damage? Water damage often, but not always, appears as white discoloration. Think rings on a piece of furniture.
- Is there insect damage? Typically, old insect damage will appear as small holes, possibly with dirt or dust embedded within. With newer insect damage, the holes will still have fairly crisp edges and may be a little lighter than the surrounding wood. You may see frass, which typically looks like coarse dirt or sand and can be light to dark brown, depending on the insect. You may see the actual insects or their casings, but you are more likely to simply notice the damage.
- Are there areas that appear to have once been repaired? Repairs are sometimes noticeable because they are a slightly different color than the rest of the object.
- If the object contains any metal parts, check to see that the metal hasn't caused staining and that the attachment areas are not under stress.
- Do not forget to examine the support structure and/or interior areas of the object.
- If this object will be displayed elsewhere, it's helpful to provide packing and handling notes along with installation requirements directly on the condition report.

GLOSSARY

Condition Terms

Abrasion: A worn area as if something has scraped across the surface of the object.

Alligatoring: A hexagonal pattern of cracking in the surface finish of an object; often caused by improper curing of the finish layer, or by not allowing sufficient drying time between coats.

Bleaching: Overall lightening of an object.

Blister: A raised area of the finish, generally enclosed; the risk is that this raised area will break and the underlying area will be exposed or the finish will deteriorate further.

Buckling: Bent or curled, often applied to veneer that is still attached in some areas, but lifting between those areas.

Burn: Furniture and utilitarian objects occasionally will have burn marks from cigarettes or other accidents; may appear to be a small stain or discolored area.

Check: A split across the annual rings of a piece of wood caused by the natural stresses of the drying process; generally checks do not cause structural harm.

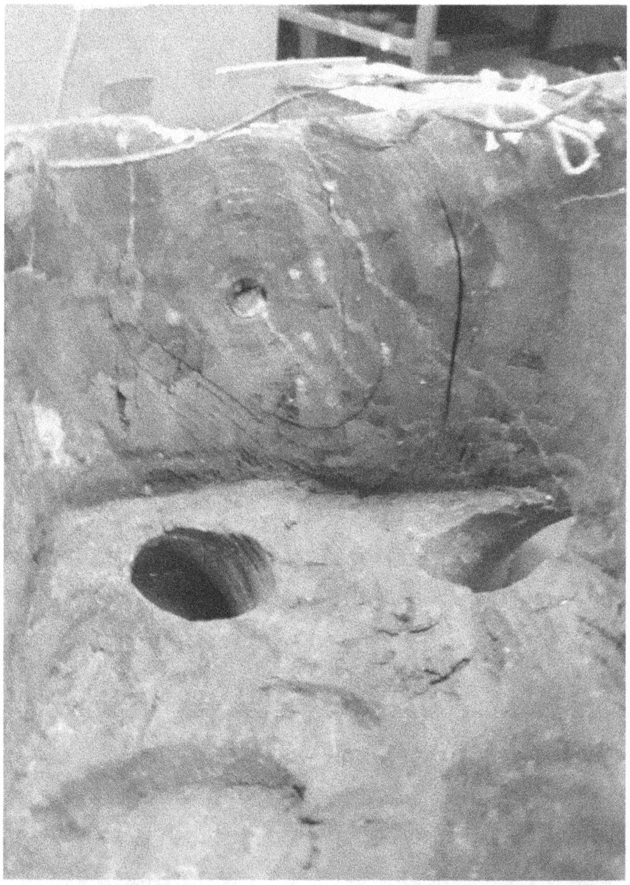

Figure 21.1. Checks (cracks) resulting from the natural drying process of wood. Source: Katherine Steiner

Chip: Small loss to the edge of a piece or to the veneer.

Crack: A narrow break.

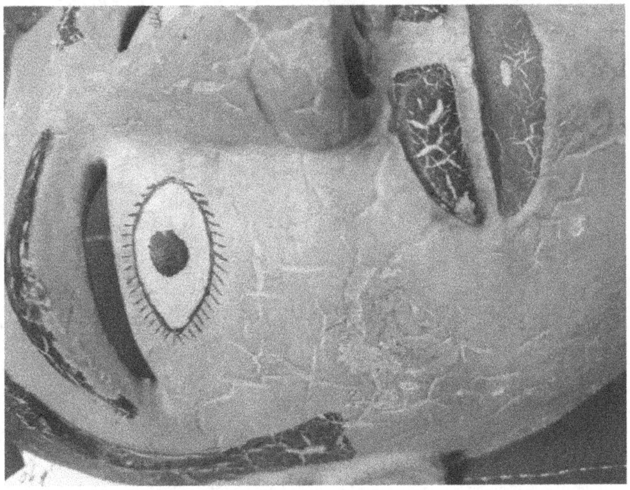

Figure 21.2. Traction cracks or alligatoring.
Source: Katherine Steiner

Cupping: A specific type of warping that causes a flat area of wood to become concave.

Darkening: Typically caused by light damage to surface treatments like varnish, or by dirt and oils on untreated wood.

Delamination: Separation between layers.

Dent: A depression in the surface usually caused by a blow; use when the fibers have been compressed rather than broken.

Expand: Become larger; typically used to note cracks, checks, or splits that have widened over time.

Flaking: Breaking into small loose particles; sometimes occurs with wood finishes like paint.

Insect Damage: Used to note small holes and discoloration made by insects; monitor insect damage carefully unless you are sure it is old to make sure you do not have an active infestation.

Lifting: Use when parts of inlaid surfaces or veneers pull away from the rest of the material.

Patina: Surface appearance that occurs with age.

Scratch: Mark in the surface finish.

Scuff: Abraded area.

Shrink: To become smaller; in wood this typically occurs under dry conditions.

Split: Divide along the grain.

Traction Crack: See Alligatoring.

Warping: Distortion caused when the moisture content of parts of an object change at different rates.

Water Damage: May take the form of white discoloration in the finish; more serious water damage may have caused other issues like warping, splitting, or lifting.

Yellowing: Discoloration caused by aging or chemical staining.

Useful Terms Related to Wooden Objects

Carved: Cut in a precise or decorative way.

Ebonizing: A black finish, obtained through a chemical reaction, usually between iron oxides and the tannins in wood.

Gilding: Application of gold leaf to wood.

Grain: Longitudinal pattern in wood.

Graining: A finish meant to imitate wood grain.

Inlay: Decorative pattern set into the surface.

Laminate: Multiple thin layers of wood glued together.

Lacquer: Term used for a hard, often shiny, surface finish.

Paint: Coloring applied to the surface.

Polychrome: Decorated with multiple opaque surface colors; generally used when referring to objects that are not modern.

Shellac: A surface finish and filler made from a resinous secretion of a specific insect.

Stained: A penetrating, colored finish.

Turned: Created on a lathe.

Varnish: Surface finish for wood, generally clear, but may contain pigment.

Veneer: A thin layer applied to the surface of an object, often of superior quality to the substrate.

Figure 21.3. Over time, joints may become loose and glue releases. Source: Katherine Steiner

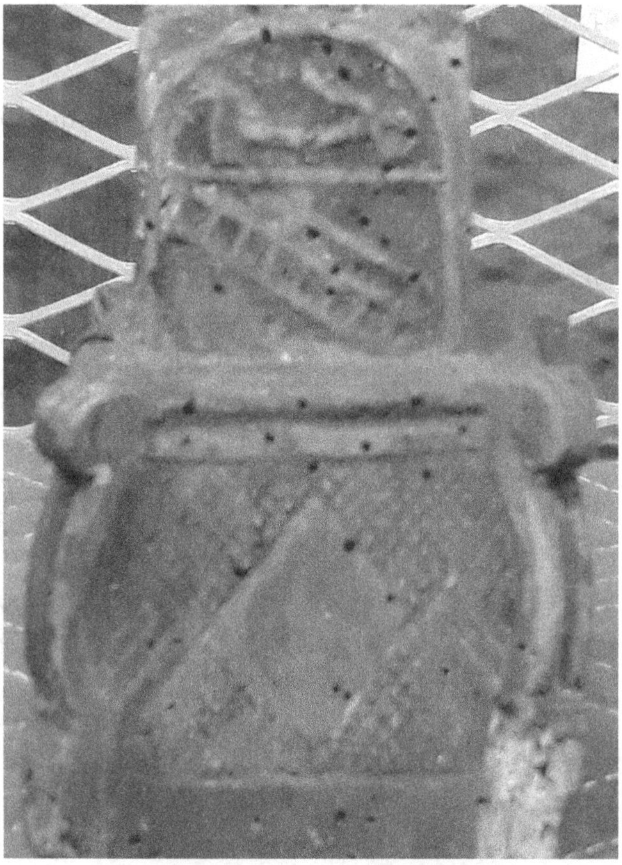

Figure 21.4. Most likely old insect damage. It is preferable when unsure of the cause simply to describe the damage without trying to identify the cause.
Source: Katherine Steiner

Figures 21.5 and 21.6. Be very careful to check for parts that may not be permanently attached.
Source: Katherine Steiner

Figure 21.7. Turned wood vessel made out of laminated sheets of wood. The darker areas may indicate wood of a different density from the remainder of the layer. Those areas may be fragile.
Source: Katherine Steiner

Figure 21.8. Slight yellowing caused by the wheat paste used for labeling. Source: Katherine Steiner

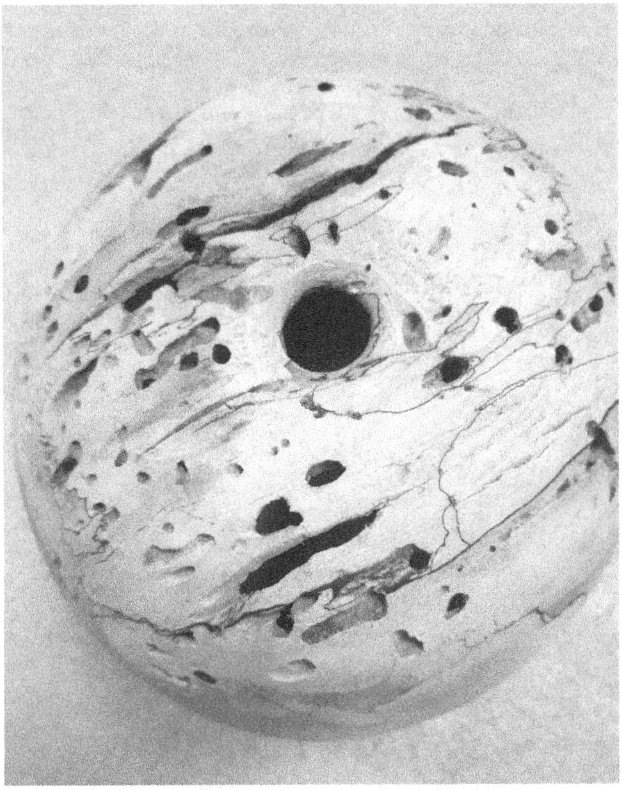

Figure 21.9. This particular type of wood has many holes and hairline cracks throughout. Some of the areas that look cracked are different wood densities and may not be cracks. This object is very stable, in spite of its appearance. Source: Katherine Steiner

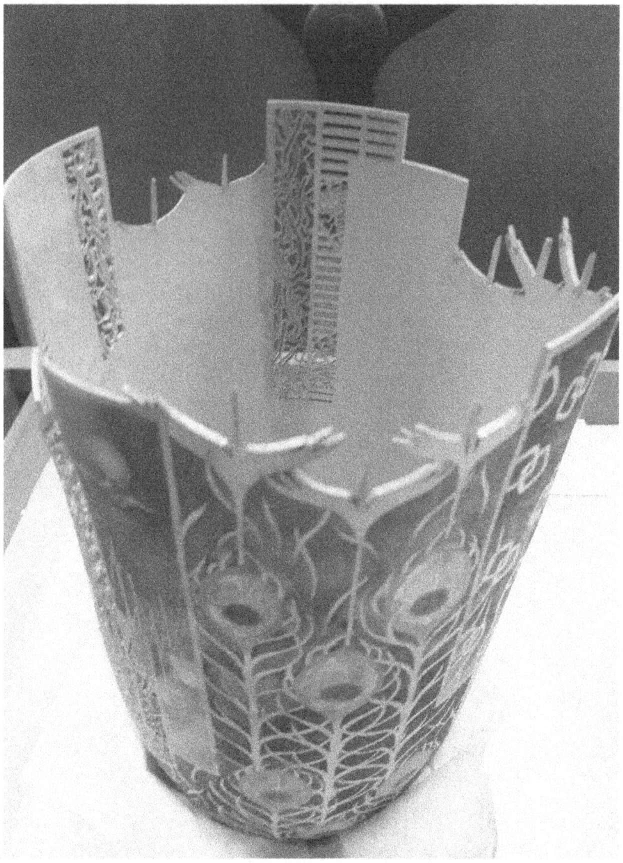

Figure 21.10. Wood artifacts can feature delicate details. Check these areas closely for damage or deterioration. Be mindful of these delicate areas when moving and examining the artifact.
Source: Katherine Steiner

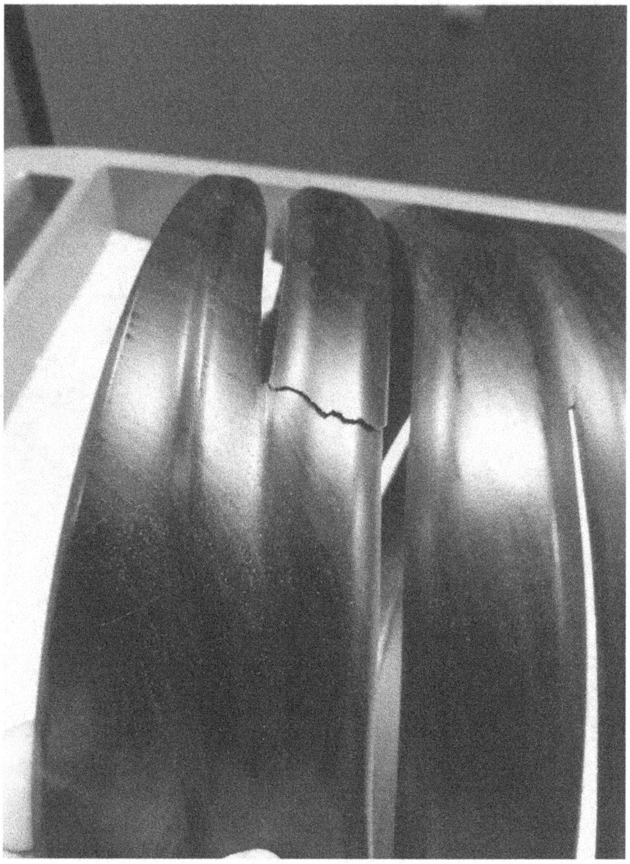

Figure 21.11. Mishandling of this thin section of wood has led to a break through the object.
Source: Katherine Steiner

Figure 21.12. The interior section of this book sculpture has expanded more rapidly than the laminate attached to the surface resulting in the delamination and cracking of the "spine."
Source: Katherine Steiner

BIBLIOGRAPHY

"Glossary for Furniture." *The Fine Arts Conservancy*, www.art-conservation.org/?page_id=1192. Accessed 31 Mar. 2021.

Jenkins, Kathleen McClain, and Marie Demeroukas, editors. "Furniture." *Basic Condition Reporting: A Handbook*, 3rd edition, revised, Southeastern Registrars Association, 1998, 53–63.

Levitan, Alan. "Upholstered Furniture: Agents of Deterioration." *Conserve-O-Gram,* National Park Service, vol. 7, no. 4, www.nps.gov/museum/publications/conserveogram/07-04.pdf. Accessed 30 Mar. 2021.

Murray, Courtney VonStein, and Rebecca Kaczkowski. "Plant Materials." *AIC Wiki,* American Institute for Conservation of Historic and Artistic Works, 2011, www.conservation-wiki.com/wiki/Plant_Materials.

"The Merriam-Webster.com Online Dictionary." *www.Merriam-Webster.com*, www.merriam-webster.com. Accessed 30 Mar. 2021.

Index

About the Southeastern Registrars Association

The Southeastern Registrars Association (SERA) is the affinity group for collections specialists in cultural institutions across the Southeastern United States. Founded in 1978, SERA encourages high standards of museum practice and fosters professional growth among museum registrars through the promotion, exchange, and dissemination of information and ideas via educational seminars, publications, and other means. SERA initiates and supports activities that create an atmosphere of cooperation among registrars, other museum professionals, and those in related service fields, and pursues further development of professional practices in the field.

About the Editors and Contributors

ABOUT THE EDITORS

Deborah Rose Van Horn has been working in museum registration and collections management for over twenty years. Deb holds a master's degree in museum science from Texas Tech University and a bachelor's degree in anthropology from the University of Georgia. Deb has served on the board of several regional and national organizations such as the Southeastern Registrars Association and RC-AAM (now CS-AAM). She has published several articles and books, including *Basic Condition Reporting: A Handbook*, 4th edition and *Registration Methods for the Small Museum*, 5th edition. Deb has worked for several museums in Georgia, Texas, Kentucky, and Florida. Currently, Deb works as a curator for Walt Disney Imagineering.

Corinne Midgett is registrar of the High Point Museum in High Point, North Carolina. Corinne has a graduate certificate in public history and a bachelor's degree in classics, both from UNC-Greensboro. She has served on the board of the North Carolina Preservation Consortium and serves as chair of the Southeastern Registrars Association.

Heather Culligan is the registrar at the Tampa Bay History Center. She has over ten years of experience in collections management and registration in history museums and historic structures. Heather is a former co-instructor of Collections Management in Museums at the University of West Georgia, a former board member of the Southeastern Registrars Association (SERA), and served as a co-editor of *Basic Condition Reporting*, 4th edition.

ABOUT THE CONTRIBUTORS

Kyle Bryner is a seasoned museum professional with over twenty years of experience in museum collections management and registration. She holds a BA in history from Shepherd University, an MA in history and museum studies from the University of North Carolina at Greensboro, and a postgraduate certificate in Museum Collections Management and Care from The George Washington University. She served on the boards of the Collections Stewardship and former Registrars

Committee of the American Alliance of Museums, the Southeastern Museums Conference, the Southeastern Registrars Association, the North Carolina Museums Council, and the North Carolina Preservation Consortium. She has volunteered her time as an Institute of Museum and Library Services grant reviewer and as an American Alliance of Museums, Museum Assessment Program peer reviewer.

Mary Coughlin is an associate professor in museum studies at The George Washington University, where she teaches preventive conservation and is head of the online graduate certificate program in Museum Collections Management and Care. Before teaching full-time, Mary worked for five years in the Objects Conservation Laboratory at the Smithsonian's National Museum of American History, where she conserved diverse objects including FDR's leg braces and C-3PO and R2-D2 from *Star Wars*. She has a special interest in the conservation challenges of plastics in museum collections.

Robin P. Croskery Howard is currently the objects conservator at the Ah-Tah-Thi-Ki Seminole Museum in Clewiston, Florida. In addition to caring for over two hundred thousand indigenous cultural heritage objects, Ms. Croskery Howard is an educator who works with Seminole youth through various internship programs to foster students in areas of history, chemistry, and the care of cultural objects. She is a graduate of East Carolina University with a master's degree in maritime studies, concentrating in the Conservation of Waterlogged Material Objects, and she was a fellow at the North Carolina Museum of History from 2014 to 2016, specializing in objects conservation.

LaToya Devezin is an archivist with the National Archives and Records Administration at the Jimmy Carter Presidential Library and Museum in Atlanta, Georgia, where she preserves records related to the thirty-ninth president of the United States of America. She has an MLIS in Archives Management from Louisiana State University and an MA in Museum Studies from Southern University at New Orleans. After graduation, she's worked in libraries, archives, and museums in a variety of roles over the last decade. Devezin enjoys the role she plays in preserving objects of enduring value for the next generation.

Michelle Gallagher Roberts received her bachelor of science degree from Central Washington University and graduated from the University of Denver with a master's degree in anthropology and a specialization in museums studies. Working in museums since 1997, she has worked in all aspects of registration, collections management, and exhibitions. For over twelve years, she was the head of registration and collections at the New Mexico Museum of Art (Santa Fe, New Mexico). She is a contributing author on several books related to museums, including *Sustainable Revenue for Museums: A Guide* and *Rights & Reproductions: The Handbook for Cultural Institutions.* Currently, Michelle is the deputy director at the New Mexico Museum of Art.

Stephanie Gaub Antequino has worked with Planet Hollywood's memorabilia collection since 2013. She started out as memorabilia archivist and was promoted to curator in 2019. She also worked at the Orange County Regional History Center in Orlando, Florida, as collections manager and photo archivist. Prior to moving to Florida, Stephanie worked at the Erie County Historical Society and Erie Maritime Museum, both in Erie, Pennsylvania. Stephanie received her BA in anthropology from Gannon University, Massachusetts, in historical administration from Eastern Illinois University, and a graduate certificate in Museum Collections Management and Care from The George Washington University. She lives outside of Orlando with her husband and two children.

Erica Hague is the collections manager at the Atlanta History Center (AHC), communications chair for the Southeastern Registrars Association (SERA), and she co-teaches the Collections Management class for the University of West Georgia's Public History program. Erica values honesty, inclusion, and creativity. When she is not managing the sixty thousand museum items and seventeen thousand linear feet of archival items at the AHC, she's plying her co-workers with baked goods, hermiting with a good book and her knitting, or plotting her next adventure as a #travelinfool.

Kara J. Hurst is the National Curator and Native American Graves Protection and Repatriation Act (NAGPRA) coordinator for the U.S. Department of the Interior, Bureau of Reclamation, headquartered in Denver, Colorado. Prior to that, she held supervisory positions for the Smithsonian's National Museum of the American Indian, the Bureau of Land Management, the Natural History Museum of Utah, and other museums and libraries. Ms. Hurst taught Museum Collections Management as an adjunct faculty member in the Anthropology Department at the University of Utah, and she has lectured on the intersection between museum and legal responsibilities. Active in national, regional, and state museum organizations, Ms. Hurst has served as the chair of the Registrar's Committee of the Mountain-Plains Museums Association and was a board member on the American Alliance of Museums (AAM) Registrar's Committee. In *Museum Registration Methods 5* (2010), Ms. Hurst authored the Repositories chapter and was an invited speaker on that same topic for the AAM Museum Essentials webinar, *Step-by-Step Collections Acquisition.* She earned her MA in museum science from Texas Tech University in Lubbock, Texas, and a BA in anthropology from Pacific Lutheran University in Tacoma, Washington.

Mary D. LaGue holds a BFA from Longwood College and an MA in art history/museum studies from Virginia Commonwealth University. She has served the Taubman Museum of Art since 1990 as registrar, keeping collections records and assisting with the logistics of exhibitions and supervising object care. Ms. LaGue serves as conservation advisor to the Roanoke (Virginia) Arts Commission; was president of the Southeastern Registrars Association; served as Southwestern regional director, then treasurer, on the governing council for the Virginia Association of Museums; and served on the Southeastern Museums Conference governing council.

Elise V. LeCompte is the registrar and coordinator for museum health and safety for the Florida Museum of Natural History. She has served as collections manager, exhibit registrar, and conservation technician, and consultant for museums throughout the southeast. She has several publications on collections management and artifact conservation and has organized and presented at workshops on related topics. She serves as an accreditation and museum assessment program reviewer for the American Alliance of Museums, council member and coordinator of the Southeastern Museums Conference Career Center, board member and secretary for the Association of Registrars and Collections Specialists, and travel grants coordinator for the Society for the Preservation of Natural History Collections. She is an adjunct professor for the University of Florida Museum Studies program and holds an MA in archaeology and chemistry from the University of Florida and a BA in anthropology from the Johns Hopkins University.

Jillian Matthews Bingham is the director of collections for the Culture & Heritage Museums located in York County, South Carolina, overseeing all three-dimensional objects and artwork spread across the organization's four sites. Her role with the organization also includes being an expert on all things related to Vernon Grant, the artist best known for his creation of Kellogg's Rice Krispies' Snap, Crackle, Pop gnomes in 1933. Jillian did her undergraduate studies at Central Michigan University, graduating through their dual enrollment program with a bachelor of arts in history and art history and a bachelor of sciences in social sciences and museum studies. She also worked at the university's Museum of Cultural and Natural History for two years, interned at the university's Clarke Historical Library, and worked as a research assistant for an art history professor. Jillian received her master of arts degree in museum studies from the University of Oklahoma, completing her graduate research project at the Bechtler Museum of Modern Art in Charlotte, North Carolina. She is a co-founding member of the Piedmont Area Cultural Resource Emergency Network (PACREN).

Laura Mina is the associate conservator of textiles and head of the textile lab at Winterthur Museum, Garden & Library and an affiliated assistant professor in the Winterthur/University of Delaware Program in Art Conservation. She has published articles on conservation ethics, aqueous cleaning techniques, modern knit fabrics, and integrated pest management.

Dixie Neilson has over twenty years of experience assisting museums nationwide with object management issues. Dixie is a past-chair of the Southeastern Registrars Association (1995–2000) and has recently retired from her latest position as director of the Matheson Museum.

Nicole Passerotti is an art conservator who specializes in objects. She is currently the program associate for the Andrew W. Mellon Opportunity for Diversity in Conservation at the UCLA/Getty Graduate Program and recently an assistant conservator at the Field Museum. Her prior conservation experience includes a Samuel H. Kress Fellowship at the Philadelphia Museum of Art and work at the Pitt Rivers Museum at Oxford University, the Kaymacki Archaeological Project in Turkey, the Smithsonian National Museum of the American Indian, the Cantor Center for the Arts at Stanford University, the de Young Museum, and the Textile Museum of Oaxaca. She holds an MA and a certificate in advanced study in art conservation from SUNY Buffalo State College and a BA in English from Oberlin College.

Fran Ritchie is an art conservator specializing in natural science materials and historic artifacts. Prior to her current position as objects conservator at the National Park Service Harpers Ferry Center, Fran was a conservator in the Natural Science Collections Conservation Lab and the Anthropology Objects Conservation Lab at the American Museum of Natural History in New York. She has also worked for the Smithsonian National Museum of the American Indian, Peabody Museum of Archaeology and Ethnology at Harvard University, and Biltmore Estate. Fran holds an MA in museum anthropology from Columbia University, and an MA and CAS in art conservation from SUNY Buffalo State. She is a Professional Associate of the American Institute for Conservation.

Tommie Rodgers is the registrar at the Lauren Rogers Museum of Art in Laurel, Mississippi, and has worked in the field of registration, collections care, and exhibit design and installation for over thirty years at LRMA. She holds a bachelor of fine arts degree from The University of Southern Mississippi and received a certificate in collections care from the University of Delaware in 1995. Rodgers appreciates working with fellow staff members and has enjoyed various tasks, including the reinstallation of the Native American basket collection in 2005, co-supervising a 2013 building addition, completing several collection inventories, researching improvements for a ninety-eight-year-old building with collections care in mind, and managing photography and tombstone information for five publications featuring the museum's collections.

Rodgers's experience in digital condition reporting began during the 2013 building addition and grew from the need for speed and efficiency when juggling the collection in various locations.

Rachel Shabica is supervisory registrar at the National Museum of the American Indian, where she has overseen the registration department since 2017. Prior to joining NMAI, she spent eighteen years as registrar at the Textile Museum, where she ultimately directed the move of the collections to a new facility as the museum partnered with George Washington University and moved to the university's campus. She holds a BA in history from Haverford College and an MA in history and a certificate in museum administration from Tufts University. She is a past-chair of the Registrar's Committee for the Mid-Atlantic Association of Museums and is currently a peer reviewer for the AAM's Museum Assessment Program.

Katherine Steiner has a master's in liberal studies with a Certificate in Museum Studies from the University of North Carolina, Greensboro. She has been a registrar since 2000 and currently serves as the chief registrar at the Mint Museum in Charlotte, North Carolina.

Misty Tilson Jackson has over twenty years' experience as a museum registrar. She was head registrar of Premier Exhibitions, Inc. She has previously worked as head registrar of the Anthropology Department of the Field Museum and the Augusta Museum of History. Misty received her Master of Arts degree in museum science from Texas Tech University. She currently lives in Lilburn, Georgia, with her husband.

CPSIA information can be obtained
at www.ICGtesting.com
Printed in the USA
BVHW062056090122
624477BV00002B/4

9 781538 150597